THE POOR HOUSES

A Story of Atlanta's Almshouses

By

Henry M. Hope

TO MY CHILDREN,

SHARON HOPE HANSARD, and
HENRY MELVILLE HOPE, III,

Together with their Spouses,

All of whom exhibit by God's grace Christian faith and
steadfast commitment to
purpose so reminiscent of those same qualities possessed
by Dr. Robert Lawson Hope.

CONTENTS

AUTHOR'S FOREWORD

For more than one hundred years, Atlanta, Georgia had an alms-house for the rescue of indigent people. Sometimes called the "Poor House," it cared for the helpless with Christian charity ministered by dedicated public servants. Their caring required much exertion, planning, and constancy, yet the tale of all the poor houses more resembles a series of heroic romances than an account of unrelieved drudgery.

The "Atlanta almshouse," really the Fulton County Almshouse, was open to all kinds of individuals. To have peeked inside was to have seen the chronically destitute, the sick, the mentally deranged, the temporarily jobless or homeless, and African-Americans as well as whites. Eventually, there was even a convict section.

The number of similar poor houses eventually exceeded 2,000 nationwide,[1] but Atlanta's was unique. Thirty years into its work, the city's leading newspaper could pronounce this almshouse "the finest institution of its kind in the South." The man who made it so was its director and resident physician, who strode colossus-like across three decades of poor house history. Most of the written material still available concerns him and the Poor House during his era. How to replace him when he should pass from the scene? When at last that happened, there were other heroes and determined workers who were equal to the task.

To "make the angels sing" however, poor houses had required a preparatory history of struggle. There was a process of refinement in the older Christian nations before the almshouse concept could achieve its ultimate usefulness. This is that story as well.

Newspaper sketches of Poor House
inmates and of the building

CHAPTER ONE

A POOR HOUSE INDEED!

"Blessed is he who considers the poor.
The Lord will deliver him in time of trouble."
- Psalm 41.1

The doctor drove his one-horse black buggy three and a half miles north along the rutted clay of the Piedmont Road. In three quarters of an hour he reached the spot where the road intersected the Peachtree Road, just a mile northeast of the little crossroads known as Buckhead. The rays of the late afternoon sun glinted through the trees as the doctor stood, tall and gangling, to stare at the infelicitous sight before him. There stood the jumble of miserable shacks which passed as Fulton County's almshouse. What a mess! A *poor* house to be sure!

The year was 1881, and Robert Hope had just been appointed director and resident physician of this institution. He had not yet assumed his responsibilities, but he was familiar with the almshouse. Often he had seen it, as he made wide-ranging house calls during brief service as a country doctor in the area. It was plain to him that massive renovation was needed, if the almshouse was to fulfill its purpose.

For now, the picture it presented was a poor one. The looks of the run-down institution for which he would be responsible surely made his shoulders sag. He crossed the road to make inspection, and confirm that the place was indeed miserable. Let him tell it:

> "It was then located on the Peachtree Road, and consisted of several two-room little shanties – about seven of them, I believe, in all. They were nothing but rude hovels, and the floors and walls were broken with large rents and fissures which exposed the inmates to the severity of storms, without sufficient cover or protection to guard against them."[2]

The Fulton County Grand Jury, at this time the body in charge of the almshouse, was the obvious culprit for the rundown condition.[3] The men of the grand jury ought to have been shame-faced. They met regularly only seven miles away, in downtown Atlanta. It would have taken small effort to keep abreast of the condition of the Poor House.

Grand Jury members were elected for two-year terms, divided into four half-year segments. Each April and September, or sometimes more often, members made report on the various county services under the authority of this or that jurist. On the basis of these reports, they made recommendations for praise, for redress of wrongs, or of measures to be taken for progress. These reports and recommendations were then taken to the dark-paneled, musty Fulton County Superior Court for confirmation and action. Shockingly, the almshouse had been a neglected stepchild.

After walking around and through the "little shanties," Robert got up on his buggy again, snapped the reins, and clucked his horse towards his Rock Spring home. His mind was full of pity for the poverty-stricken victims of almshouse neglect, and of anger against the faceless perpetrators.

The next morning, the youthful physician was up early, and was on the Piedmont Road again. This time he headed south, four miles to Atlanta. The grand jury was not in session, but Robert located three members of it, and got them together for a meeting of his own. He questioned them, and their answers held little surprise: there had been negligence by previous grand juries; hard times, too, had been suffered. There was no money following the late war of 1861-65, and some previous almshouse directors had given poor management.

The consensus of the three was to wash their hands of the problem, and toss the whole matter into the lap of the new director. "You have to do it," they said. "Nobody else can pick up the alms-house and carry it forward. It's the director's job."[4] By thus washing their hands, they appeared to be shirkers, but it was quite sensible counsel. Only the director could direct. But, for the moment, how to do what needed to be done was a mystery to Dr. Hope.

*   *   *   *   *

Now for the time being, abandon Robert Hope to ponder his problem. Go across the Atlantic Ocean to visit the almshouse scenes of origin. What was the background of the poor houses?

Care for the poor and helpless was an obligation deeply rooted in the Judeo-Christian ethic. When Mary of Bethany lavished an expensive perfumed ointment on Him, Christ's treasurer, Judas, protested that the cost of it could have been spent on the poor. The Bible's editorial comment on his protest is that Judas cared nothing for the poor, but that he was a thief, who wished to steal the money put into the disciples' money box, and did. In response, Jesus answered, "The poor you have with you always" (John 12.8). He was not advising against charity, however, but was simply arranging priorities. The corporeal presence on earth of the very Son of God should occasion unusual celebration.

Instructing the inquiring Rich Young Ruler of the way to his personal salvation, Jesus discerned that the man's wealth was his idol. Money was the roadblock preventing this seemingly earnest soul's acquisition of eternal life. Jesus therefore said, "Sell what you have, and give to the poor" (Matt 19.21).

Again, when Jesus opened His public ministry, He quoted Isaiah 61.1, applying it to Himself, when He announced in the synagogue that He had been anointed "to preach the gospel to the poor" (Luke 4.18).

In the so-called Sermon on the Plain He declared, "Blessed are you poor: for yours is the kingdom of God" (Luke 6.20).

In four more places in the Gospel of Luke (7.22; 14.13-21; 18.22; 19.8), charity towards the poor is commended.

In addition, Christ praised the poor widow, whose small gift was worth more spiritually than the larger gifts of the rich, because it was all that she had (Luke 21.2-3).

In all these teachings, the Lord was echoing what had been taught among God's people throughout the Old Testament. In the Book of Leviticus, and in a number of passages in other books of the Pentateuch, the Law of Moses had commanded or recorded provision for the poor. God saw that this instruction was repeated, especially in The Psalms and the Prophets.

It is evident that God intended for His holy people to reflect His own love and compassion towards all people. Goodness to the poor was emphasized because of sinful man's tendency to discount them, and all other people who are powerless.

*   *   *   *   *

Christians and Christian churches followed their Savior in compassion for all, including the poor and the weak. This appealing love was a key element in the rapid spread of the Faith.

As Christianity continued to grow and spread in the Roman Empire, it was influenced by some elements from outside the Faith. One of these was the philosophy of Platonism, which eventually provided the developing church with a Greek framework of thought. Platonism, brought into the service of the Bible, enabled the great creedal statements of the church's first five centuries to be built. This philosophy remained the lingua franca of the church's theologians until well into the Middle Ages, when the philosophy of Aristotle replaced it.[5]

Platonism was not an unmixed blessing. The pagans who adopted it used the Platonic theory to downplay the importance of the physical creation, including the human body. Platonism guided the Manichaean religion and other Gnostic religions from the East, resulting either in sexual license or in asceticism. The body could either be given free rein, or be neglected, since only the spirit was important. It was a mistaken and disastrous route to spirituality.[6]

Yet many Christians, also, who wanted to be serious and undisturbed in their relationship to Christ, fell into asceticism, under the spell of Platonic thought. They moved out to lonely places, as individuals, away from corrupt civilization, both to pray, and to mortify the flesh. They were mystics, ascetics, and hermits.[7]

Hidden in this movement was God's blessing for the poor. In Egypt, Anthony, called, "Saint Anthony," became a hermit at fifteen, and reputedly lived so for eighty-five more years, until 350 A.D. Early in the 300's, he entertained brothers who came to him seeking instruction, and on this scanty evidence, he is credited with establishing the first monastery.[8] No longer content to be hermits, these earnest men would live and worship together.

Once established, it was the monastic system which eventually provided an effective mechanism for the relief of the poor. By the time it did, the Christian community was already considering itself divided into clergy (the spiritual people), and the laity (the carnal, or common, people). The grace of compassionate ministry to the poor was still practiced in the form of individual Christians' alms, but more substantial help began to be institutionalized in the monasteries.

After its Fourth Century elevation by the Emperor Constantine, first to toleration, then to official state religion of the Empire, Christianity was granted one hundred years of relative peace. After this time, the German barbarian nations flowed across the Rhine and Danube, and over the next half-century dismantled the Empire piece by piece.

Mostly because of missionary efforts of the Eastern Roman Empire, the Visigoths, the Ostrogoths, and the Vandals had been brought into at least a superficial, heretical Christian faith. Even this smattering of Christianity meant that their invasions and settlements of Western Roman territory turned out to be mild compared to the actions of the Vikings later.[9]

After the German nations conquered the Empire, the Gospel conquered the Germans, from 400 to 800 A.D. Once this happened, the High Middle Ages saw the monasteries' almsgiving reach its greatest development.

The incursions of the pagan Vikings of Scandinavia were very different from those of the Germans. Unlike the Germans, the Vikings had not been touched by Christianity. Their ships' sails began appearing off the coasts of France, Britain, and Ireland. Whenever they did, raids or full-scale invasions would follow. These huge, fierce, fair-haired men were filled with the Devil's blood-lust. Their especial delight was to leap over the sides of their ships, slosh through the shallow salt water, run up the beach in their scores and hundreds, and massacre all the inhabitants of a monastery.

It was a nightmare era. Howbeit, the gospel's power conquered even these enemies, from 800 to 1200 A.D., and transformed them into the Christian kingdoms of Denmark, Sweden, and Norway.[10] Their monasteries were active in the care of the poor, along with those in the rest of Europe, notably of France, but also of England.

$$* \quad * \quad * \quad * \quad *$$

In England the development of almshouses got mixed up with politics. It is a fascinating drama. One could wish, focusing on the plight of the poor, that it were altogether the story of sincere men laboring to bring about good in their country. But, in truth, it may be partly a classic example of the work of a personal malevolence in the world, scheming behind the scenes to *prevent* good.

The account begins as a handsome young king sits in earnest conversation with the dean from Oxford University. Henry the Eighth and John Colet were discussing the ideas that had been advanced by Colet in his lectures and writings.[11] Colet, like Sir Thomas More, was a disciple of the New Learning, based on the thinking of the Italian Renaissance, very popular in the England of the 1500's.

Both Colet and More strongly advocated moral reform within the English nation and church. The latter, in his half-jesting "Utopia," had criticized the overwhelming authority of the king, and the notion that "the king can do no wrong." Ultimately, he sealed his words with his blood on Tower Hill.

The interview between King Henry and Colet went on and on. Colet admitted his denunciations of the luxuries and low moral state of the clergy. He even confessed that some of his remarks about kings had not been very nice. As they talked, however, Henry broke with his precedent, deciding that he liked what he was hearing. Colet might be used! The Bishop of London had charged Colet with heresy, and had denounced him to the king. But Henry now told Colet, "Go boldly on." He told his intimates afterwards, "Let every man have his own doctor, but this man is the doctor for me!"[12]

Henry had great natural gifts: a keen mind, a physical frame taller and larger than anyone else's, superb ability as a horseman, huntsman, jouster, and wrestler. All of this was undermined by his boundless selfishness. Even in these early days of his monarchy, his protection of Colet was motivated only by the opportunity to use the dean to weaken the bishops, who were his rivals for power.

The almsgiving monastic orders of the land had already passed their zenith, by the time that Henry was reaching his. The monks still had a program of caring for the poor, but the former fire and fervor were gone. They were now little more than wealthy landowners, often quite self-indulgent ones. Moreover, since they were necessarily allied with the bishops, their antagonists were both Colet's New Learning and King Henry's monarchy.

Henry had neither zeal to save the monasteries from themselves, nor any spiritual power to do it. "What the king wants from the abbeys is not goodness but gold," it was whispered.

Despite the corruption within the abbeys, the nation at large did not yet desire the utter destruction of the monastic system. As the rain poured outside, Parliament met behind grey stone walls, and debated long and bitterly. One speaker insisted, "Only a third of the houses in the land are fairly and decently conducted!" But another reported, "In the north of the realm, where some of the greatest abbeys are located, the brothers are on good terms with the country gentry, and school their children."[13]

Parliament finally struck a compromise. An Act was passed which provided that all religious houses whose annual income fell below 200 pounds should be suppressed. Thus, at a single stroke, 400 of England's one thousand abbeys were dissolved, and their revenues given to the Crown.[14] Alms to the poor were lessened, and the government's takeover of the task of almsgiving was not far off.

Indeed, in 1538, just two years later, Parliament completed the job, wiping out the remaining 600 abbeys.

Henry's other exploits are more or less well known: divorce of Catherine of Aragon, beheadings of two other wives, loss of another in childbirth, and divorce of another two; scheme to claim rulership of France; excommunication by the pope; retaliation by having Parliament enact the Act of Supremacy (1534); and finally, forcing his enemies, the bishops, to acknowledge him "the only supreme head of the Church of England."[15] With all of his activity, he is not known ever to have had a serious intent to extend help to the poor.

This complex man hanged and beheaded Catholic political traitors who were loyal to the pope. Yet, with some frequency, he also burned Protestants at the stake. He claimed, to the end of his life, to be a devout Catholic.

CHAPTER TWO

FROM THE VIRGIN QUEEN TO THE WIDOW AT WINDSOR

"The time is out of joint; O cursed spite,
That ever I was born to set it right!"
Hamlet - William Shakespeare

After Henry's death, the stage was set for gains to be made in benefits for the poor and suffering. England was prosperous and able, but, although experience can be a great teacher, men have to be willing to learn. The nation had not learned enough about relief of poverty. So the poor and needy were, as always, the pawns of politics.

It must be kept in mind that the Christian religion, of one stripe or another, was the most important factor in the running of the nation in the 1500's. Religion, ever present in the human heart in affirmation or denial, was magnified in day-to-day matters at this time, because all the nations of Europe had union of church and state.

Two of Henry's children enjoyed brief reigns before Elizabeth I ascended the throne. With her coronation, the land was not only well-to-do, but was blooming with creativity. Marlowe wrote his plays, and Shakespeare built on them; Sir Francis Bacon spun his philosophies, and suddenly England was "a nest of singing birds."[16] The political climate, too, began to change. The Protestant Reformation had come to England – not Henry's personal, selfish rebellion, but the genuine Reformed truths. Eventually, this would help the cause of almshouses; initially, it hindered them.

The influx of religious refugees from the Continent assisted the new doctrines to catch on.[17] Persecuted in France, the Spanish Netherlands, and elsewhere, these people moved in large numbers into the towns and villages of the island, and taught their faith to others.

Englishmen returning from studies on the Continent were also importers of Calvinism.

Cambridge University became an early supporter of Puritanism and its Calvinist theology. Oxford at first claimed staunch adherence to Rome, but then flip-flopped, and became a hotbed of Calvinism.[18]

Even before Elizabeth got to the throne, Protestantism was replacing Henry VIII's religion. The king's only son, Edward VI, became king at age 10, and died at sixteen. The Lord Protectors who ruled for him favored Protestantism, and re-fashioned the church in that direction in many ways. Mary I, daughter of Henry and Catherine of Aragon, repealed those laws, seeking to restore Catholicism. Her laws were in turn repealed by her half-sister, the red-haired Elizabeth, who became one of England's greatest monarchs.

As the new queen, Elizabeth knew her political position was fragile. She wanted to, almost *had* to, steer a middle course for the Church. By this strategy, she hoped to please as many of her subjects as possible, in order to build her power. She was willing to run the risk that *half-pleased* constituents might turn *displeased*.

Elizabeth was under attack by the pope, who regarded England as his most dangerous foe among the northern European Protestant nations. On the other hand, Elizabeth looked on the Calvinists as her most hateful enemies within the English realm. Thus, in Elizabeth's reign, and with her blessing, the English church took on very much the hybrid, Protestant-Catholic appearance that it has today. At the same time, the political and religious climate forced patience on the queen. For years she was denied the blander, liturgical, Arminian church she desired.

It happened in this way. The Catholics were weak, and Elizabeth kept them down mercilessly. At the other end of the spectrum, she was helpless to stem the steady advance of the Calvinistic Puritans within the Church of England.

The problem for Elizabeth was that the bulk of the country gentlemen, the wealthy traders, and three-quarters of the general population, were now Puritan sympathizers. If she were to continue to prevent a Catholic resurgence, she would have to go along with Puritanism to some extent. Her compromise involved the need to replace the Marian bishops with staunch Protestants. But a zealous Protestant was almost inevitably a Calvinist. The queen was forced to fill the English bishoprics, quietly and steadily, with men whose creed in almost every case was Calvinist.[19]

Initially, most of the lower clergy were left undisturbed, but as the older parsons died out their places, too, were in most cases filled by Puritan successors.

With a developing Calvinist Church of England had come the final emptying of the monasteries in 1538, and that brought about the unintended finish of church-controlled alms for the poor. The English church swung back and forth between Rome and Geneva for a hundred years. Four times the images were taken out of the churches, and four times they were brought back in. During this period, under alternating threats and approval of the royalty, Calvinistic Pilgrims and Puritans emigrated to New England, while the Anglicans, at that time officially Calvinist, came to Virginia.

Finally, Parliament decided to allow denominations other than the established church to exist in England. By this time, the now state-operated poor houses had been shaped by the English "Poor Laws."

*   *   *   *   *

The Poor Laws became necessary since the Church of England was no longer equal to the task of caring for the indigents. The Tudor statesmen took on the job of relieving the poor in England. The numbers of the vagrants and the "idle and disorderly" had increased, before and during the reigns of Henry and Elizabeth,[20] because of social and economic changes of the late 1400's and throughout the

1500's. Parliament now scrambled to pass measures to deal with the bad situation.

In 1601, the forty-third year of Elizabeth's reign, Parliament codified the various laws that had been enacted. This measure was called, "The Act For the Relief of the Poor."[21]

By this Act, the government used the many parishes of the church only as convenient units to accomplish its work. Each parish was ordered to collect "rates," as the local taxes were called, which were gathered to relieve the poor.

The rates were put to use in several ways. One of them was the apprenticeship of poor children. If poor parents could not support their children, the Crown's agents caused the children to be put out to work for someone else as apprentices. The parish rates supported them while they learned their trade. Child labor laws? Unheard of.

The rates also subsidized the able-bodied adult paupers. These men were compelled to work, but without subsidies they could not make enough money to live. This was because the government previously had fixed the wages of farm laborers and artisans, and fixed them very low. To have raised wages would have discomfited the upper and middle class employers. So the great majority of the nation, the working lower classes, were getting the short end of the stick. In Seventeenth Century England, it seemed quite natural and right, and, in the case of the paupers, it was thought more than generous.

The rates were used as well to assist those persons who were unable to work because of age, sickness, injury, or war wounds.[22]

Though flawed, this system would have been absolutely impossible in, say, Hindu India. There, the underclass could expect no help at all, and, indeed, received only severe and daily despite. In Christian England, even an impersonal government's care for the poor was not only possible, but was highly organized.

Observant Englishmen soon began to protest that the system was far from ideal. The able-bodied paupers were often under the thumb of harsh and imperious magistrates. These insensitive men, like the worst caricature of prison guards, delighted in reminding their charges of their lowly status, and their misery, and did so pitilessly. Moreover, the laborers could not leave the land that they worked.

They were therefore once again back to the position of serfs, but lower still. Unlike the serfs, they had no rights to the land on which they labored.[23]

This relief Act, later called "The Old Poor Law," nevertheless worked fairly well for a generation, but problems with it grew with the English Civil War. The problems only increased after Cromwell died in 1658.

Cromwell's successor was weak, and London was only too glad to welcome Charles II from France in 1662. This turnaround was called, "the Restoration." The Puritan short-haired "Roundheads" were out, and the "Cavaliers," with their luxurious, flowing locks, were in. No more Puritan bleakness! London was wide open. Anti-Puritan looseness was exaggerated, and flaunted. The theaters reopened, with new touches such as footlights, curtains, painted scenery, and women on stage for the first time.

The dramatists now delighted London audiences with comedies that poked fun at Puritan virtues. Poet John Dryden, turning his back on his Puritan background, hailed the new regime, writing that 1666 was "annus mirabilis":

"Methinks already, from this chymic flame, I see a city of more precious mold."

But Roundhead sympathizer, John Milton, a former government secretary, now blind, simply retreated to his home in London. There he finished "Paradise Lost."

Amid all the gaiety, care for the paupers again lost ground. A "law of settlement" was passed which sent poor transients back to the parishes whence they had come. What a windfall for cheaters! Like politicos elected by dead men's votes, some parish officials cooked the books by counting removed paupers as if they were still on their payrolls, and simply pocketed the money.[24]

This disgrace began around 1670, and was going on throughout the last three decades of the century. With the arrival of the new century, reform was attempted again. A kaleidoscope of measures spanned the next hundred years. There were workhouses, originally milder than the later horrors of Dickens' *Oliver Twist*. There were contractors who got the able-bodied poor from the government, and rented them out as workers. Then the system was modified to cut out the contractors as middlemen.

In England at large, the so-called "Classical Age" was developing, 1740-1780. Art, elegance, the humanistic Enlightenment, and religious tolerance, were keynotes of the times. The pinched-faced paupers languished in their grime, but for the rest, wealth and leisure were more widely shared than ever. In towns and in the open countryside commoners built comfortable, beautiful Queen Anne and Georgian homes. They were furnished with the designs of Chippendale, Sheraton, and the Adam brothers. English handi-craftsmen provided their exquisite china, glass, and silver plate.[25]

Men were moving about in bright-colored silk coats, waistcoats, and breeches. Women wore hooped skirts and high pompadours. Reynolds, Gainsborough, and Romney painted the fashionable uppercrust. Hogarth was less exclusive; in his paintings many of the common people appeared.

Alexander Pope's genius and bitter satire had been combined in his no-regrets farewell to London:

"Dear, droll, distracting town, farewell! Thy fools no more I'll tease:"[26]

But Samuel Johnson's was the sanguine spirit of the age:

"The happiness of London is not to be conceived but by those who have been in it. I will venture to say, there is more learning and science within the circumference of ten miles from where we now sit, than in all the rest of the kingdom."[27]

However, if one were looking only for worldly glory, "all the rest of the kingdom" was a fair measure of greatness also. The happy race of men on their island were undisturbed by their frequent wars, since the professional armies that fought them were small, and the wars were fought elsewhere.

Success was not unbroken. After the German kings, the Hanoverian George's I and II, had only played at being king, George III came on strong. He was determined to be the ruler, and got rid of Prime Minister William Pitt, to prove it. This was perhaps the most blundering of George's mistakes. Pitt was the Seven Years' War leader, who had vastly extended Britain's empire by overseeing the discomfiture of the French in Europe, America, India, Africa, and on the high seas. In place of this wizard, Britain got only the posturing king.

However, George's loss of the American colonies in the Revolutionary War proved not to be a great disaster for Great Britain. There was an impact to be sure, on the treasury and on trade, but the nation had become so strong that it shook it off the hurt.

Britannia still ruled the waves. With almost a thousand ships in the Royal Navy, her sailors and merchants built a second British Empire mightier than the first. Weak on land in comparison to Napoleon Bonaparte's legions, the British were blessed with those twenty-two miles of Channel that separated them from the awesomely powerful French army. The nemesis of the Napoleonic Empire remained Great Britain.[28] Even so, English mums and nannies stilled their little ones with the warning, "Mind you behave, or old Boney will get you."

The cause of England's prosperity and shared wealth, and of its growing democracy and tolerance, was a spiritual leaven. The government cared little for reform, but individuals throughout the realm did care. They began to be more and more concerned for the wretchedness of the poor. The concern originated, not in some vacuum, but in the Wesleyan Revival. God had once again stepped in, to help the helpless.

* * * * *

John Wesley was a godly man, a fine preacher, and an excellent organizer. His and George Whitfield's Methodist movement, based on the infusion of Pietism, swept Britain, and leaped the ocean to America. The movement's success was won despite the public's persecution and vilification endured both by Arminian Wesley and Calvinist Whitfield.

William Wilberforce was converted while on a trip to France in 1787. When he returned to England, he was convinced he should seek holy orders, but the Calvinistic Pietist John Newton talked him out of it. "Get into the House of Commons," he said, "and serve your Lord there."[29]

Only three days before his death, 88-year-old John Wesley himself added his own advice that Wilberforce should fight to rid the nation of the slave trade, and of slavery itself, "that execrable villainy which is the scandal of religion, of England, and of human nature."[30]

Wilberforce took the words of his counselors to heart. In Parliament, he led the battle to end slavery, and after twenty years of struggle, he finally succeeded in passing his zeal to the younger MP's. Voters for his side were steadily gained in Parliament. The bill to abolish slave trading was voted in 1807, by 283 to 16. It was a notch up for the oppressed.

Twenty-six years later, a month after Wilberforce died, Parliament ordered the release and permanent freedom of 700,000 slaves throughout the British Empire. Wisely authorized was an indemnity, adequate for the era, of 20 million pounds, to be paid to the former slave owners. Consequently, the Empire avoided any rebellion that might have contested the emancipation, as later wracked North America.

Few victories for righteousness have been so resoundingly won as this one in Britain. And it was won in the Name of Him who came to free the slaves.

If the paupers in England still languished under a government that seemed to care more for slaves abroad than it did for them, deliverance was at hand. The same year that the slaves were freed, Parliament authorized the "New Poor Law."

In the 1700's varied attempts at reform had bounced back and forth. The one measure which had offered poor people a real break, had been one which made no fiscal sense for the government at all. It had been ordered that the paupers be paid almost unconditional doles! It was "welfare without limits," and quickly proved so expensive that it fell of its own weight. This triggered the complete reorganization of the parish system.

The new system, instituted by the "Poor Law Amendment Act," of 1834, was nicknamed, the "New Poor Law." The formerly independent church parishes were grouped into Unions with elected boards of guardians, and all under the central authority of the Crown, to enforce uniformity.

The New Poor Law's cardinal principle was the subsidizing only of able-bodied workers and their dependents. Costs quickly went down, and King William's accounting gnomes were happy. The same could not be said for the diseased and lice-ridden folk who were simply abandoned to the grim prospect of begging or starving.

But better things were on the way. Charles Dickens' novel, *Oliver Twist*, with its nightmarish elements, appeared in 1838, just four years after the passage of the New Poor Law, and a year after Victoria ascended the throne. The Victorian Age would see the zenith of Britain's power, and Dickens' very alarm was only effective as the fruit of the nation's softening, more compassionate society.

No doubt both the nation and its system of support for the paupers were badly flawed.

With the Twentieth Century's arrival, the Victorian Age soon began to be thought of as a time of crassness towards the poverty-stricken. One reason for this was the image created by the suspension of what had been called, "outdoor relief." All the poor laborers, men and women, were confined to unhealthy workhouses, where they could be more carefully superintended.[31] These workhouses were feared more than prison.

A general outcry caused the workhouses to be improved. They continued, nevertheless, to be so bad that a public investigation was made by a royal commission as late as 1905-1909.[32]

English poverty relief then continued to be adjusted and readjusted. Already, however, the Old Poor Law of England had been, for a long time, the basis for the poor laws in the several states of the United States of America.

CHAPTER THREE

POOR HOUSES IN AMERICA

"The three problems of the age – the degradation of man by
poverty, the ruin of woman by starvation, and the dwarfing
of childhood by physical and spiritual night."
                                                    - *Les Miserables*
                                              Victor Hugo, from its Preface

It was onto Plymouth Rock, says tradition, that the Pilgrims
stepped in 1620. They were Calvinist Separatists, rebels against
the established church in England. On their heels in 1630 came
other Calvinists, the Puritans, to the same New England area. The
Puritans, scrupling against the semi-Romish worship of the Church
of England, had nevertheless remained within that body.

The Puritans continued to come in their thousands, and the
few hundred Pilgrims were soon (1630) absorbed into their ranks.
Amalgamation with the outnumbered Pilgrims might have been
expected to turn Separatists into Puritans. Curiously, it had the
opposite effect of turning the American Puritans into Pilgrim-type
Separatists from the Church of England. This successful separation
was of course mightily assisted by the English king's inability to get
at them across the wide Atlantic Ocean.

With their "Protestant Work Ethic," the second and third generations of Puritans built their prosperity, but suffered spiritually. The
first Puritans had come to America to find a safe place to practice

their Biblical, no-nonsense worship of God. Now many had ceased to attend church. God was little needed by people who were apparently getting along quite well without Him.

Another human wave, also, was hitting the shores of New England. These newcomers had little interest in the church. What they wanted was material wealth, and Massachusetts Bay Colony was the base from which to obtain it. They came, and the character of the general population changed. John Winthrop, only four decades after the Plymouth Rock landing, was asking, "Where did all these ungodly men come from?"[33] He was seeing the region's hallmark change from Puritan faith to Yankee self-reliance.

There began to be liberalizing adjustments of the rules governing admission to the local church, especially in the "Half-Way Covenant." It was an effort to preserve Puritan numerical dominance in New England. But these polity changes were mere stopgaps. Eight decades later, and another eight decades after that, the celebrated First, and Second Great Awakenings did a deeper, a truly spiritual work. Society at large was blessed. With the rapid population growth, however, two persistent ogres, poverty and vagrancy, still haunted the scene.

The first almshouse in America was established in Massachusetts in 1660. This colony and others were slow to establish more until 1700. Once the almshouses caught on, they were considered to be the best method of relieving poverty. The colonists were in correspondence with England, and knew something of the ups and downs that had been the fate of the various English experiments.

The almshouses usually handled all manner of cases. Sick people, including those who were extremely ill, were usually there in great numbers. But so were the merely "infirm," the aged, the insane, children, the feeble-minded, and vagrants.

All of the colonies later became states. The almshouses, in those states which had them, were in the charge of some unit of government. Legislation tended to be lenient, and it was left to the appointed authorities in charge to decide whether the poor houses should be enlarged or improved.

The New England states had "selectmen" of townships, who cared for the poor. Later, as populations continued to increase, the job was given to special "Poor Relief" officials appointed by the townships or the cities.

* * * * *

Poor houses came into vogue somewhat later in the largely agrarian South. A proper grasp of the practical operation of a poor house may be gained by considering the one which, in time, became the best. That one was established in Atlanta, Georgia. Much material on its day-to-day operation is extant, and its story is inspiring.

In the southern states, the county was the governing unit. Relief of the poor, therefore, was nearly always managed on a county basis. Whatever governing board the county happened to have elected or appointed, was the administrative authority. In Fulton County, Georgia, the county in which Atlanta was located, the almshouse served the city, but was not under its authority. Instead, the responsibility belonged to the Fulton County Grand Jury.

Under the systems at work in many states, an almshouse had great autonomy. In Atlanta, the system did not allow this. At the very outset, the Grand Jury declared that it would exercise complete control over the institution. An annual report from the almshouse director would be required, with review by the Grand Jury following.

In 1837, the railroad stake was driven which marked the terminal point of a projected railroad. This railroad gave birth to Atlanta, originally called, simply, "Terminus." Only twenty years later, the need for an almshouse began to be felt.

The town grew in those first two decades to a population of almost 7,000. Most of the citizens were hard-working, and some were already quite prosperous. In the hobo havens in green wooded areas near the city, however, existed a dark underside. Seamy-faced men dressed in rags boiled their soup over little fires whose grey ashes betrayed to the vigilant sheriff the tramps' sometime presence in the vicinity.

Atlanta from the beginning was peopled both by white people and African-Americans, but was overwhelmingly white. Perhaps their sheer numbers caused the white paupers to be noticed. The few blacks were house slaves who were cared for, or freedmen, or poor people who were unnoticed because blacks were *expected* to be poor. Poverty of course affected both races. Notwithstanding, the "poor" of Atlanta, just now, were mostly the thin, pinched and pale Caucasian wraiths who lived in the out-of-the-way gullies, in cracker box hovels. They were men, women, and children, who peered out of the shadows of the railroad trestles beneath which they slept. Their dirty countenances contrasted with the well-scrubbed appearance of mainstream white Atlantans who glanced at them, shuddered, and hurried their carriage horses forward to work or church.

Businessmen of the fledgling city pressured the Fulton County Grand Jury to make a statement. It did so in the second week of its April, 1857 term:

> "- - the subject of the poor in our county is one that demands consideration and action."[34]

These words were little more than an acknowledgement, but following them, the Grand Jury added more – a glimmer of the extraordinary stature that an Atlanta almshouse might attain:

> "The central position of the county, together with the usual facilities of access from every direction has tended, and continually tends, to concentrate many who are unable to provide for their own support - -."[35]

The Grand Jury's statement held the germ of a grand idea, first draft blueprint for an institution to serve, not just Atlanta, but all of Georgia. Not only was the location right for it, but also the governmental structure posed no obstacle. In some states, the city/county relationship was delicate and complicated, but not in antebellum Atlanta. From the first, Fulton County's almshouse was to be the *Atlanta* almshouse as well.

Not much imagination was required, either, to envision an almshouse. As the oldest public welfare institution in America, the almshouses were written into many state constitutions, particularly those of New England. What was visionary in the report was the "thinking big."

More than pure benevolence was involved in the Grand Jury's concern for the poor.

Vagrants made the solid citizens nervous. The Grand Jury almost, but not quite, voiced the fear and the nuisance:

"- - Many, who though able to work, are far from willing, so long as they can drag out a miserable existence upon the charities of the public."[36]

Charities, yes, but thieveries and burglaries were what mostly haunted the thoughts of shopkeepers with their goods at risk.

The Grand Jury's report continued with a portrait that wrenches the heart even yet: children of the unfortunate poor running the streets without control or restraint. This situation was a harbinger of the much larger postwar orphan problem that was only eight years away. But the pre-war problem seemed bad enough. Albeit Atlanta was only a tiny town in 1857, a certain segment of the Victorian culture expressed its horror at the way things were. A town should be a moral community of people!

Of the street waifs of Atlanta the Grand Jury opined that they were the makings of an abundant future crop of candidates for the jails, penitentiaries, and gallows[37] Conclusion: there should be a county poor house.

The men of the Grand Jury knew that the ball was now in their own court for action. If anything were to be done this year, they were the men to do it, either now, or in the October term. Nevertheless, they did nothing in either term, other than make the statement. At least the need had been marked.

If the Grand Jury was hesitant to move, the leaders in Atlanta at once embraced its ideas. Two factors, as well, gave impetus to the poor house: a good financial year, and the election of Governor Joe Brown.

CHAPTER FOUR

JOE BROWN, MONEY, AND WAR

"Cincinnatus was ploughing his four jugera of land
upon the Vaticanian Hill – the same that are still known
as the Quintian Meadows, - when the messenger brought
him the dictatorship, finding him, the tradition says,
stripped to the work."

Natural History, Book XVIII
Pliny the Elder

Sixty days after the Grand Jury had revealed that an almshouse
was on its wish-list, Joseph Emerson Brown, of the little town
of Canton, Georgia, received the Democratic Party's nomination for
governor.[38] Amazingly, Judge Brown, thirty-six years old, was not
even present at the convention which nominated him. Cincinnatus-
like, he had spent all of that hot June afternoon in his field on Town
Creek near Canton.. He and his field hands were cutting wheat.

Brown went home at sundown, and was shaving and making
ready to wash for supper, when a horse galloped into his yard, bearing
a gentleman whom he knew. The visitor was Colonel Samuel Weil, a
Canton attorney, and he was bursting with excitement: "Judge, guess
who has been nominated for governor, down at Milledgeville?" He
waited for an answer. Brown played the game, and made an honest
guess: "I think it must be John E. Ward." "No," said Weil, "the
nominee is Joseph E. Brown, of Cherokee County!"

The convention, down in the state capital in Middle Georgia, had been one of the hardest fought in Georgia history. Colonel Weil had been in Marietta when the telegram came through announcing Brown's nomination. Losing not a moment, he had ridden hell-for-leather twenty miles north to break the news.

A better advocate for an almshouse could hardly have been chosen. In the election which followed, Brown was elected over thirty-four year old Benjamin Harvey Hill, the candidate of the Know Nothing Party. Georgia's rich and powerful were unhappy that power had slipped from their grasp, and Brown soon proved that it had. In office, he became "the Andrew Jackson of Georgia," and the poor white people caught a break. They always identified with this man who was so obviously one of them.

Joe Brown had grown up in a family that never had the service of slaves. Even so, as a Georgia legislator, and governor, he became a staunch supporter of slavery, and stood firmly for the rights of the South. Born in Pickens County, South Carolina, he had moved to the Georgia mountain county of Union, and later to Canton. He always did hard manual labor, growing up, for he was an important part of the family's work force. A chief duty for Joe was to plow behind oxen.

Union County was remote from cultural centers, and education also was sketchy. Nonetheless, at age nineteen, with only the barest learning, Brown set out for Dr. Waddell's school in South Carolina, driving a team of oxen. The oxen were then given to the school in part payment for Brown's tuition and board.

The future statesman proved to be an outstanding student, and was afterwards able to borrow money to study law in Connecticut, at Yale College. Back again in Georgia, he began law practice in 1846, and in 1849-50 represented his district in the state legislature.

Brown's years in the legislature came just at America's beginning of sorrows. The old thorn of slavery was festering as never before. Politicians North and South were starting their decade-long tilt at name-calling, which emotionally prepared both sections for the vast blood-letting of 1861-65. Possibly Brown's involvement in that slanging match as a legislator worked to crystallize his pro-slavery attitude. For whatever reason, Brown followed the path of most Southern politicians of the era, never including African emancipation in his list of reforms favoring the poor. All the same, like "Old Hickory," he was a man in touch with the common folk, who loved him. At the outset, the aristocrats hated him, but the Civil War caused them to rally behind him.[39]

Joe Brown, after his 1857 election, retained the governor's chair until 1865, leading Georgia right through the war years of invasion, death, and destruction. The Atlanta almshouse, variously called, "Poor House," "Poor Farm," "County Farm," and "County Home," had Governor Brown's strong approval. The forward march of the almshouse towards opening day, owed a lot, in 1857 and 1858, to the governor's advocacy.

$$* \quad * \quad * \quad * \quad *$$

Besides the election of a sympathetic governor, the almshouse idea profited by the financial year enjoyed in Atlanta, and in Georgia generally, in 1857. The Panic of 1857 was a landmark in U.S. financial history, but it affected only the northern, not the southern states. In Atlanta, an almshouse could be afforded.

The Panic began to be set up when gold was discovered in California in 1849. This led to much speculation, overcapitalization, and over-building of railroads, in the next eight years. The Ohio Life and Trust Company failed on August 24, of the fateful year, and the panic spread. Less than two months later, on October 14, banks in general suspended specie (minted coin) payments of gold and silver.

The South was virtually untouched by the Panic of 1857. The cotton crop was exceptionally large. The price of cotton was high, because England and France were buying tremendous amounts of it. Not one Atlanta business failed, the banks did not have to suspend specie payments, and Atlanta merchants owed less than their counterparts in the North.[40]

All of this increased Southern confidence. The Panic was a Yankee thing; need for cotton would always keep the Europeans on the side of the South. "If the Yankees press us into secession, their mills will lose our cotton altogether." The Yankees had better mind their manners!

Meanwhile, the Fulton County Grand Jury was busily defining what the almshouse would be: It ought to have more than a merely adequate amount of land around the living quarters, to give the inmates productive outdoor work to do. The almshouse would have the high moral purpose of helping people in need; on the other hand, that should never preclude its being self-supporting. Labor would be put in by the able-bodied inmates to raise crops. By that method the place would be sustained.

Progress on the Atlanta almshouse was deliberate. Not until over two years had passed was a cluster of wooden structures erected. These were placed a mile and a half beyond the western limits of the little city. They were built on the location of the present grey granite main gatehouse of Westview Cemetery. Soon, in 1861, the Grand jury would be commending the director, Mr. James M. Cook, for his good work. But first came the fateful year 1860.

*   *   *   *   *

Eighteen-sixty! What a year! Year of tumult and shouting, year of dire portents. If Abraham Lincoln were elected president, some Southern states were sure to secede from the Union. The Abolitionists were very strident. Never mind that Lincoln's own strategy had been quite moderate, despite his stated belief the nation must be all slave-holding or all free. He was "the Abolitionists' man," and the Southerners had had enough. Vitriol had been spewed at them for ten years, by the "self-righteous Northern moralizers, and religious zealots," so ran their argument. The abolition of slavery issue had been brought to the boiling point.

Southern "fire eaters" replied to the Abolitionists with injured self-defense, and countercharges. If these generally had not quite the Yankees' sharpness of insult, their sting lay in the very real threat: "If these abusive attacks, and the menace of changing the South do not cease, we will secede."

The issue was complex, as war issues often are. Complications besides slavery included Lincoln's run for office as the "high tariff" candidate. Charging foreigners the high tariffs meant that their goods would cost U.S. consumers much more. In simple terms, a pair of shoes or trousers made in Boston would cost Southerners aplenty, but not as much as the artificially inflated goods from London! The high duties would keep dollars in the U.S., but would punish the English sellers and Southern buyers. Since the goods in question included all sorts of tools, vehicles, clothing, and horse-drawn machinery, a multitude of Southern small farmers would be ruined. That fear haunted the South, almost as much as did Abolitionism. Moreover, the Southerners long had complained that not enough was being paid for Southern raw materials that went into the Northern factories.

All of these factors added up to a Southern belief that the South was being plundered by the "imperial North."[41] The way to freedom from this economic oppression was secession.

The North, too, claimed its grievances. Not only did the pure humanitarianism of the abolitionists, but also economic self-interest, motivate many Northerners. Their charge was that every other interest in America was being sacrificed to accommodate slavery, as long as it existed.

The South insisted that continued slavery was necessary, to preserve the peace and balance afforded by its social organization. To protect the institution, it hid behind the "local autonomy," embodied in guaranteed States' Rights. The Northern abolitionists continued to attack viciously, yet always from the high moral ground that slavery was wrong, wrong, wrong.

Exasperated by insult, and goaded by fear, the South wound up defending a terrible institution, though eighty percent of whites did not own so much as a single slave. Only five percent owned one of the large plantations, where most slaves were held. Moreover, despite postwar justifications of the conflict from both sides, slavery probably was an institution in its death throes. Patience, however, was not in anyone's vocabulary at this time.

Lincoln was elected, and one after another the states of the Deep South, then those of the Middle South, tumbled into secession. The whole series of events was set into motion that would bring war to the Atlanta area. Battle here would result in the physical destruction of the first Poor House, only four years after it had been built.

*   *   *   *   *

The fearsome invasion was still four years in the future. In 1860, in spite of all the national uproar, the Poor House plans were not allowed to lag. They were completed, the dwellings were built, and the Fulton County Almshouse had its grand opening. The area where it stood was one of rural woods and fields, with a few scattered farms. Later, as Atlanta expanded, the territory between the city and the location of the original almshouse was developed into the West End residential and business section. By that time, the original almshouse structure had been a victim of the Civil War, and the institution had been established elsewhere.

One of the buildings of the original Poor House was utilized as office space, and the others were the homes of the inmates. The doors of the facility were always open to both black and white, although within it, the races were kept segregated.

For many indigents, of course, the Poor House was their last home. In addition, it was the nearest thing to an entitlement program in a society which as yet had no Public Welfare or Social Security.

Many unfortunates went to the Poor House when it was impossible to do better. Too old or sick to support themselves, and without a supporting family, they needed a poor house desperately. On the other hand, there were people who were only temporarily in great need, and whose stay at the Poor House was not going to be of long duration. To them, the Poor House was only a shelter, much like the shelters provided in Atlanta today for the homeless, in severe weather. The Poor House kept off the rain and kept out the cold.

CHAPTER FIVE

THE POOR HOUSE DESTROYED

Heckler: "Before the war, you said we could whip the
Yankees with cornstalks!"
Toombs: "Yes, and we could have, too – but they wouldn't
fight that way!"

> - General Robert Toombs, late
> 1860's, during a speech on the
> square in Marietta, Georgia.

In 1864, the four-year-old Fulton County Poor House stood
exposed in the middle of an open field, in what would become the
West End section of Atlanta. By July of that year, all of its inmates
had been refugeed away. Sherman was coming. The almshouse
would be in harm's way.

William T. Sherman, general commanding, had an army group
of three Federal armies maneuvering and fighting in North Georgia,
with Atlanta their goal. Sherman, by calculation or happenstance,
was certainly the right choice to lead the invaders. As a first lieutenant in the U.S. Army, he had visited this very area at age twenty-
three, in the year 1844.[42]

On January 21 of that year, the tall, red-haired lieutenant received
an order to leave Charleston, South Carolina, and report to Marietta,
Georgia. He was unable to leave until February 14. When he finally
did, he wisely took the train. The train made good time, passing

43

through Augusta, and on to Madison, Georgia, where the rail line ended.

Lieutenant Sherman caught a horse-drawn mail coach and continued west. He passed through the village of Terminus, renamed, "Marthasville," just the previous year, on a motion by legislator Daniel Johnson. The tired Sherman got to Marietta, and reported to a Colonel Churchill, February 17, a full three days after he started out from Charleston.

Churchill was Inspector General of the Army. He told Sherman that he was to assist in taking depositions in upper Georgia and Alabama. The purpose of this was to reimburse volunteers from those two states who had just fought in Florida against Chief Osceola in the Second Seminole War. In that war, the U.S. government had failed to supply enough forage for the troops. This omission had cost the troops many horses, and much equipment was worn out, as well. The government wanted to make good on the ex-soldiers' losses, and Congress had appropriated money for the purpose.

Churchill told Sherman what he was to do, after which the young officer fell into bed exhausted. He was up early the next morning, though, and rode northward to begin what was to be a six-weeks' task.

During the six weeks, he used his spare time to scout the countryside, traveling several times to Kennesaw Mountain. From its summit, he could plainly see Allatoona to the north, and Lost Mountain off to the west. He rode through the northwest Georgia area again and again, making notes, and remembering what he had seen. Twenty years later, Sherman used his knowledge of the topography as his troops battered their way south from Ringgold to Atlanta, the "Marthasville" of his early career. He may have known the ground better than did his Confederate opponents.

*   *   *   *   *

The inhabitants of the Almshouse were fortunate to be non-resident when Sherman's troops made their incursion into the vicinity of Atlanta. The inmates had been evacuated. The general doubtless would not have intended to harm those helpless people, but one never knew what he *would* do.

Mistrust of Sherman was a safe policy. After all, when the fighting around the Poor House was over, and his subsequent battles were won, resulting in the capture of Atlanta, Sherman directed that the few Rebel civilians remaining in the city (1,644, out of a wartime population estimated at about 22,000) must leave. Later, on November 14, he issued the infamous order to torch the city. When the fires burned out on the 15th, only 400 out of 5,000 dwellings and other buildings remained.

Moreover, prior to the completion of this victorious North Georgia campaign, it had been demonstrated that Sherman's *idée fixe* was to reach around the enemy army to get at the civilian population. He would break their will to resist, and shorten the war. Better, then, for the non-military persons to flee, as Sherman came on.

And come on, he had. With 110,000 men at the start, Sherman enjoyed a better than two-to-one numerical superiority over his skilful opponent, Joe Johnston. The heavier numbers enabled the Yankees to flank the counter-punching Johnston out of one defensive position after another. The whole chess match between the two, from Dalton down to Peachtree Creek, cost Sherman some 27,000 men, shot or taken. Johnston, alternately fighting and withdrawing in good order, had suffered only 10,000 casualties, according to one source, though another says the figure was 14,700, plus 2,500 deserters. Replacements for both sides had ultimately maintained Sherman's two-to-one advantage virtually unchanged.

One thing *had* changed. The Yankees were now at the gates of Atlanta, instead of 100 miles away. Confederate president Jefferson Davis liked neither the situation, nor Johnston. On July 17, he replaced the ever-retreating general with a known fighter, Kentuckian John Bell Hood.

Davis' decision has been called one of the worst mistakes of the war. Atlanta, key rail and munitions center, and unofficial capital of the Confederacy, must be held. Perhaps this would have been impossible for any commander to do, faced with the odds. Even so, if Atlanta *could* hold on for three and a half months, until the war-weary North voted Lincoln out of office, a negotiated peace could be won.

The city's fortified lines were the strongest ever prepared on the North American continent, and might have held out against the certain battering, but Hood chose not to remain within them. He knew he had been given the command in order to fight. His four battles around Atlanta were, in military language, "sallies from fortress," and he lost all four. The third conflict, known as the Battle of Ezra Church, was fought in the present West End section of Atlanta, a mile outside of the fortifications. It was the battle in which Atlanta's first Poor House was destroyed.[43]

The Poor House structures had the misfortune to be located at the site of the present stone entrance to the vast Westview Cemetery. Marching to the spot along Lickskillet Road, now called, Martin Luther King Drive, two understrength Confederate divisions used the Poor House as the dividing landmark between them. Brown's division in the open meadows on the left, and Clayton's on the right, along what is now Westview Drive, formed a concave basket. In that basket, General Hood hoped to catch and crush Sherman's right wing, O.O. Howard's Army of the Tennessee, as it moved south. The effort would be helped by Hood's corps of A.P. Stewart, which would swing wide to the west, take the Federal line in rear and break it up.

At crunch time, Hood failed again, with a characteristically good plan whose intricacy required coordination too exact to work. The Yankee artillery, in contrast, worked very well. General Howard had seen with his own eyes how hard-pressed was Logan's Fifteenth Corps. They could scarcely stand their ground against the Rebels' onslaughts. So Howard brought up more artillery to help. The guns had little effect in the wooded areas east of the Poor House, but they wreaked havoc on the butternuts in the open spaces.

The Poor House had little chance as Howard swept the meadows with his cannon.

The flimsy wooden buildings were shattered by solid shot, and set alight by explosive shells. After the crashing explosions and crackling fires had ceased, only forlorn, blackened chimneys were left.

Before the lamented destruction of the Poor House, it rendered one, last, melancholy service, that of sheltering a wounded general. It happened in this way: When A.P. Stewart's corps had arrived belatedly on the field, the bluecoats were not quite where they were expected to be, besides which, they had been reinforced with fresh floods of troops. When the Confederates desperately pressed their attack anyway, they lost four generals, including corps commander Stewart himself.

On the present School Place, a block south of Martin Luther King Drive, a determined Stewart spurred forward, and was struck in the head by a spent bullet. The blow was enough to unhorse him. He was carried unconscious by aides, back down the road to the still intact Poor House. Inside, he woke up a few minutes later with a splitting headache, and was out of the battle for the day.

The Battle of Ezra Church was a resounding Federal victory. Today, three or four blocks northwest of where the church stood, the jumble of streets have names memorializing the fiery Rebel attacks, and the stout Yankee defense: New Jersey Avenue, Yonkers Avenue, Westchester Boulevard, Chicago Avenue, Detroit Avenue, Illinois Avenue, and Dixie Hills Drive.

*   *   *   *   *

A few days prior to the Battle of Ezra Church, a future director of the Poor House was involved in Atlanta's general disaster. He was the same Robert L. Hope with whom this narrative began. He was, at the moment when Sherman came, a five-year-old living temporarily in the area between Decatur and Atlanta.

A native of the little crossroads village of Dawsonville, in the north Georgia foothills, Hope had been taken on a fourteen-mile carriage ride every Sunday, to the Methodist church at Dahlonega. Once war came to Georgia, he was given a longer journey, traveling to the Atlanta area to live. This move was made for safety's sake, after his father had been called up for military service. The Federal forces had occupied Georgia at its mountainous northwest corner. This was far from Dawsonville, yet no one knew whether a cavalry raid, or Sherman's whole force, might come east and sack this very town. Better to get away, and live with relatives.

Ironically, little Robert was directly in Sherman's path when, six months later, his army group began to fight their way south towards Atlanta. After the Confederates unsuccessfully attacked them on the northern approaches at Peachtree Creek, the Yankees circled to the east, where the so-called "Battle of Atlanta" was fought, mainly in the present Inman Park and Little Five Points sections.

It is not known exactly when the blue soldiers arrived at Robert's house, but it is believed to have been on July 21. This was just the day before the big battle, as McPherson's Army of the Tennessee was moving west from Decatur towards the conflict.

The humidity of that midsummer day was matched by the warmth of soldierly belligerence. Although any Georgia home was endangered by the presence of marauding Union troops, this was especially true of one with young children on the premises. They, with only their mother present besides, were a dead giveaway that the absent father was off fighting for the Confederacy. That thought incensed the troopers, but they were also acting under orders to destroy buildings that might give shelter or succor to Rebels.

Thus it was that Robert, with his older brother George, sat hunched glumly, chin cupped in hands, watching the enemy at work. The soldiers dragged chairs, couches, and bedsteads into the front yard, to be loaded onto wagons and taken away. Any mattresses and pillows which were not confiscated were ripped open, and their feather stuffings scattered to the wind. In malevolent glee, the men then torched the house, and burned it to the ground.[44]

Young Robert was afterwards refugeed away, by a convoluted route eastward, then northward, ending in the Dawsonville-Dahlonega area again. He thus missed the ensuing siege of Atlanta.

CHAPTER SIX

RESURGENCE

"- - it made itself a nest of twigs of spice-trees, on which it died, by setting the nest on fire, and burning itself alive. From its body, or its ashes, or the nest, which it had fertilized, came forth another phoenix - -."

> \- "Phoenix," *Encyclopedia Brittanica*
> article on the mythical bird.

To treat at length the epic events of the siege and fall of Atlanta is a task far outside the purpose of this book. Likewise, Sherman's deportation of the relatively few citizens (fewer than 2,000 of 22,000) who had chosen to remain in the city, and the conqueror's celebrated "March to the Sea," will not be detailed.

It must suffice only to relate a few of the hardships of the sufferers in Atlanta during the siege. Amid that soul-wracking month, the people within the fortifications must have felt themselves in the anteroom of Hell! Solid shot and explosive shells rained into the city. Two heavy siege guns were railed down from Chattanooga, to be added to the field artillery trained on Atlanta. Federal hot-shot furnaces heated solid cannon balls until they glowed red, then were rammed into wet-wadded cannon, to be fired. As they arched into the city, they set fire to whatever flammable object they hit.

Among the many stories of personal tragedy during the siege is the one about the little, four-year-old girl, who was the first civilian casualty. She was playing with her puppy when a Federal shell fell that morning of July 20, at the corner of Ivy and Ellis, and blew her to Kingdom come.[45]

Most civilian deaths were caused by the huge Rebel-Yankee artillery duel on August 10. The popular African-American barber, Solomon Luckie, was wounded fatally by Union cannon fire at the corner of Whitehall and Alabama. The superintendent of the gas company, Mr. Warren, and his six-year-old daughter, were killed together in a house at Elliott and Rhodes. A woman ironing clothes in a house on Pryor Street, near the present Candler Building, was slain. A young lady on her way to the Car Shed (the old Union Station) was struck in the back and mortally wounded. Many others were blasted into eternity on this most awful of days.

As in beleaguered Vicksburg, Mississippi, the year before, old men and women, mothers and children, took shelter in cellars, and in shebangs dug into the sides of hills and railroad embankments. They were desperate to escape the fire-bursting death.

*   *   *   *   *

In peacetime, a Poor House, like the one which had just been destroyed near Ezra Church, is the concern of the kindly, and the salvation of the needy. But what if everyone is in the same boat of misery? What if there is little or no help? That was the plight of the fewer than 2,000 civilians who remained in Atlanta in summer, 1864.

As has often been remarked, the scarcity of non-combatants in the city means that the frantic, mass flight depicted in the movie, "Gone With the Wind," never happened. Almost all of those who had not previously left, stuck it out to the end.

But another image created by the movie was fact. For, under the shelling and the broiling sun, thousands of wounded Confederate soldiers lay in the railroad yard around the Car Shed, and in other open spaces. For them there was little or no anesthetic – morphine, chloroform, or other pain-killer. Doctors were scarce. Elderly people, and some younger women gave some help. Occasionally, since the routes to the south had not yet been cut, some wounded were put on trains, carts, wagons, or drays, and sent away.[46]

Through all of this, Sherman was intransigently Sherman. To Hood's written protest of the shelling of civilians, Sherman penned three answers. The first two made some sense: (1) War was "the very science of organized barbarism" (thus it is all right to bombard innocents); (2) Atlanta was an enemy fortress, not a haven for civilians.

Sherman's third answer made no sense at all. He said that shells that fell in Atlanta were only incidental to the fighting that was taking place in the outskirts. In other words, he was aiming at the Confederate soldiers, not civilians. If stray shells hit noncombatants, that was too bad. This absurd fiction is contradicted by Sherman's own order of August 1, 1864, to General Schofield: "You may fire 10 to 15 shots from every gun you have in position into Atlanta, that will reach any of its houses. Fire slowly and with deliberation between 4 P.M. and dark - -."

The above directive, which is on the official record, was issued before the shelling reached its height. It is plain that the general's intention was to make the siege as hard on Atlanta as possible, with no regard for the citizenry. They continued to be killed and maimed, both day and night.[47]

This measure, with his later insistence on having the captured city cleared of its people, and his still later order to burn the city, did not endear Sherman to Atlantans. Some of his Union Army colleagues thought him "crazy." In the eyes of the people of Atlanta he was demonic, and they have forgotten this only with difficulty, despite Sherman's postwar expressions of support for the rebuilt city.

One thing can be agreed by all, about this man of nervous and insecure temperament: he was an excellent military commander.

*   *   *   *   *

The conflict moved inexorably to its close. In Virginia, Grant paid an exorbitant cost in blood to wear down Robert E. Lee at last. Sherman marched with seven leagued boots down to Savannah, and up through the Carolinas, to final victory.

For its part, Atlanta rebuilt rather quickly after the war. Contrasting with the sleepy cotton markets to the east, south, and west of it, the city was railroad-centered, money-driven, and atypically Southern. Prospect of its recovery was a sure thing.

When Sherman started his March to the Sea, Atlanta's civilian refugees flooded back into the city almost immediately. The dramatic fluctuations of the city's population tell a tale. When the Civil War began, Atlanta had only 7,000 people. The war developed it into the high-priority munitions center that it became, and workers swelled the population to 22,000. As mentioned above, Sherman's siege fell upon fewer than 2,000 who had remained in the city. Seven months after Appomattox, Atlanta again had 15,000 inhabitants. That figure climbed to 21,000 just a year and half later, as former plantation slaves had begun to arrive, seeking livelihood.

There was frantic activity, but the Poor House had to wait its turn. Construction was now the major industry, but its object was the replacement of the homes and businesses that the war had destroyed, not the building of a Poor House.

The sounds of saws and hammers filled the streets By December, 1865, seven and a half months after Lee's surrender, and a year after Atlanta's citizens had come back en masse, three hundred and thirty-eight new business firms had been established. The railroad companies were repairing their lines, and rebuilding depots and shops. Ten new foundries and machine shops were started, and a new rolling mill was built. The war rubbish was cleared from the streets. The city limits were extended to enclose a circle three miles across. In short, the place was jumping, but the Poor House concept was, for the moment, neglected and forlorn.

*   *   *   *   *

The need for a Poor House could never be entirely forgotten, however. Citizens returning saw black children here and there, appearing from the corner of some charred or smashed house. In those corners several sheets of tin roofing often had been propped up overhead, to form a wretched place to live. The children were dressed only in tow sacks, with openings cut at the corners for armholes.[48]

The plight of white children and widows was little better. By some estimates, the Confederates had enlisted three quarters of a million men in their armies. The Union had enrolled two and a half times that number. To both sides, the war's butcher's bill was shattering, in this bloodiest of America's wars. The South lost 258,000 men killed outright, or dead from wounds or disease, while Yankees going the same way numbered 360,622.

Georgia, as one of the heavier contributors to Confederate manpower, suffered proportionately. After hostilities ended, fifty thousand children in the state were fatherless, and another ten thousand had neither father nor mother.

The great bulk of the parentless children were spared a homeless future. In their thousands, they were adopted by relatives, or other kindly people who took them in.

Almshouses seemed less needed in the rural districts than in the city, where population was denser, and street waifs multiplied. For those young unfortunates, help was often not available.

Atlanta's city fathers argued over what form the help should take. The need was urgent, but the delicate subject was brutally overruled by the lack of money. Wishful thinking: "It would be nice if the Poor House were not gone," but gone it was. To erect a new one, with facilities to care for a variety of kinds of inmates, young and old, was clearly beyond the capability of Atlanta's budget, or that of the county. It would remain so until 1869.

Instead of a Poor House, Atlanta's solution for the time being was a school for the orphans. In 1867 a local lottery was conducted to raise funds to establish the Orphans Free School, which would be simply an orphanage. The rallying cry, sounded in the business houses, churches, and homes of the city, was, "Care for the children!" The cry sounded almost patriotic.

The whole city swung behind the appeal, and the lottery was a very big success. The live-in Orphans Free School was built. The children had a haven.[49]

By a singular coincidence, a future director of the soon-to-be-revived Poor House lived in the orphanage. Robert Hope, now only eight, was forced to live there for several years. With his two brothers, one older, the other younger than he, Robert lived in the Free School through his childhood years.

As a free spirit, the eight-year-old future director, on a day when a circus was in town, was puttering about his own concerns, at some distance from the main house. He was called repeatedly to come in, but ignored the calls. When everyone left for the circus, he was left behind. He learned what he had missed, and wept bitterly. He told the story many years later, as an object lesson of the harm of perverse behavior.

An independent nature was useful to an orphan, however, and also to a Poor House director, later on. As the children lived in the long-timbered, congregate institution, they faced a daily challenge. It happened that the matron in charge was not cruel, but she was cold in manner. She and the other employees ran a rather eccentric, insular institution. Without much external oversight by the city, they largely bypassed whatever struggles any of the children may have had.

The Orphans Free School had its failings, but its overall success rose far above them.

In its very existence, the Free School generated a new confidence all around. By the creation of the school, and by other measures, Atlanta was regaining its feet.

If a Poor House could at last be established, the poverty problems of many groups could be alleviated. One of those groups had always been "outsiders" – the African-Americans.

CHAPTER SEVEN

AFRICAN-AMERICANS

"Everywhere the human soul stands between a hemisphere of light and another of darkness on the confines of two ever-lastingly hostile empires - - Necessity and Free Will."
Goethe's Works, quoted by
Thomas Carlyle

The realization grew and grew that the Atlanta Poor House must be restored. The city's impoverishment and the swarms of orphans were only part of the problem. Many white people had resumed their residence in the city with Sherman's departure in November, 1864. After the Confederate collapse in spring, 1865, many newly freed black slaves had begun to come into the city as well. A lot of them were very poor. An almshouse was going to be needed which could care for blacks as well as for whites.

The scale of the migration was unprecedented. Fulton County, in 1860, was seventy-five percent white, twenty-five percent black. By 1867, Atlanta, with the bulk of the county's population, had seen its own numbers shift to fifty-four percent white, forty-six percent black.[50]

The reason for the change was simple. The counties to the south and east of Atlanta had been plantation counties. They formed a concave curve 200 miles long and 100 miles thick. Without exception, the populations of these counties were over fifty percent black.

When the Federal soldiers appeared, bringing freedom, many of the slaves at first simply wandered the countryside in groups. Often they were looking for relatives who had been sold to other plantations. They were happy that liberty gave them the opportunity to move from place to place. But Atlanta was a magnet that eventually drew a lot of them. The city offered the fellowship of the crowd, and a certain kind of security.

Not all of the ex-slaves chose to migrate to the cities. Some chose to remain on the plantations as paid servants and workers, or as sharecroppers. As for those in the cities, what would they do, once they got there? As unskilled laborers, never having faced the realities of providing for themselves, some were going to be candidates for residence in a Poor House, unless they changed and grew.

* * * * *

Many former slaves did change.[51] In city life for the first time, newly freed people caught on quickly. They rolled up their sleeves and joined the whites in rebuilding. Black men could be seen wielding picks and shovels, working on the city streets, not as slave labor, but as paid workers.

In the pick-and-shovel men, one could recognize the unlettered former field hands. There were others, though, who found a ready market in Atlanta for the skills they had learned on the plantations. Carriage drivers got jobs at the livery stables. Carpenters, plasterers, and blacksmiths worked to restore the war-torn city.

Seamstresses found employment, too. Former house servants, both male and female, became the domestics in the urban setting. Skilled mechanics from the plantations were also in great demand.

A heartbreaking development at this time was the false "forty acres and a mule" promise made to the freed slaves by Northern carpetbaggers.[52] It is said that this story got started on Hilton Head Island, South Carolina, where it had some legitimacy of truth. But it quickly spread to all parts of the South, and deceived a multitude of black people, for a short while. The line was one of agrarian reform: "Come Christmas, 1865, the white men's lands will be divided up, and every one of you will get forty acres, and a mule to plow it!"

When Christmas came, and Santa Claus did not, the hoax was exposed, and disillusionment set in. But for a few months, as the hoax was operating, and the something-for-nothing land redistribution was expected, the hucksters, white and black, had a field day. Votes for candidates were obtained by the dangling of this carrot. On almost every downtown street corner in Atlanta, there were ex-plowboys, idle and gullible. They heard the message that they should insist on extravagant benefits before they agreed to work for a white employer.

Here was great tragedy. The postwar building boom begged every day for laborers, but some ex-slaves were choosing to be loiterers. They sat looking, refusing to enter the open door for wages. They would be content to live in one of the lean-to villages that had sprung up around the city's fringes. They would live on handouts from the U.S. Freedmen's Bureau, for as long as that remained. Then, one day, some would come to the Poor House.

*   *   *   *   *

Pity and compassion are the right emotions with which to view these people. Not only did they face race prejudice, but they also had to try to adjust to a completely new life situation. To most of the half-million ex-slaves in Georgia, freedom was hardly understood. Entrance into the great, wide world meant mobility, and above all, *no work to do.*

The "no work" feature has to be kept in mind, to understand those recently freed. They came to the city like country-come-to-town bumpkins. Very many were childlike, naïve, accustomed to master's providing the meals. Slavery had been a sorry, oppressive institution, but food at least was a positive benefit.

The difficulty of getting food raises a question. If it was going to be so hard to come by, why take the risk of leaving the safety of known surroundings? They found reasons to do so. One was that they naturally loved a crowd, and came to the city because others were coming. And what a relief, just to get away from the plantation, at last! Who would not have felt the same?

In those early days of freedom, those hungry African-Americans followed different courses of action. Pious souls who had a genuine relationship with Christ were praying to the good Lord to provide for them. Others were resorting to vagabondage, raiding unprotected cornfields and hen roosts in the rural sections.[53]

Long after he became the Poor House director, Dr. Robert Hope looked back on those days. He wrote:

"Before we censure these people too harshly for their thievery, we should remember that they had never owned anything at all. Everything was their master's, and all they had came to them from his hand. It was natural for them as freedmen, to expect to continue to take freely from the white man."[54]

* * * * *

The future comeback of the Poor House in Atlanta was affected in 1867 by two events. One was positive, the other negative.

The first event was the beginning of planning for the Atlanta-to-Charlotte Air Line Railroad, later known as the Southern Railroad. Not completed until 1873, the railroad was set to run just east of where the prominent Lenox Square Mall was located many decades later. The course of the railroad would be one major reason to put the revived Fulton County Poor House where it was placed. The Poor House would be at the corner of Piedmont and Peachtree roads, and a scant half-mile from the new railroad.[55]

The other development was the arrival in 1867 of something that would temporarily halt Atlanta's promising growth. That year, in the spring, came radical Reconstruction. With it, the city ceased to resurge, and the idea of a new Poor House was put on hold for two years.

In the eyes of its authors, Reconstruction of the governments of Southern states was an absolute necessity. Without it, the four years' bloodshed of the Civil War would have proved nothing. The Radicals in Congress meant to make certain that there would be no disguised "Slave Power" rising in the place of the previous one.

CHAPTER EIGHT

RECONSTRUCTION: WHO NEEDED IT?

"What's one man's poison, signor,
Is another's meat and drink."

Love's Cure,
Beaumont and Fletcher

With a new Poor House fairly begging to be built, Atlanta and the rest of the South had yet to be pulled through another political knothole. "Reconstruction," as it was dubbed, would have been better named, "Restructuring," because it was a rearrangement of governmental power in the states that had been in rebellion.[56] Atlanta's comeback, and any chance for a renewed Poor House had to be put on hold until the Reconstruction dust settled.

Lincoln had counseled, concerning the former Confederate states, "let 'em up easy," and his two leading generals, Grant and Sherman, subscribed to this view. But Lincoln was dead, and the Northern Radicals in Congress, previously called, Abolitionists, had something else in mind. They had won their forty years' fight against slavery, with a bloody and costly war at the end of it. Now the Southerners must be punished by submitting to the forcible remaking of their states.

Civil War historian Fletcher Pratt wrote that the Radicals, by their harsh terms of Reconstruction, "disgraced themselves."[57]

Atlanta's all-time leading chronicler, Franklin Garrett, also wrote of Reconstruction in colors of disgust.[58] He pointed out that the Reconstruction Act was not passed until March 2, 1867, a full two years after the war had ended. Supplements to the Act were added later in March and in July. Atlantans had thought the war was over, and were shocked to see Federal troops come back. The soldiers piled off their trains and marched into barracks as a new army of occupation, to enforce the Act.

Up in Washington, President Andrew Johnson, the Radicals' opponent, vetoed the various Reconstruction measures, only to see his vetoes overridden. He gloomily reflected that, of the war's objects, to restore peace, to bring the rebel states back into the Union without rancor, to regard the ex-Confederates as American citizens, with their dignity, and their governing power restored, all had been ruined.

*   *   *   *   *

What would Reconstruction look like? First, it would set up a new electorate. Congress said the voters must include Negroes, and must exclude anyone who had ever been disenfranchised for disloyalty to the United States. The second stricture ruled out former Confederate soldiers, especially officers. This was an unfortunate measure, for it decapitated Southern society. The men who might have provided responsible leadership were forbidden to do it. They remained in the shadows, helpless, suspect, and embittered. When the Federal military had ordered a full praise service at First Presbyterian Church, Macon, Georgia, to commemorate Fourth of July, the Presbyterians complied, but the preacher took his text from Psalm 137:3, "- - those who carried us away captive required of us a song, and those who plundered us required of us mirth, saying, Sing us one of the songs of Zion!"

From any reasoned viewpoint, however, the disenfranchisement made sense. Before the war, "gradual emancipation" had never happened, had it? Why should it be expected that pro-slavery whites would show fairness to the Negro now? A good question, for soon many excluded whites were plotting to regain control. They were thinking, "Ku Klux Klan."

So Atlanta's erstwhile comeback was effectively poleaxed. It would be a further two years before the rebuilding of the Poor House could even be authorized.

*   *   *   *   *

Reconstruction included ironies that reveal its apparent racism. Former white soldiers were disenfranchised, but blacks who had served with the Confederate armies were exempted from the charge of having been disloyal to the United States. They were therefore eligible for service in the postwar state governments.

The histories of wars are written by the victors. So it is no surprise that much is made, today, of the 186,000 blacks who entered the Union Army and supposedly "fought for their freedom." They were segregated, however, just as U. S. Army blacks were in World Wars One and Two, the vast majority serving only as noncombatant laborers.

Little or nothing is mentioned of the even greater number of blacks who served with the Confederacy. Like the black soldiers on the other side, they were mostly noncombatants: fortifications builders, wagon drivers, cooks, butlers. Many were irregular soldiers, traveling with their masters as "body servants." Often they were illegally given rifles and expected to shoot at the Yankees. Other blacks were regulars. The existence of a uniformed, 3,000-man black Louisiana brigade violated the wishes of the Confederate congress, but gave a good account of itself in pitched battle. Union soldiers were surprised that a few Confederates captured at Gettysburg were black.[59] Yet Afro-Virginians fought for the Confederacy at First Manassas, Seven Pines, and were in all of the battles right up to the end of the war.

Why would blacks fight for a slave-holding society? Some certainly, were coerced to do so, but others were simply patriotic. They fought from love of their country, despite the less-than-ideal conditions at home. After the war, some Southern states recognized them, giving military pensions to black veterans just as they did to white veterans.

*   *   *   *   *

Reconstruction promised to receive a state back into the Union if it followed a rather tortuous, seven-step route.[60]

First, a new electorate should be created, including African-Americans, and excluding most of the former Confederate soldiers. Opponents called this, "the black electorate."

Second, the new set of voters should be called to a general election, to elect delegates to a constitutional convention.

Third, the convention should draw up a new state constitution, whose most important feature should be Negro suffrage.

Fourth, the new electorate should then have another general balloting, to give statewide endorsement to the new constitution.

Fifth, the same electorate should return to the polls one more time, to actually put the new constitution into effect, electing a new state legislature.

Sixth, once all the above was done, the next move would be that of the U. S. Congress, to decide whether to approve the new constitution.

Seventh, the state's new legislature should ratify the Fourteenth Amendment to the U.S. Constitution.

Anything in this series of steps might go wrong. The carrot extended to the state was, "faithfully execute these steps, and you will be eligible for readmission to the Union, representation in both houses of Congress, and the withdrawal of military rule."

*   *   *   *   *

For the white majority, this seemed a nightmare time.[61] There had been defeat in war, manful resurgence, then galling military reoccupation, racial humiliation, and loss of political power. It was a time of indignation at the steps that must be taken to satisfy the Congress, so as to return to the Union they had so disliked; a time of disgust that illiterate blacks were receiving Republican money which bribed them to vote. It was a time of bitterness as the rigged electorate easily won an almost totally Radical representation to the constitutional convention; a time of madness, as Republican Radicals railed trainloads of blacks from county to county, to make sure their 1868 gubernatorial candidate, Rufus Bullock, was elected; a time of grim determination, as the Ku Klux Klan became very active and successful in the rural counties, frightening the blacks so that Democratic majorities began to be achieved by intimidation, in county after county; a time when virtually *every* white man began to say that, "for once, I *have* to be a Democrat." "For once - -." For always. It was the beginning of racist Southern politics, and the "Solid South."

* * * * *

Amazingly, Georgia fared much better through the trauma of Reconstruction than she expected.[62] The constitutional convention was rather mild, not controlled by blacks and carpetbaggers. Instead, the dominant voices were those of Yankees who had lived in Georgia for decades, and truly cared about the state. They were joined by the "scalawags" – white Southerners who favored Reconstruction. The convention disappointed the outsiders and the blacks, for the revolution to turn society on its head had not happened.

The measures enacted by the convention were compliant enough to satisfy the U.S Congress, which readmitted Georgia to the Union on July 15, 1870. It was a short-lived Reconstruction, and much of the readmission credit belonged to Georgia's former, wartime governor, Joe Brown. He led the majority of white conservatives to accept the Reconstruction terms.

No credit at all was due the current governor, Rufus Bullock. As a Republican Radical, he realized that the continuance of his power depended on Reconstruction's being prolonged. That did not happen, and Georgians also found that Bullock's governorship was scandal-ridden. Deciding that they had had enough, they elected a conservative legislature in 1871. Bullock fled the state, and in 1872 Georgia again had a conservative governor, James M. Smith.

*   *   *   *   *

Reconstruction was a failure, in the sense that the state reverted to white conservative control as soon as the Federal army of occupation was gone. Washington Radicals were foiled.

The blacks were not benefited in the long term. They got four anemic years at most, followed by many decades of Jim Crowism, the new slavery.

And whites lost their freedom of choice. Thenceforth they would be Democrats, and often, Klan members, or else.

Arguably, Reconstruction's real winner was the white middle class. Land and slaves had given way to other measurements of wealth and social prestige. Sectional dominance shifted from the coastal and midland Georgia cotton belt to the uplands. Atlanta was growing dynamically, amid American egalitarianism, independence, and vigor of thought. The outcome of the war made it inevitable that eventually, over a century's time, the South would be remade somewhat in the North's image. That image was not at all bad.

With the end of Reconstruction, the stage was again set for a host of new improvements. One of those was a new Poor House.

CHAPTER NINE

THE POOR HOUSE REOPENS

"He has filled the hungry with good things."
St. Luke 1:53
Words of the Virgin Mary

With the shift of real power to Atlanta, before, during, and after Reconstruction, things were happening fast. The Atlanta business community was thriving. It would be too much to say that Atlanta businesses had not wished for secession, but many of them had wanted it less than did other areas of the state. Once it was an accomplished fact, they had kept quiet.

Business opportunities abounded. In May, 1867, the same year that Reconstruction began, a twenty-year-old native of Kashau, Hungary, named Morris Rich, borrowed $1,000 from his brother, William. With it, he rented a rough-hewn, one-storey wooden building. It measured only twenty by twenty-five feet, and fronted on an unpaved street at 36 Whitehall. Morris was all business, and from this unimposing start, he grew the sprawling, Rich's Incorporated, department store empire. It became Atlanta's queen of stores, was much beloved for its motherly treatment of customers, and had a book written about it.[63] It existed for thirteen decades before being bought out, and merged into Macy's, of New York.

The following February, 1868, an old idea was implemented. The state capital since 1807 had been the city of Milledgeville, down in middle Georgia. Atlanta citizens had tried, in 1847, and 1854, to have their city made the capital. They were unsuccessful. Now that the center of gravity had changed, it was a different story. Atlanta, very populous, and the premier rail center, became the capital.

*   *   *   *   *

But what about an almshouse? Ever since the 1864 destruction of the old Poor House, Atlanta had had none. The Atlanta business community wanted one. Since Atlanta was Southern-controlled once again, the businessmen felt their restored influence. The Yankee bayonets were gone, and their puppet, Governor Bullock, had left the state in ignominy. It was the businessmen who pushed the Fulton County Grand Jury to report, in May, 1869:

> "Under the recommendations of previous grand juries, the worn-out and timberless tract upon which the Poor House was located (the present Gordon Road) has been sold and the proceeds reinvested in well timbered land of much better quality for the same purpose. This tract is about seven miles from the city on the Air Line Railroad. Comfortable houses for the poor have been erected on it - -."[64]

Thus the Poor House had abandoned the neighborhood which later became Atlanta's West End. Its transfer to the north side put it a mile beyond Buckhead village at the northwest corner of Peachtree and Piedmont roads.

The mayor and city council of Atlanta controlled and supported the Poor House until 1877. However, on February 26 of that year, Atlanta would be relieved of any responsibility and expenses for the Poor House. Fulton County at that time assumed full oversight.[65]

Fortunately, enough land had been purchased for it, in this 1869 acquisition, to ensure that the Poor House could become a self-supporting farm. Starting at the Peachtree-Piedmont corner, the property spread northeast, embracing the present Tower Place, and northwest across the present Georgia Highway 400 and Ivy Road. There was also some acreage on the Buckhead side of Piedmont, mostly north of the present Mathieson Drive. The whole area comprised 230 acres, later increased to 336.

All of this territory and more had been formerly in the possession of the so-called, Native Americans. It was the Creek Indians who, much earlier in the century, had occupied it.[66] It was the northernmost part of their lands, bounded by the powerful Cherokee Nation still farther north. The Creeks had ceded the land by successive treaties to the white men when the pressure of numbers forced their hand, again and again. White settlers were pouring in, and little could stop them from encroaching across the boundary of a previous treaty.

After the white men took possession of this area, the rest of the state was surveyed. This had earlier been done to the eastern portion of it. The whole state was divided into huge rectangular "land lots," which were in turn divided into smaller "plats." The plats were intended to accommodate private homes, farms, businesses, or whatever. So it was that the new Poor House property, whose location is described above, lay largely in Land Lot Number 62, with a smaller portion in Land Lot Number 98, adjacent.[67]

*   *   *   *   *

Prospects for the Poor House looked more than fair. It was only six and a half miles from the downtown station in Atlanta, and was easily reached from there on the Airline Railroad. Today, the tracks of Metro Atlanta Rapid Transit Authority run parallel to the railroad tracks, and carry passengers to the famous Lenox Square Mall.

As proclaimed by the Grand Jury's report, the new site had been chosen for its physical goods also. The richness of its soil, and the luxuriousness of its forest, were blessings of the new Poor House, matching its accessibility as key advantages.

In May, 1869, then, the new Poor House seemed ideally situated, even though its buildings were small. The "comfortable houses for the poor," to which the Grand Jury's report referred, were only seven duplex dwellings. However, they were imagined (or mis-imagined!) to be mostly for short-term occupancy, and were more than adequate for that purpose. Among the fourteen duplex units, one was reserved for the director and his family. In the other thirteen, families of three, or even five persons, could live in fair comfort in each.

Once again, as in the West End Poor House, this one would be a place where the poor who could work would do so, to earn their keep.

Through the remaining thirty months of Reconstruction, the Poor House operated. It reached peak capacity soon after Governor James Smith came into office in 1872.

*   *   *   *   *

Sad to say, the Poor House during the Seventies failed to live up to its potential. A good start had been made, and for two or three years thereafter there was obvious progress. To develop the farm, plots of ground were cleared for the raising of corn and vegetables, so the place had a food supply. Healthy inmates were promptly put to work on the property. There was no salary for these people, but they were physically well cared for.

In 1873, or thereabouts, a decline set in, as the new Poor House was in only its fifth year. This was caused by two unhappinesses. First, there was a lack of proper oversight from the Fulton County Grand Jury. The Grand Jury, busy with Atlanta's and the county's growth, simply seems to have been looking in other directions. It was taken for granted that the Poor House was "all right."

Second, two years later, the situation got worse, as the Poor House leadership succumbed to human failings. Especially in the years 1875-1880, weaknesses included drunkenness, mistreatment of inmates, and misappropriation of funds. It should cause no surprise that it was the last of these sins which finally got the attention of the Grand Jury.

By this time, the physical structures of the Poor House had gone far into disrepair.

Evil reports of the Poor House buzzed through downtown. The Grand Jury voiced its concern, but was unable to solve the problems. Wishing to help, they ran up against one blank wall after another. There were a couple of hirings and firings as new directors were engaged, then let go.

The Grand Jury, agreeing among themselves that it was an awful pity to have to fire people repeatedly, saw this also as a devastating rerun of 1860-64. In those years of the first Atlanta Poor House in West End, there likewise had been a rapid turnover of directors. The Civil War battle's fury had not yet come to Atlanta at that time, but the Poor House teapot had had its own tempests. The Grand Jury had said it in carefully restrained words: "We are unable to say that the management of the Poor House reflects the utmost credit on its keeper, Mr. Jesse M. Cook."[68] And who could say that this was anything other than a chaste statement that hid a ton of mismanagement?

Now, to the Grand Jury's chagrin, the same unhappy process was being repeated in the 'Seventies.

CHAPTER TEN

A NEW DIRECTOR

"Too many devious paths lead down the land
And I shall need in that strange, vast unknown,
Thy hand upon my hand."

- Poetry quoted by
missionary Jim Elliot

After the Poor House' troubles had dragged on for some time, Judge W.L. Calhoun succeeded Judge Daniel N. Pittman as ordinary for Fulton County. He was immediately confronted with the Poor House problem. He could hardly have dodged it. It was the talk of Atlanta.

Moreover, like his predecessor, Judge Calhoun had been deputized by the Grand Jury to keep the Poor House directorship filled. As it turned out, Calhoun had a young friend, Captain George M. Hope,[69] who said that he knew just the man who could handle the position.

Young George Hope had already become quite a man about town. He had considerable business acumen. He had been partner in a downtown Atlanta grocery business for several years, and was getting into other businesses as well. By the end of his life, in 1927, he had become an insurance executive of wealth and influence. He also served, in the 1920's, in the non-lucrative position of President of the Board of Atlanta City Schools. Judge Calhoun had courted his support as a political ally. At this moment, in 1881, Captain Hope looked the judge in the eye, and suggested, "Hire my brother."

"Brother" was the man with whom this story of the almshouses began (see Chapter One). He was twenty-two-year-old Dr. Robert Lawson Hope, the gangling young man whom many on the Grand Jury would consider *too* young for the Poor House task. It was a demanding responsibility to be sure, but Dr. Hope had done a lot of living, and learning, in his two-plus decades of life. Moved to the Atlanta area from Dahlonega in the middle of the Civil War, he had arrived at age five in time to see his house burned down by the Federal soldiers (see Pages 47 and 48). He had lived for several years in an orphanage, then was given room and board by an aunt, as he attended public school. He had worked in the grocery store in downtown Atlanta, faithfully saving his dollar-a-week salary. Ultimately, he attended and graduated from the Georgia Eclectic Medical College.[70]

The Medical College, later merged into Emory University's medical school, had prepared Robert well. He had been an excellent student. Moreover, he knew both the allopathic and eclectic methods of medicine, which had been at war with each other, decades before the Civil War. He had also been prepared to be a surgeon. For the year and a half which followed graduation, though a mere stripling, he had been a country doctor. His days had been spent making house calls in the area extending roughly from the present Morningside residential section to Buckhead.

The humble young physician might have been inclined to decline the Poor House job, had not his brother gotten to him before Judge Calhoun did. Captain Hope's advice was, "This is your opportunity to benefit *individuals* – isn't that why you became a doctor? But besides individuals, you will benefit the whole community, too."[71]

Few, admitted his younger brother, could spar with George Hope in debate, and Robert seized his point. He agreed, and was signed on, as the new director. A few months later, a new entity, the Fulton County Board of Commissioners, was organized, and was given oversight of the Poor House. The commissioners promptly confirmed the judge's appointment of Dr. Hope.

*   *   *   *   *

The director's salary of $400 per year was enough, Dr. Hope thought. In 1881 it was a living wage. The pay was especially adequate for a young man who only a few years before had worked in a grocery for a dollar a week, and saved all of it.

Hope's predecessor, J.B. Mayson, had drawn a salary of $750 per year. The Grand Jury decided that the new director's youth and inexperience dictated the smaller starting salary. The salary would stay at that level for five years, until in 1887 it would be increased to $900.[72] The hire was the best deal that the Grand Jury had made for itself, for they had acquired a man who would fill a two-in-one job. He would be resident physician as well as director of the almshouse.

Robert Hope had more on his mind than the size of the Poor House salary. He was faced with the upgrading of the rundown place that he now viewed with jaundiced eye. And despite its shabby condition, the Poor House had forty-five inmates. Robert must meet all of them, and acquaint himself with their various physical conditions, good or bad.

This was also the year of Dr. Hope's marriage. He had courted the red-haired Della Plaster, a descendant of a rather prominent family of early settlers in the neighborhood. When Della's great-grandfather had died in 1836, he had left a thirteen-hundred-acre plantation stretching from the present Rock Spring-Morningside area to south Buckhead. To his heirs he bequeathed this property and twenty-five slaves. His was the oldest recorded will of DeKalb County,[73] out of which Fulton County and Atlanta were later carved.

The marriage of Robert and eighteen-year-old Della, at the Rock Spring Presbyterian Church, was a love match, and it lasted until his death fifty-seven years later. Even so, Dr. Hope's alliance with this heiress of Benjamin Plaster could not hurt his political standing in the community, either.

*   *   *   *   *

What could be done about the eyesore that the Poor House facility had become? Robert was an idealist, a little trait which endeared him to some on the Grand Jury, and was the despair of others. The latter were cynics who advised, "You just sit back and wait for him to destroy himself." Such pessimism was in part a natural response to a new superintendent, since previous men had failed. Self-destruction might, in fact, be the result if Robert pushed too hard, too soon. All the same, the new director quickly let his wants be known. Within the existing facilities, he said, his tasks would be very hard to manage. He hoped that monies would be allocated to improve the place.

Regardless of the difficulties, some duties awaited. The superintendent and resident physician must treat and care for sick inmates, generally manage and oversee the place, seeing to its sanitary condition and the personal habits of the inmates. In addition, he must keep records of admissions, dismissals, and deaths. Lastly, he would direct the cultivation of crops, so as to make the farm self-sustaining.

After his first thorough survey of the institution, Dr. Hope said that he could forecast his life of daily rounds, and urgent calls in the night to attend the sick. Did he also foresee his role of father-figure to many aged "second childhood" people among a big household?

All of the responsibilities together added up to quite a handful, and the doctor knew it going in. It was not to get any less demanding. A few years after, one of the city's newspapers would call him "one of the busiest men in the county,"[74] while another said that he was "the busiest man in Atlanta."

If the young doctor stood ready to tackle a tough job with a whole heart, and with optimism, that attitude was not born of his limited professional experience. It was the fruit of his experience with God. Years before, in early childhood in the north Georgia hills, he had been taken to church each Sunday. Later, in the orphanage, he had felt the presence of God very strongly. This was not just a notion of "God in general," but of God's Son in particular. He was conscious that many people claimed belief in "God," but somehow "never got around to Jesus Christ."

Robert did get around to the only Savior, and only five years before, at age seventeen, he had professed Him publicly in the Rock Spring Presbyterian Church. He was then baptized there.[75]

A life of hard knocks had prepared this young man for the long odds which he now confronted. He believed that just as God had found him, and had drawn him to Himself, He had also arranged the Poor House opportunity for his life. God, who would use him, was more than equal to the odds.

There is a legend in the family lore. It is told that on that first day, when he looked on the Poor House as its new superintendent, he rededicated himself to God. Fear no doubt prompted him. In any case, he knelt and renewed his commitment, on the almshouse property, as the sun sank behind the oaks, elms, and ashes, over Buckhead way.

CHAPTER ELEVEN

POOR HOUSE MEDICAL CARE

"- - some patients, though conscious that their condition is perilous, recover their health simply through their contentment with the goodness of their physician."

Precepts, Chap. 6
Hippocrates

The Poor House, having suffered at the hands of superintendents who had mishandled the place, desperately needed a "kinder, gentler" approach. Robert Hope turned out to be the catalyst to bring it about. The young doctor genuinely hated to see anyone suffer, and those he treated felt that he was deeply concerned for them. The seriously ill knew it, and no doubt many of them pulled through, partly because of that conviction.

The training that the young physician had received was at the Georgia Eclectic Medical College, located at Easton, Georgia. The hamlet of Easton, whose post office was phased out in 1904, was only a shade over two miles north of Atlanta's northern limits. Today, this is the site of the Ansley Mall, at the corner of Piedmont Avenue and Monroe Drive, Atlanta. In 1877, it was a little crossroads community with six businesses, two physicians' offices, a justice of the peace office, the post office, and, of course, the medical college.

Georgia Eclectic Medical College had arrived in a relocation from Macon, Georgia in 1874, three years before the 1877 enrollment of Robert Hope, who was a recent graduate of the little school which became Atlanta Boys High.[76] A jump from high school to med school was by no means unusual. As late as the first decade of the 1900's over ninety percent of doctors in the United States did this, having no training at all, at a conventional college or university.

The medical community in Georgia had not received even its medical training within the state until the first half of the Nineteenth Century. Until then, educated physicians had been imported from elsewhere.

In the 1800-1850 pioneering days, two schools of thought and practice vied for acceptance, though they had much in common. The "Allopathic" faction gradually became known as the "regular" school.

The "Eclectic" school, also called the Thomsonian, or Botanic, school, used the procedures of the "regular" school, including extensive use of surgery. However, the Eclectic school relied more heavily on manipulative arts in the treatment of muscular and skeletal ills. Robert Hope, casting his lot with this school, was able to be of more help to aged and disabled inmates at the Poor House, than would otherwise have been possible.

In the field of internal medicine, the Eclectics made more use of remedies with a directly herbal base. The Allopathics also used these, if to a lesser extent.

Hearing the debates between the two, the state legislature scratched its collective head, and approved both factions, making it lawful for both to receive individual licensure and practice medicine for remuneration.

Colleges for the "regular" faction were set up in Augusta and Savannah. The Savannah Medical College, incorporated, 1838, was phased out of existence in 1880. The Augusta Medical College lived on, becoming the medical department of the University of Georgia, and is thriving yet today.

The college of the Eclectic opinion, originally named, "Georgia College of Eclectic Medicine and Surgery," was opened at Forsyth, Georgia, in 1839.[77] It was moved to Macon, seven years later, and is said to have graduated several hundred physicians prior to the Civil War. When the conflict came, all medical colleges were closed, since their student bodies had simply marched away to war. The Eclectic school reopened in 1867, and stayed in Macon until 1874, when it moved to the vicinity of Georgia's new capital city, Atlanta. In this more influential setting Georgia Eclectic Medical College continued to operate, at Easton, until it was absorbed by Emory School of Medicine.

* * * * *

To continue to call the Eclectic school, "Georgia Eclectic Medical College," after it moved to Atlanta, is accurate only for the years 1874-1886. In 1884, three years after Dr. Hope graduated, Georgia Eclectic Medical College absorbed another very similar institution. The College of American Medicine and Surgery had been founded by the brilliant writer and medicinal dispenser, Dr. S.F. Salter. His college was "closely allied to the Thomsonian and the Eclectic Schools of medicine."[78]Upon his death, Georgia Eclectic Medical College obtained his charter, and received his students. It then reverted to its original, 1839 name, "Georgia College of Eclectic Medicine and Surgery," and so it was known for the rest of its existence.

* * * * *

The work at G.E.M.C. was very hard, and it trained Robert Hope in the kind of care that he would be giving to the inmates at the Poor House for almost 30 years.

The medical training began with study of the body's structure and formation. Human anatomy was carefully studied. Histology, which is the science of the microscopic structure of animal and plant tissues, also had to be mastered. Embryology, the study of the embryo, its formation and development, was covered as well. Dr. Hope became quite adept at delivering babies, and later did this many times over the years, for younger inmates in his years at the Poor House.

At about the same time as these courses on body structure and composition were given the students, they had to tackle studies relating to the body's functioning. The courses were in physiology and biochemistry.

Physiology, simply stated, is that part of biology which teaches the functions of the organs and tissues of the body. The budding physicians learned the life processes of the living being.

Biochemistry was not called by that name, at the time that the future Poor House superintendent was in school at Georgia Eclectic Medical College. It *was* taught, however, and rapid advances had been made in the field, especially since 1870. Biochemistry, which is actually one of the oldest branches of chemical science, was developed by Antoine Lavoisier, at the end of the Eighteenth Century.[79] He showed clearly for the first time that the life-processes of the animal body can be investigated by chemical means. This would later determine what Robert Hope would allow Poor House inmates to have to eat and drink.

Not far behind all of this was the study of pharmacology – the treatment of various illnesses by means of medicines. In his pharmacological work, the future Poor House doctor would mix up his potions, and analyze their chemical content. Much later, in his retirement years, he would joke, "a Creek Indian medicine man might have helped me a lot."[80]

* * * * *

The physicians-to-be had to devour their textbooks, reading, reading. There was never any surprise, when, in their various dwellings, the light was seen under their doors in the wee hours. It was only a wonder that their reddened eyes did not fall out of their heads, with all that studying.

The great day for all came when they observed the dissection of a pasty-grey cadaver.

Even though this was a malodorous event, for most it was more joy than trial. Watching surgery done on a dead man was to the students a celebration of the human machine: "So *that's* how it works! How fascinating!"

When the students took up the tools of surgery in their own hands, and did what the teacher had been seen to do, they were tense, but not trembling. It was a thrill, an exercise that explored a new continent, or that examined the intricacies of an engine. It would be a challenge, to restore this apparatus to running order in a living person.

*   *   *   *   *

The second year's study was more difficult than the first's had been, although, in large part, it was "more of the same." Robert Hope's daily schedule as a student was always a close run thing, since he had a job to keep up with, along with his studies. In another couple of years, he reminded himself, he would have his sheepskin diploma from the medical college, and would be propelled into his life's work. Almost all that he had studied would be applied at the Poor House, day by day.

CHAPTER TWELVE

MEETING THE PEOPLE

"The setting sun is reflected from the windows of the alms-house as brightly as from the rich man's abode."

- *Walden, XVIII*, Conclusion
Henry David Thoreau

The immediate task facing the recently elected Poor House super-intendent was to interview his charges, and see what might be done to help them. That job would be more or less routine for a physician.

Next, however, the Poor House itself, with its sad facilities, would have to get in line for change. That change must be, at the least, a thorough renovation, and perhaps a rebuilding on the grand scale. There was not much margin for error. The superintendent would need to plan carefully, if the Poor House were to be built as inexpensively as possible. The county's budget would have to be expanded, in any case. At the same time, the buildings ought to be good enough to conform to the superintendent's pristine vision: "I must provide a haven for the paupers that will give them a manner of life that will bless, not burden them."[81]

The existing Poor House could not justly be called a burden, but it was certainly a much less comfortable home than was originally intended. Personnel and inmates were housed in the seven wooden duplex shacks. Whether those had been built as temporary or permanent structures is not known. But, there they were, having stood for ten years. They were patterned after the buildings of the first Poor House, which would argue that they were meant for permanency. After all, the buildings of the first Poor House had survived until the Battle of Ezra Church did them in.

Robert Hope judged that the county had stopped short of the best that it could do for its indigents. The buildings surely needed great improvement, if not outright replacement. The young superintendent said this to the Grand Jury once, then backed off, to wait and see if anybody had been listening.

*   *   *   *   *

The building problem would have to wait. First, the new superintendent had his new job to learn, and had already hit the ground running, learning as he went.

He went around to meet each of the forty-five inmates, white and black. About a third of them had some sort of chronic ailment which he would be caring for, long-term. There was usually a nurse on hand to assist. Most of the burden of actual medical care, of course, fell on Dr. Hope. This included the making and applying of prescriptions and treatments. From the week that the doctor took office in 1881, the weight of that burden bore on his thin shoulders. These poverty-stricken people were seldom out of his proximate vicinity, and could never be out of his thoughts.

Some of the inmates were, to say the least, unusual. Take Jim Hill, for example. By 1894, he would be the oldest inmate in point of residence. He was described by a visiting newspaper reporter as "a dwarf in size, and little better than half-witted."[82] Still, he was useful around the place. He was the chap whom Robert appointed to bring wood into the kitchen, and having that responsibility pleased him no end. Little Jim was fond of his pipe, and smoked it incessantly.

Jim Hill had been on the place since its inception at the Buckhead location ten years before. Previously, he had taken a shine to a young woman with whom he traveled over the country for a time, on a "poor man's holiday." More of that later.

After Dr. Hope had been serving for a year, the female convict camp was made part of the Poor House conglomerate. Jim Hill's earlier escapade had indicated his interest in the fair sex. He now got a crush on one of the female convicts, a woman called, "Missouri." This led to a cruel practical joke's being played on him.[83]

Mr. Jim Collins, the son and namesake of an Atlanta pioneer, had been clerk of the superior court since 1873. When he learned of Jim Hill's *affaire du coeur*, Mr. Collins told little Jim that as soon as he could get him a marriage license, he could marry Missouri! Of course Collins was thoughtlessly having some fun at Hill's expense. He was far wiser than to seek a marriage license for the likes of Jim Hill. When the license was not forthcoming, little Jim was very much hurt and irritated. But he was a harmless sort, and very useful at chores.

*   *   *   *   *

Another very special inmate at the Poor House was S.F. Billings.[84] "Billings and his cigars" was the common saying that conjoined the man and his hobby. Billings did not smoke cigars, he made them.

Some official visitors called at the Poor House one day, and Dr. Hope conducted them on a courtesy tour of the place. Billings was sitting in his room chatting with a guest when the knock came at the door, and the superintendent and his visitors were admitted. When they entered Billings' room, they saw several bunches of tobacco leaves hanging about the walls. Plainly, they had been hung there for the purpose of drying them, and the mellow odor of the plant pervaded the apartment.

As Billings and his friend got to their feet, the superintendent said, "Mr. Billings, here are two visitors who would like to make your acquaintance."

"I am glad to see you," said Billings, fingering his beard, and wreathing his face with a bright smile. He stumped forward on his wooden leg, extending his hand in greeting.

One of the visiting men, eyeing the peg leg, said, "You seem to be an old soldier."

"Yes, I belonged to Longstreet's corps, and I lost my leg in one of his charges. I have had a rather hard time of it, since the war, and things have not prospered with me, but I guess I ought to be satisfied."

Dr. Hope broke the ensuing silence. "Show the gentlemen your cigars, Mr. Billings."

The old veteran immediately pulled up the lid of a stout, old-fashioned trunk, reached to the bottom of it, and lifted out a box of fragrant, golden-brown cigars. His eyes twinkled as he saw the admiration on the visitors' faces, and heard their praises.

"Yes, I understand this work. I have made cigars off and on ever since the war."

Indeed, Billings had been in the cigar business in Atlanta, with Mr. Charles Beerman.

*   *   *   *   *

One phenomenon of the Poor House that the superintendent quickly observed was the extreme retiring nature of so many of the inmates.[85] This feature caught the eye of visitors as well. An individual like old Billy Waters would be standing outside his room, but as visitors approached, he would withdraw and quickly shut the door. What was the problem? Billy was beset by a complex. He feared unpleasant scrutiny by someone who might have known him in Atlanta, back in his days of solvency. Poor, fearful soul!

So it was with whole groups of inmates as well. If they saw strangers coming, their conversation would cease, and they would scatter.

"They are almost all like that," was Dr. Hope's comment.[86]

*   *   *   *   *

The sick and the aged were dosed up with herbal potions, teas, pills, and mustard plasters. After he had been settled into the work for some time, Robert described his routine to an interested newspaperman. He had established a schedule that took him into the city every few days, "to replenish his stock of medicines," said the paper, "and to attend to such business connected with his work as may require his presence in the city."[87]

To make these Buckhead-to-Atlanta trips, he could go through the little hamlet, and thence down the Peachtree Road, but he often preferred the route along Piedmont Road. Traveling that way, he could pick up some medicine from the dispensary at Easton.

Easton was situated at the present corner of Piedmont and Monroe Drive, where today the most prominent landmark is Ansley Mall. It had been at Easton, with its post office and stores, that Dr. Hope had studied the medical profession. Later, as previously mentioned, the Georgia Eclectic Medical College was merged into Emory. When the Easton post office was closed, the place name passed into history.

From one of the rooms of a hut in the Poor House cluster one might often whiff the odor of camphor and menthol vapors. A peek inside would have revealed the source – a coal scuttle and pan contraption in the center of the floor.

Not only those physicians of the "Eclectic" school, but most others also, were responsible to prepare many of their remedies by formula. "Natural" medicines were made of purchased plants and herbs which were ground up into bottles, then placed in solution. Robert worked at night on these.

Five decades later, his grandchildren saw the potions that he continued to prepare and keep.[88] This was well into the Twentieth Century, and well into the superintendent's years of retirement. He still believed in these home-prepared medicines. They were on shelves in the rambling, two-storey house that he had built the year after he retired. The remedies were bottles of green and brown liquids, with dark solids which seemed to be twigs or leaves, settled at the bottom. In the Poor House years of service, such homely creations were only part of the superintendent's arsenal. Robert would some-times give his patients medicines in the more concentrated pill form. Neither did he flinch from doing surgical operations, if those more drastic measures seemed called for.

The medicines were good and helpful to the patients. The constitutions of people like peculiar little Jim Hill, lady law-breaker

"Missouri," cigar-making Mr. S.F. Billings, and shy, reclusive old Billy Waters, and many others, were benefited.

Some moderns may disdain the use of the kinds of balms and healing juices that the Poor House kept on hand in great quantities. Usually, the objection is to the weakness of the solutions as compared with the pill-compressed antibiotics. There is seldom any accusation that the liquid solutions are in the category of "snake oil," but only that the medicine is so diffused that it may have much less potency.

A certain degree of reassurance about the homemade remedies, though, is found in their proven antibiotic content. Although antibiotics did not enter the field of medicine until the Twentieth Century, they were already present in the potions. The ancient Egyptians and Greeks, in fact, had them in many of the medical concoctions that they prepared from molds and herbs.[89]

When Robert Hope was interviewed by a newspaper reporter in 1895, after fourteen years at the Poor House, he was able to say,

"As the result of this individual care of the inmates and the general superintendence which I have given to the sanitary condition of the farm, no disease of any kind has broken out,[90] and not a single death has occurred during the last ten years except from old age or chronic disabilities. At present we have in the house several old men and women who are over eighty years of age, and have been inmates of the Poor House ever since the (Civil) war."

This statement may be taken in evidence that the Poor House was doing something right. American life expectancy as late as 1900 was just 47 years.[91]

Above – Poor House personnel with Dr. and Mrs. R.L.
Hope at center, with almshouse in background
Right – Mrs. R.L. Hope with husband's
picture on her cameo

At a rear corner of the Piedmont Poor House, about 1903,
left to right, Hollis, Dr. Hope,
Della holding baby Martha, and Lucien

CHAPTER THIRTEEN

MAKING THE PLANS

"Unless the LORD builds the house,
they labor in vain who build it."
Psalm 127.1

As Robert Hope became more and more sure of himself in the Poor House job, he became less and less tolerant of the living quarters of the inmates. Something simply had to be done for this shabby excuse of a public home.

More property had already been acquired at the director's urging. Most of the huge tract of Poor House land that was not under cultivation was covered with timber, and tangles of bushes and brambles. The area around the paupers' cabins was the exception. There, both in the white and black sections, was bare dirt. Clouds of dust filled the air around the cabins whenever there was movement during the dry, parched seasons of the year. Grass must be planted over a rather extensive area, to hold the soil, and pathways must be established to see that the grass was undisturbed.

Robert was working manfully to get more of the land in shape for the crops it needed to raise. When additional acres were cleared, plowed, and sowed, their produce would go far to make the Poor House pay for itself.

He was also wrestling with the budget. He figured that once his projected farm expansion was complete, the food grown would almost victual each inmate. By his arithmetic it would cost eight-and-a-half cents per day, per person, above what was raised on the farm.[92] Including meals for him and his wife, the sum would come to $4.00 per day, $28.00 per week, and about $1,500 per year, with no margin. Although $1,500 was a lot of money in 1881, the super-intendent knew the Grand Jury would like it. The Poor House had been costing them more.

But there were the Poor House buildings. They were an all too present need every single day! Dr. Hope reported to the Grand Jury that one inmate had recently injured his leg when a rotten floorboard broke.[93] The board was replaced.

The young director was faced with a tough Gordian knot that must be cut. The need was there, but all he heard was that there was not enough money available to meet it. What he really wanted to do was to build a grand main house, with the white inmates' quarters there. Because of the policy of racial segregation, the blacks would not be allowed there. So, then, build another main house for the blacks. No, the members of the Grand Jury told the director, county resources would not be able to provide more than one main house.

It was clear that the racism which controlled the politics of the time reached into all areas, extending even to the benevolent institutions. Within the parameters allowed him, however, Robert began to imagine something that would upgrade the blacks' situation as well. The houses that were now occupied by both whites and blacks would be re-plastered inside, bricked outside, or even completely rebuilt if necessary. Then the African-American people would get all of those quarters, giving them more space, and a far more comfortable living area.

The director went to the members of the Fulton County Grand Jury, told them the need, and his ideas:

"It *will* take considerable money, but not as much as you think. The convicts on the chain gang can be put to making brick and working on the buildings, under strict supervision. That will cut costs. In the meantime, the able-bodied among the paupers will have greater incentive to work (in the fields).

This will permit us to make enough money on the food we raise, to be self-supporting."[94]

The plan sounded good to some on the Grand Jury, but some doubted. The proverbial difficulty of coming to one mind in committee is well known. No matter the proposal, at least one committee member will drag his feet. Thus, in the U.S. Congress, the usual method of effectively killing a measure is to send it to committee.

To at least accomplish *something,* Robert could wish that the more activist account of committee procedure might be acted out. It ran, "be sure to appoint at least three men on a committee, so it can complete its report. One of the three will surely be ill, the second out of town, and the third will attend the meeting and write the report!"

In this case, a slow-moving Grand Jury was not the only roadblock. By the time the young superintendent brought in his recommendations, some members already were entertaining a prior idea. It was based on the approach of Atlanta's biggest event in a long time, the International Cotton Exposition.

The Cotton Exposition, the equivalent of a world's fair, was to be held in Atlanta at old Oglethorpe Park in this same year, 1881. It was truly a big thing, with steering committee representation not only from Atlanta, but also from New Orleans, and four of the great cities of the North. This was the most notable event that had happened to the city since Sherman captured it.

An interesting sidelight on the Exposition was that General William T. Sherman was a large monetary subscriber to it. He personally attended the event. This time, he who had once ordered the city burned, sat on the platform as an honored guest. During the festivities, he made a speech to the Mexican War Veterans present, most of whom were Georgians or men from other Southern states. He said, in part:

"I have come today to look upon these buildings where once we had battlefields. I delight more to look upon them than to look upon the scenes enacted here sixteen years ago. I say that every noble man and kindly woman over this broad land takes as much interest in your prosperity and in this Exposition as do those sitting in this presence, and that we are now in a position to say, every one of us, great and small, Thank God we are American citizens."[95]

The significance for the Poor House was the interest that the Exposition drew to Oglethorpe Park, on Marietta Street. The park was only two miles northwest of the center of Atlanta. Some on the Grand Jury thought that it would be a good idea to secure new property near the park, and erect the new Poor House buildings there. They agreed with Dr. Hope that new buildings were necessary, but were firmly convinced that the securing of a brand new site was desirable. Should the almshouse stay where it was, or should it be moved? Obviously, the location had to be settled first, meaning that the building project would be further delayed.

The Fulton County Grand Jury traveled in a body to the Buckhead location. The <u>Atlanta</u> <u>Constitution</u> newspaper reported their findings:

"(They) found the almshouse well kept and the inmates seemingly well contented. The buildings are declared to be mere shanties, sufficient perhaps for summer shelter, but wholly inadequate for winter. They recommended new buildings, but first suggest that the 300 acres now owned be sold[96] and 50 acres purchased near enough to the city to admit of frequent visits from humane and benevolent persons who would be glad to contribute to the comfort of these unfortunate inmates."

On the surface it sounded good enough. No doubt horses and buggies from those grand homes downtown could easily run over a couple of miles to Marietta Street. It was harder for the vehicles to bounce, groan, and squeak six miles "over the hills" to the Buckhead Poor House.

But something was rotten in the state of Denmark. Influenced by certain political considerations, but even more by economy, the Grand Jury was on the verge of making a very poor decision. The

City of Atlanta already owned the 50 acres mentioned by the news article. Its transference to the Poor House, and the sale of the 300 Buckhead acres would make a little money for Fulton County, but was the location right?

Decisions with long-term effects must be made very carefully. Rarely does an institution benefit when its location is chosen simply for its low purchase cost, or because the property is offered as a gift. The Commission of Roads and Revenues was not satisfied with the Grand Jury's projected plan. On the same day that the Grand Jury voted it, the Commission, in a lengthy meeting, overturned the plan. They decided that something else would be done with the 50 acres.

The <u>Atlanta Constitution</u> had it all, in a story that appeared next day:

> "- - the county already has 50 acres of land near the Exposition grounds, but the alms house will not be placed thereon. The commissioners intend to put the convict camps on that property, and after a long consideration of the matter will let the alms house remain where it is, namely, on the land north of Buckhead. The commissioners do not consider it wise to let the paupers live so near the city, as it will be rather too convenient for them to steal away and spend their time loafing around the city."[97]

The commissioners likely cared more about keeping the streets clear of vagrants, than about the inmates' morals. They had a point. In recent years, the late Mayor Maynard Jackson, and current Mayor Shirley Franklin have wrestled with the problem of street people in Atlanta. So the 1880's inmates would be kept north of Buckhead, not tempted by the bright lights to be idle nuisances. At the Poor House, those able to would work.

The way seemed open to proceed to build. The Grand Jury had already spoken in favor of its being done. Yet now considerable time was spent reviewing what they had decided. The decision was confirmed, but next, additional months must be consumed to establish the convict camp on Marietta Street. Always delays! And, as

1882 dragged into 1883, the Poor House still had nothing more than its less-than-adequate cabins on Peachtree Road.

The superintendent of course continued to wish to spur the plan, and see it through.

On his frequent buggy rides over to town, he would stop in to lobby with a Grand Jury member. He would remind the man of the pitiable state of the Poor House buildings. He now had the advantage that the men had seen the buildings with their own eyes.

Availing himself of his older brother's advice, the superintendent also went by to see George in his downtown office, every three or four days. This brother, though only twenty-six, had been a full partner in the grocery business for five. He was well known in the city as a promising young man. His influence could only do the Poor House good.

Dr. Hope's plan was unfolded to the Grand Jury. There should be a large central building, replacing the small one built on the same general location. The central building would look somewhat like the grand resort hotels of the day. The director and his family would reside here, along with many of the white inmates who were to be housed in its multi-roomed accommodations.

The provision for the black inmates was not extravagant, but they were not forgotten. They would inherit all of the existing cabins, including those which the whites vacated. These cabins would be thoroughly renovated. Outside, they would be brick-veneered. Inside, all cracks, rifts, and holes would be sealed. The inside walls would be plastered, to make them suitable all-weather dwellings.[98]

The bigger and better Poor House would be much more of what the area needed. The expansion of living space would allow 50-100% more inmates to be accommodated.

Not until the spring of 1884 would things really begin to move. In the meantime, the commissioners of Roads and Revenues made a group visit to the Poor House, to begin planning the building arrangements. Mssrs. Gramling, Hunnicutt, Murphy, and Colonel Grant were accompanied by Mr. Bruce, the architect who would draw the building plans. With Robert Hope, they walked over the thickly timbered land, as well as the cleared areas. Then they met with him, and made their projections.

The commissioners agreed that at the appointed time they would send a squad of convicts to the farm to make brick for the main house, and the lesser buildings. They reaffirmed that white inmates would live in the wings of the main building, if they needed close medical attention, while others would be housed in new cabins to be built a short distance beyond. The black inmates would continue to reside in their present cabins, and also the ones which would be vacated by the whites. All of those cabins would be completely rebuilt to the superintendent's specifications.

The rest of the plan also contained other things that Dr. Hope had yearned for. A windmill to pump water would be built. A grassy lawn, and shrubbery would be put in place, to make the establishment much more pleasant.

Now the superintendent could believe that the Millenium was just around the corner!

But before that corner was turned, there would be a virtual Battle of Armageddon to be fought. He would have to fight it, just to keep his job.

CHAPTER FOURTEEN

TRIAL BY GOSSIP

"No sooner is a temple built to God but the Devil builds a chapel hard by."

- Jacula Prudentum
George Herbert

W hile plans were maturing for the Poor House expansion, the seas of life were not untroubled. The doctor's wife, Della, bore a baby – stillborn. Less than a year later there was a miscarriage. The couple were still childless. Then, over the years, they contrived to produce twelve more offspring, for a total of fourteen pregnancies. Of these, nine of the children died in the womb, in infancy, or in childhood – an appalling mortality rate in the home of a physician, though there was a special reason. Later, in 1886, Della would contract polio. The young woman would begin a life of wearing metal braces on her paralyzed legs.

Irrespective of the superintendent's personal heartache, he moved forward on the Poor House expansion. Plans were revised and corrected, and were maturing fast. Already, though, in April, 1883, Robert, at the helm for only two years, had been accused of mismanagement of the almshouse.

It began merely as a distant thundercloud on the horizon – somebody else's trouble.

County commissioner G.T. Dodd had been keeping close watch on the management of the county jail. He publicly accused sheriff A.M. Perkerson of spending too much of the county's money to feed the prisoners. Dodd made his attack through the newspaper's regular complaint column, entitled, "Let the Responsibility Rest Where It Belongs." In the column someone was always in trouble, and this time it was Perkerson.[99]

Dodd charged that Perkerson was spending 25 cents per day to provide food and blankets for the prisoners under his watchcare. This amount is ridiculously small, but it was not so, 124 years ago. Dodd said that it was an exorbitant cost. Instead of simply leaving his complaint at that, he went on to compare the 25 cents with the daily mere eight-and-a-half cents per inmate that Robert Hope was spending at the Poor House. Willy-nilly, the innocent Poor House director was dragged in, although in the process he had received a compliment.

Dodd was not finished. He offered the information that a responsible firm in Atlanta had offered to furnish Army rations, including vegetables, at a cost of fourteen and two-thirds cents per prisoner, per day. Why could not the sheriff avail himself of this opportunity? "This we think would give the sheriff a fine profit."

The commissioner perhaps intended to say that the *jail* would be given a fine profit, but the statement was poorly worded, and easily capable of misinterpretation.

Mad as a hornet whose nest has been knocked, Sheriff Perkerson rebutted by putting a reply in the same gripe column of the newspaper. His article contained phrases such as,

> "- - another voluntary epistle by Dodd - - in which he labors to show that the sheriff is not doing the clean thing - - the repeated harangues of Dodd (who appears to have jail on the brain for some reason)."

Perkerson's letter thus revealed that this contention was not the first instance of wrangling between the two. Whatever their history had been, they certainly did not now like each other.

If Dodd had gone unnecessarily far in his letter, so Perkerson did also in his. He wanted to conclude by explaining why it took 25 cents per prisoner to do the daily feeding at the jail. Since Dodd had compared the jail's expenses to the smaller ones of the Poor House, Perkerson next lit into the Poor House superintendent. Here were his words, written in the heat of anger:

"As to his reference to the expense of keeping the inmates at the almshouse, I have only to say that if the statement be true that these unfortunates who are unable to support themselves and who are real objects of charity (if not they should not be there) are fed on 8½ cents of food at the present market value, the fact is sufficient to damn its author in the estimation of every man, woman and child who has a soul as large as a mustard seed.[100] 'Let the responsibility rest where it belongs.'"

Robert Hope replied in an open letter in the press, headed, "To the People of Fulton County." The tone of his letter shows that he was hurt, yet he wrote with restraint. His purpose, of course, was political: to defend his operation of the Poor House:

"A.M. Perkerson, sheriff of this county, in his card of December 11th, to Commissioner Dodd, in regard to feeding and furnishing blankets, etc., to the prisoners of the jail, made a very unkind and unjust remark in regard to the feeding of the inmates at the almshouse, of which I am superintendent. I am instructed by the county commissioners to buy all necessary provisions and supplies for the inmates, and I have done so to the satisfaction of the inmates without complaint, to the satisfaction of the commissioners and the satisfaction of the grand jury of the county, composed of such men as Henry Porter, E.P. Chamberlin, John Stephens, T.M. Clarke and other of the best citizens in the county; and a committee from the grand jury examined for themselves and were satisfied as well as the county commissioners, and my expenses were 8½ cents per day for each person. I raise vegetables on the place, and have a cow, which enables me to feed them cheaper; and for doing this I don't feel that I deserve to be 'damned' by the public for feeding these unfortunates well, though I do it for such small cost to the county. The sheriff may think differently. Respectfully, R.L. Hope."[101]

Dr. Hope had pressed the one key point: Food was *produced* on the Poor House farm, but *not* in the jail. No fair comparison of their expenses could be made.

An unfortunate weakness of human beings in a nation of freedom is their propensity to launch political assaults on public officials. Out of the blue, they wash dirty linen in public, before ever conferring with their offender. This public slashing is excused by the assertion that public problems demand public solutions. This unfair process mistreats people, but, "that's politics."

Robert Hope's letter had a positive effect, but failed to get him entirely off the hook.

Total exoneration took another month or so.

Smelling a story ready to be told, the <u>Atlanta</u> <u>Constitution</u> began sending reporters out to the Poor House on a regular basis. This practice continued for many years. The papers discovered that readers were as curious about the inmates' diet as a modern operetta's King Arthur, concerning, "What do the simple folk do?"

The reporters' assignment was always to question either the doctor or his wife, as well as the white and black inmates, thus to close in on the truth. Two such investigators found the average meals simple, but nourishing and adequate.[102] In abbreviated form, this is essentially what they caused to be printed in the paper:

For Breakfast: Coffee, Bread, Bacon, or other Salty Meat, Grits or Rice, with Gravy.

For Lunch and Dinner (the reporter, in Southern fashion, called them "Dinner" and "Supper," respectively): A Second Cup of Coffee, Assorted Vegetables, White Beans, Meat, Beef Soup, Bread, and Syrup.

He reported that the noon and evening meals were served to the inmates at the same time. They took both to their rooms, to dine alone, and re-heated the latter meal when they were ready for it, at about five or six o'clock.

All of this was printed in the <u>Constitution</u>, and people around the city read it, and grinned at each other. "They're eating as well as I am. Maybe I'd better 'go over the hills to the Poor House,' myself!"

The criticism sputtered out with a few guffaws.

* * * * *

Of a much more serious nature was a sensational report that got onto the street right on the heels of the food cost complaint. Two inmates, it was said, had died in the Poor House under mysterious circumstances.[103]

The story went that one of the two, an insane black man, had a convulsion resulting in his death. During the fit, he had fallen into the fire in his room, and had been burned to death. Another man was reported to have frozen to death. The two tales hit the public's ear on the same day, as one narrative.

Right away, County Coroner F.A. Hilburn reacted, for the deaths had occurred without his being notified. Understandably wishing to clear his skirts as coroner, he sent a letter to the <u>Atlanta</u> <u>Post-Appeal</u>, stating what he surmised had occurred. He thought that the deaths had taken place, and he knew that he had not been called for an inquest in either one. Burials had been made anyway – presumably illegal burials.

Hilburn's letter was of course interpreted as a condemnation of the Poor House superintendent. It was the only conclusion to draw, if the matter really happened as the coroner said.

A newspaper subscriber made a published reply to Hilburn, however, in which the subscriber defended Dr. Hope. This defense called forth a second letter from Hilburn. The coroner said, in all humility, that he had not wished to reflect on "that gentleman," the Poor House superintendent, "or anyone else," but had wanted only to relate the events.[104]

He might well have concluded his letter right there. He did not. Instead, he went on to speculate whether one or both of the deceased inmates might not have been murdered! In the case of the insane man, he said, someone could have slipped in, cut the man's throat, and then have thrown him into the fire in an attempt to conceal the evidence.

Why all this graphic speculation? Because the coroner, using his detective's imagination, was illustrating to the public the reason for a coroner's existence. But, unfortunately, the letter did nothing to clear the name of the superintendent. Indeed it only served to intensify curiosity. Had the superintendent committed the illegality of outlaw burials? Was he a bad man?

At this hinge moment, Mr. J.T. Cooper, chairman of the County Commission, stepped forward like the surprise rescuer in a stage play.[105] He revealed that neither of the deceased inmates had even been *at* the Poor House at the time of their deaths! Furthermore, he, Cooper, the ranking member of the Commission, had ordered that there be no inquests. He had trusted the investigations made by Dr. Hope, and had told him not to bother the coroner. Since Cooper held precedence over both the Poor House superintendent, and the coroner, his decision would stand. Robert Hope was exonerated in full.

Cooper's letter of explanation to the Atlanta Post-Appeal was so conclusive that the editors headed it, "The Matter Settled." The text of that letter was the following:

"Editor, Post-Appeal: It gives me no pleasure to appear in print, but the articles published in your paper of the 26th and 27th instant attempted to involve the official integrity of Dr. R.L. Hope, the superintendent of the Alms House, whom I know to be a good and humane man, and a competent and reliable officer, and who is at his post of duty, attending to his business, seven miles from the city, and not likely to see and read the little insinuations directed at him. Wherefore I feel constrained to give the history of this little 'tempest in a teapot' in his behalf.

"Dr. Hope reported the cases of the insane negro and the man who froze to death to the Board of County Commissioners through me, their clerk.

"It was so clear that 'nobody was to blame' for the cause of their death, that I told Dr. Hope that if he was satisfied, after an investigation by him, that the facts were as stated as to the cause of their death, that it was unnecessary to put the county to the expense of holding inquests over them. If anyone is to blame in the matter of not having inquests held, I am that man and not Dr. Hope, for I advised him to that course.

"The 'insane negro' was not an inmate of the Alms House at the time of his death. He had left its 'bed and board' and sought other quarters and other companionship without the consent of the Alms House authorities. He was not insane, but was subject to fits.

"The man who 'froze to death' had been off to Decatur during the day on a 'spree' without the consent of the Alms House authorities, and on his return had 'fallen by the wayside' and there met his 'quietus' at the hands of the cold north wind.

"The abode at the Alms House is entirely voluntary, and there is no authority to keep the inmates in confinement without their consent. All that can be done in that direction is to have 'disciplinary rules' which we have endeavored to enforce. There is no guard to prevent the ingress and egress of inmates, nor has there ever been.

"I hope this little matter is now settled to the entire satisfaction of all.

Yours Respectfully,
John T. Cooper[106]
Atlanta, April 30, 1883"

No doubt Robert Hope had asked Cooper to write the letter. He had read the insinuations against him, and always kept close tabs on whatever went on over in Atlanta.

This letter was the end of the matter. The superintendent continued to stand tall.

The criticisms of his detractors now seemed like the yelps of a row of little yellow dogs, barking at the moon.

This incident was not the last attack, however. An official investigation was only three years away, but that one would end even better. In addition, the road to progress had already opened wide.

CHAPTER FIFTEEN

BUILDING BLOCKS OF PROGRESS

"No man is born into the world whose work
Is not born with him; there is always work,
And tools to work withal, for those who will;
And blessed are the horny hands of toil."
                    - A Glance Behind the Curtain
                    James Russell Lowell

Questions about the Poor House had been so lacking in substance that building and progress were possible even as the news-paper gossiped. Some further plans were made by the Commission, and duly reported in the dailies. Then came another delay, which stretched across the summer. The problem was one of procurement. Materials of all kinds had to be ordered by the Commission, which unfortunately had many other matters to attend to at this time.

The superintendent, too, was kept busy - - so busy that he never minded the check that was being imposed on his dream.

When September and October rolled in, one more delay loomed. The convicts were being employed on prior projects elsewhere. After a couple more months, they were free from those duties, but by that time, some of them had served out their sentences, or got special pardons for Christmas. A partially new crew of prisoners would have to be trained, even for menial jobs.

At last, in the early months of 1884, most of the elements needed had fallen into place. A force of sixteen convicts was brought to the Poor House property to live there temporarily, under guard.[107] A number of tents and lean-to's were erected for them, and for the officers in charge. They would be there until the job was done, fed by the Poor House, as were the inmates. Care for their health also fell to the superintendent.

The tasks of the convicts were to make brick, then build a new "main house," and some new smaller quarters, as well as to brick up the old ones. The target date for completion of the entire project was summer, 1885.

It was a huge undertaking. The work was there to be done, and from scratch. Could it be completed in the time specified, or anywhere near it? The superintendent took a fair look at it, concluding that it was possible to finish by that time. Nonetheless, he acknowledged to himself that it might not happen, and his mental burden because of it was very heavy.

It was during this period that Della sometimes glimpsed his spare, lank figure from a window, as he moved about the grounds. A sleepless moonlit night was a good time to walk and talk with God.[108]

Spring months seemed to come quickly, then summer. Day by day, oppressed by a merciless summer's humidity at its height, Robert Hope, tall, shirt-sleeved, was outside for some hours. He was supervising preparations for a more permanent camp for the convict crew. Lumber for it was sawed right there on the place. Plans of the architect, Mr. Bruce, were reviewed, and re-reviewed, with the gentleman himself present. The brick-making, and brick-laying would be a hard and crucial part of the job.

* * * * *

Irrespective of his private doubtings, the superintendent turned a face of optimism towards the public. In autumn, 1884, the <u>Atlanta Constitution</u> reported,

"Dr. Hope, superintendent of the county almshouse, was in the city yesterday, and a <u>Constitution</u> man asked him how he was getting on with the new quarters for the inmates. Said the doctor:

'We are getting on very well. There is a force out there of sixteen convicts, and they have cleared off the brickyard, and are preparing to make the brick that we will need. The lumber has been prepared for the construction of camps for the convicts, and plans for the new almshouse have all been drawn up and we are about to get fairly started in on the work.'

'How fast will you progress with it?'

'We will have to make 400,000 brick and you know winter is coming and that will interfere with our work. We will fix up the present white quarters before winter so that they will be comfortable before one more winter. We expect to finish the new quarters by the middle of next summer. The new quarters will then be given to the white paupers and the quarters now used by the whites will be turned over to the colored inmates.'"[109]

The Commission had dictated this plan, though with no desire to injure or insult the African-Americans. In the social context of the time, it simply never entered their heads that a lower order of humans should rate anything but the leavings.

*   *   *   *   *

In November, the making of brick got started, and an interesting process it was.[110] The requirement was that 400,000 bricks be made by the convicts. Today, a large brick plant may turn out 150-200,000, or even 300,000 per day, but without large, sophisticated modern machinery, 400,000 was a mountainous chore.

The clay used was found in abundant quantities on the Poor House property. It was composed of hydrated silicate of aluminum, with oxide, or carbonate of iron, and various other substances. The convict force dug it out, and mule-drawn wagons pulled it near.

A load each of wetted clay and sand was poured into a large, wooden-sided floor and mixed. One can imagine the commands of the deputy acting as foreman: "Careful there, boys! There's too much sand! The bricks will crumble!" Yes, and if there were too little, they would crack. An exact balance was required of the craft.

Smoothed to level, the mix was allowed to settle. This went on for some days, the water being drained off at intervals. Then it was covered with 2-3 inches of ashes, which were mixed in, too.

The whole pudding was put into the "pug-mill." A skilled white convict, bull-necked, with muscular forearms dun-colored with drying clay, took over. He forced the mud out between two boards which formed a sort of sluice. Cut then into proper lengths, the mud bar became slightly oversized bricks, which another man popped into forms. As he did so, he sheered off the excess mud, and expertly hand-molded the oblong bricks with his fingers to fill in the crevices.

The bricks were plopped out of the forms onto wide, flat, board trays, and taken off a little distance. There they were set down, and covered with straw, to cure from three to six weeks. After that they went into the little kiln to be fired.

The clay had components in it that actually burned, really fed the fire. And as the bricks burned, they changed color. The clay, sand, and ash mixture had gone into the fire a dull, dun color; it came out a pinkish red, turned chemically by the iron oxide in the clay.

So the brick-making went, one by one, hand-molded. Using several mixing floors, the crew were kept busy each day with some part of the process. Although caught by the cold weather, which stopped manufacture for awhile, Dr. Hope had his 400,000 brick by the spring. Construction had already begun on the main house.

The main house was built according to the plan originally drawn by that competent architect, Mr. Bruce. It had been approved by Dr. Hope, followed by final approval from the Commission. The house was placed close to the Roswell Road on Piedmont. It was perhaps half a mile from the cluster of wooden duplexes which sat near the corner of Piedmont and Peachtree.

* * * * *

The main house was completed in December, 1885. Once it was up, the inmates were moved in, and there was an "open house" to show the building to the public. The place was considered a marvel of loveliness and convenience, and Atlanta visitors to it pronounced it a great source of satisfaction to them. Said the <u>Atlanta</u> <u>Constitution</u>:

> "- - a place the county may well feel pride in. The house is of splendid brick and is almost if not fully as well built as any in Atlanta."[111]

Robert Hope himself had selected the site on which the main house would be built. He had also put much care into the planning of the other arrangements for the structure. He wanted a building that would last for many years. He himself was going to stay, and this would be his permanent base.

The configuration of the new Poor House was that of a squared "U." The bottom of the "U" was the grand main house fronting on Piedmont Road. The two sides of the "U" were apartment wings extending rearward from it on either side. The <u>Constitution</u> paid its tribute:

> "It is in a beautiful location. The front is occupied as a residence for Dr. and Mrs. Hope and the paupers occupy two wings running back. In the court (in the rear, between the two wings) is a good well. The adjacent grounds are sown in blue grass. The place is exceedingly attractive, both for the surroundings and on account of the excellent new plastered rooms and clean beds. There is no hired help, but one of the pauper women is detailed to cook. The paupers eat at a common table in a long dining room. They have breakfast at eight, dinner at one, and a cold lunch at suppertime. There is a hospital department and Dr. Hope has a good stock of medicines. The inmates appeared bright and cheerful, exceedingly so when it was remembered that the company

was an aggregation of lame, halt, blind, idiots and unfortunates generally."[112]

While the quarters of the white paupers, inside and outside the main house, were complete, the blacks were not as fortunate. The cold weather of the winter of 1885-86 again halted work, delaying the bricking up of their dwellings until spring. There was even further delay, but the superintendent confidently told reporters,

"We have now on hand 125,000 brick with which to erect this summer brick quarters for the colored people. When that is done, the Poor House will be an honor to the county."[113]

He had, in the early spring of 1886, ten acres of planted garden, and was cultivating thirty-five acres in all. He said,

"I expect in two or three years to make the place self-sustaining."[114]

*   *   *   *   *

This year of 1886 was a notable one for Atlanta in a number of ways. For one thing, the aged former president of the Confederacy, Jefferson Davis, made his last visit to Atlanta from his home in Woodville, Mississippi.[115] The occasion in Atlanta was to be the unveiling of a marble statue, a monument to the late, great Georgia senator, Ben Hill.

Davis made the trip on a train, coming by way of Montgomery, Alabama. At every station along the way enthusiastic crowds greeted his train, making the journey one long celebration for the ex-president.

In Atlanta, one hundred thousand people from many communities jammed Peachtree Street. Ten thousand Confederate veterans, men still in their prime, marched down Peachtree in rank. On a platform erected for the occasion, Davis sat with other dignitaries. A murmur ran through the crowd, for it was noticed that General James Longstreet, who had been a north Georgian for several years, was absent. A coolness had arisen between Longstreet and Davis, because of the former's having turned Republican following the Civil War. Longstreet had received political favors because of his complicity with the hated Reconstruction measures of the Republican Party.

The statue had been unveiled, and several men had spoken, before the main speaker began. During his speech, the drama of the day occurred. Those who happened to glance up Peachtree Street towards the business section, saw a solitary horseman riding toward the platform. It was Longstreet, in the full grey uniform of a Confederate lieutenant-general. He reached the platform, dismounted, gave the bridle to an attendant, and walked up the steps. As he approached the canopy under which Davis sat, the latter rose and started towards him. The two embraced with great emotion, and the thousands of veterans gave a mighty shout of joy over the reconciliation of their two former leaders.

Newspaper editor Henry Grady skillfully orchestrated this Atlanta event to secure the nomination, and subsequent election to the governorship, of General John B. Gordon.

All this took place on May 1, 1886.

The "Lost Cause" legend was on a rising tide.

*　　*　　*　　*　　*

During the same month, druggist John Styth Pemberton, after trying various formulae for a year, since May, 1885, finally hit it. What he had been after was a syrup blend for the relief of headache. Now he had a concoction that included fluid extract of coca, and fluid extract of kola. It was Coca-Cola, written in the flowing script of Pemberton's chemical company partner, Frank Mason Robinson.[116]

*　　*　　*　　*　　*

On August 31, Charleston, South Carolina suffered a severe earthquake which killed fifty-seven people. The shock was very heavily felt in Atlanta also, as it was in communities to the east of the city.

*   *   *   *   *

In the autumn, ground was broken for Fort McPherson, the great U.S. Army post in southwest Atlanta, near East Point along the Central Railroad. The base was completed in 1888, and was made a permanent post in 1889. It was initially garrisoned by the U.S. Fourth Artillery, and later became the headquarters of the U.S. Third Army. Fort McPherson was named for Civil War Union general James B. McPherson, who was killed in the Battle of Atlanta. The fort made a handsome home for "the boys in blue," whose uniforms, incidentally, were exchanged, article by article, in the 1890's, for khaki.

*   *   *   *   *

The Poor House superintendent had lived through something of a civil war of his own, in 1883. He had successfully proved that all charges of Poor House mismanagement were groundless. However, he now faced another assault in 1886.

CHAPTER SIXTEEN

NEW RUMORS

"Confound their politics, - -"
From *God Save the Queen*,
British national anthem

The superintendent's spring, 1886 report, published in the newspaper, sounded very good. Progress was being made, and lots of it! But behind the scenes, not everything was roses.

Only sixty days before, just following the coldest depths of winter, an African-American man named Hamp Moss had made some sensational charges.[117] He delivered them in downtown Atlanta, against the Poor House and its administration. Although his accusations were soon exposed as gross exaggerations, deliberate lies, they caused a stir.

The manufactured untruths, aimed at damaging Dr. Hope, failed in their purpose. They did create a battle, though, which took several days to win.

One can readily see why the allegations were so interesting to the general public. Hamp Moss lived near the Poor House, and claimed to have visited it often, in the role of a Good Samaritan. The Poor House, and its development, had already received much favorable publicity. Yet here was a man who was assumed to be "in the know." He was asserting that there had been three recent scandals in the Poor House, unreported until he told of them.

Moss said, first, that a seventy-year-old inmate named Maria Wilson had rolled from her cot in an attack of illness. She had fallen into the grated fire in her room, and been burned to death!

Secondly, an elderly man, Wylie Sutton, very feeble with dropsy, had complained to Moss that his feet were very cold. When Moss then pulled off one of the old fellow's shoes, he had found ice in it! Since dropsy involves the unnatural collection of fluids in any cavities of the body, it is easy to imagine the speculation that may have gathered around this story.

The third alleged incident was supposed to have happened the week prior to the ice-in-the-shoe horror. An old blind woman, Emily Smith, had died. When the body was being dressed for the coffin, it was said that discovery was made that her toes were ready to fall from her feet because of frostbite.

Moss added a somewhat anticlimactic caboose to his train of accusations. He said that the black inmates were underfed.

Here was a pretty mess! If the charges were true, Dr. Hope was guilty of gross mismanagement. The <u>Atlanta</u> <u>Constitution</u> wanted to know. Thus, on the next morning following the afternoon that Hamp Moss burst on the scene, a reporter was sent out to the Poor House.

The reporter found the African-Americans' quarters, with the paupers themselves sunning on the warm sides of the houses in the fresh air. The man was skilled in making friends. Once he did, he had no trouble in getting these people to talk.

As they talked, Hamp Moss' stories were shredded by the plain truth.[118] Maria Wilson had not burned to death. She had been discovered dead in her room, a victim of her "dropsy of the heart." The body showed that she had not been burned at all, but had fallen in a spot where she had merely gotten ashes on her face. None of the paupers knew anything at all about an old man with ice in his shoes, or a woman with frozen toes. The paupers had no reason to lie, for no authority was around to monitor what they said. It became evident to the reporter that they were stating the facts accurately.

In the midst of the reporter's interrogations, Dr. Hope did finally show up. According to the newspaper account, he "hooted at the idea of mismanagement." He sought to prove the rumors false by telling the exact circumstances in each case. He substantiated what the paupers had told of Maria Wilson. She had died of dropsy, nothing else. No ice had been discovered in Wylie Sutton's shoes, because his old feet were so badly swollen that he could no longer put on shoes, much less have shaken ice out of them! As to Emily Smith, the toes of her corpse showed no frostbite at all.

The superintendent concluded by saying that he could definitely prove all the charges false. The reporter was convinced. So lacking was any fuel for Moss' flames of rumor that the journalist went home to write his article. He assured Atlanta newspaper readers, "The reign of terror that the sensation hunter was after did not appear to exist."[119]

* * * * *

If the wild charges of Moss had no basis in fact, what prompted him to make them?

Politics. The election for superintendent of the Poor House was rushing closer. It would take place on the first Wednesday in May.

The superintendent's political opponents had somehow learned that the 70-year-old woman, Maria Wilson, had been Hamp Moss' friend. The friendship went back to the years before circumstances had sent her to the Poor House. Moss was understandably distraught over her death, but in addition, he was nursing a racial grievance. He believed that the black inmates in general had been neglected. As he saw it, the neglect was deliberate, and was proved by the African-American cabins' renovation having been delayed past the winter of 1885-86. Moss' impulse to strike out in revenge against cruel fate, plus the payment of money to him, triggered his wild stories.[120]

Moss was discredited, but the election was not yet safe for Robert Hope. The opposition knew still that the only way to beat him was to blemish his reputation. Otherwise, the public's knowledge of the Poor House improvement and expansion made the incumbent a shoo-in. Therefore, another attack was launched, this time by a white man, C.S. Bailey, who had recently left the Poor House and now alleged cruelty against Dr. Hope – he had whipped a female inmate.

This slander did not get very far. The <u>Atlanta</u> <u>Constitution</u> called it "a queer story," and the <u>Atlanta</u> <u>Journal</u> actually wrote an apology to the superintendent for Atlanta's unwarranted suspicions:

"The sensational reports about the mismanagement of Fulton County alms house have proved to be without foundation. A <u>Journalier</u> visited the alms house and found every inmate satisfied with the treatment received and having no complaint to make. It is asserted that these reports are originated and stimulated by parties from personal motives. Dr. L.S. (sic) Hope, the superintendent, has an unblemished reputation in every respect."[121]

CHAPTER SEVENTEEN

PRE-ELECTION SCRUTINY

"There is another way to truth: by the minute examination of facts."

Shakespeare and Spiritual Life
John Masefield

The election was now drawing very near. The superintendent had been cleared, virtually, of all the irresponsible charges made against him. Still, the daily news sheets persisted in publicizing the hot story. They were not only anxious to use it to sell newspapers, but also to make themselves the channels for election campaign information. This worked to Dr. Hope's advantage, for even if he could have left his oversight of the paupers for long, in order to go and influence voters, he did not need to. The newspapers did it for him.

* * * * *

The most extensive investigation of the Poor House was conducted by the <u>Atlanta Evening Capitol.</u>[122] One of the <u>Capitol's</u> reporters had interviewed two white men, and one black woman. All three of these had recently left the Poor House, part of the institution's constant turnover of occupants. They were claiming that the Poor House food and clothing were inadequate.

The reporter suspected that the complaints were merely the all-too-common grumbles of beggars, but they were worth checking out. Accordingly, the <u>Capitol's</u> city editor and business manager decided to use Sunday morning to take a seven-mile carriage ride out Peachtree Road. Said the editor,

> "The road over the hills to the Fulton County poor house is a good one, a little steep just this side of Peachtree Creek, but in the main quite a pleasant drive. The <u>Capitol</u> party left the city at ten o'clock, but after an hour and a half's drive by blossoming orchards, pleasant attractive country houses, the home of the paupers was reached."

The newspapermen went first to the twenty-eight room, red brick main building, finished the previous December. They found Dr. Hope gone to church, as was his Sunday custom,

> "- - but Mrs. Hope kindly showed the visitors around and allowed them the privilege of conversing alone with any of the inmates - -."

Before holding any interviews, the newsmen decided to inspect the rooms. No problem there, they discovered. They subsequently wrote,

> "Every room was looked into and in each the floor was scrupulously clean; the furniture was good and the beds were comfortable and neat – there was no exception in any apartment. The large room at the end of one of the galleries (see diagram) used as a hospital, contained four or five well-kept beds and a bright and cheery fire burned upon the hearth."

But what about the Poor House food, which had been the source of the most recently expressed disgruntlement? It had been the food complaint which had brought the <u>Capitol </u>men to investigate.

"The dining room contained a long table set for dinner. The cloth upon the table was white and clean and the plates, knives and forks were better than those seen in many boarding houses. In the kitchen, a white woman, one of the paupers, was cooking dinner and the investigators had a chance of seeing what sort of food was given to the paupers. In one pot was three or four pieces of bacon; in another was about a bushel of peas boiling with fat meat, and in a number of pans were 'pones' of corn bread. The molasses was tasted and found to be of good quality. Everything in the cooking department was clean and well arranged."

What the reporters had seen was the simple fare eaten by Southern farm folk of the time. The investigators consumed some of it themselves, as it was now past lunch time.

*   *   *   *   *

The interviews with the inmates came next. The men first quizzed a wrinkled old German, baiting him with the deliberately vague remark that complaints had been made about the Poor House. The reply was favorable to the Poor House:

"You can't please everybody. We get plenty to eat, and have nice, comfortable rooms to sleep in. I live better than I did when I was working for good wages and supporting my family. Of course we are being supported by the county and mustn't expect to be placed in a palace and fed like kings and queens. I get all I want and am contented."

The next inmate, "an old grey-haired man," who had lived over in Atlanta until he became unable to work, also gave a generous answer. He said,

"I don't see what people can expect in a place of this kind than what we get. The food is not the daintiest in the world, but it is good enough and there is plenty of it. The only thing that is short is coffee. We get only one cup a day. For my part I am quite satisfied with the way we are treated by Dr. Hope. He is thoughtful and kind and gives us a good home. I am satisfied."

A paralyzed boy was accosted outside the Poor House lodgings. He said he was happy, and lived much better at the Poor House than he used to in town. He had no complaint to make about his food, and his sleeping apartments were comfortable. He did "look happy and contented," the reporter wrote next day. The young fellow had been given the assignment of gathering eggs, for some of the chickens were enclosed, but not all. The reporter watched, fascinated, as the young fellow dragged a useless limb, to crawl away over the dark brown leafy carpet. His task was to hunt for hens' nests in the hollow just below the main house.

In the Poor House hospital, the reporters talked with an epileptic. He testified that Dr. Hope treated him well, and that his food was quite good enough and bountiful.

Of all the twenty-six inmates then housed in the white section of the main house, none said anything against the superintendent, or against the way they were treated. As in the earlier series of interviews which had been conducted by the <u>Atlanta</u> <u>Constitution,</u> the inmates were under no compulsion to give "right" answers. Neither Dr. Hope nor his wife was present.

There was only one thing that any of the inmates wished could be changed: "We get short rations on coffee." Robert Hope's conviction that coffee was bad for the elderly, especially, led him to deny them more than one steaming mug each morning. Later in the day, with the second meal served them, they received a second cup. To his credit, the doctor was at least following his physician's instinct, rather than the line of indulgence. He knew that multi-cups of coffee might comfort an oldster passing the time, but he was sure that they might shorten the time that he had left! So much for the leisurely, contemplative, second cup in the morning.

* * * * *

As the Capitol reporters continued what was developing into an all-day investigation, they very much wished to get over to the blacks' quarters, fronting on Peachtree. They paused, however, to quiz Mrs. Hope, the superintendent's spouse. She was the lady described by the Atlanta Constitution reporter a few days earlier, as "his very clever little wife."[123]

Clever, maybe; outspoken, definitely. Della usually held her peace, but this time she stood in the gap to defend her absent man, and she gave the reporters an earful. She sailed right into the political opposition. First, she told the investigators something they probably already knew: The complaints against the Poor House were purely political in origin. The complaints had been noised abroad by those who for personal reasons wanted her husband removed from office.

As the reporters asked their questions, Della parried every stroke, and got in some licks of her own. On the matter of the coffee ration: The county commissioners had visited three weeks earlier, and had pronounced the one cup sufficient. On the paupers' wardrobe: If some thought them not well enough dressed, the county commissioners knew what they were wearing, and the commissioners were the men ultimately responsible.

Her most amusing response, to the reporters, was made concerning the charge of former inmate C.S. Bailey. Incredibly, he had said that Dr. Hope had taken $750 from him, and had bought a watch with it! Unquestionably he meant that a *part* of that sum had been so used, for, in 1886 no watch sold in Atlanta would have cost such an amount. Della answered laconically,

"That is not so. A person with $750 would not be a pauper, and in the second place, Dr. Hope has no watch."

One can almost hear the chuckles of newspaper readers, when they read that riposte.

* * * * *

The Capitol men left the main house with a most favorable impression. They drove their buggy over to where the African-

American inmates lived. These quarters were surrounded by a fence pierced by one gate. Entering the compound, the visitors saw no one, heard no sound. Wrote one of the reporters,

> "The place had the appearance of deserted 'Negro quarters' on an old plantation."

It consisted, now, of eight or ten duplex cabins, with two front entrances to each. The cabins sat primly, all in a row.

It turned out that most of the Negro inmates were ranging about, over the large farm, or had gotten off the Poor House grounds to visit friends.

So it was that the first living soul whom the reporters saw was old Uncle Lewis Miller, a very ancient, grey-haired, grey-bewhiskered "antebellum darkey," the newspaper called him. He was sitting in a chair, snoozing in the sun. The reporters gradually induced him to put aside his reticence to talk, and once he was fairly awake, and got started, Uncle Lewis told all.

He had been in the Poor House for eleven years, and was looked on as a sort of superintendent of the African-American division. He said that Dr. Hope had recently instructed him not to let anyone, white or black, inspect the Negro division unless the doctor himself were present. The reason was, the doctor wanted to "stop people comin' out here and carryin' tales back to town dat wasn't true" (English subdialect courtesy of the <u>Atlanta</u> <u>Evening</u> <u>Capitol</u>).

In spite of enforcing his limitation on the reporters, Uncle Lewis was at least willing to tell how the food system was operated for the blacks at the Poor House:

> "We gits our food on ration-day, tomorrow (which would be Monday). We bring it here to cook it for ourselves. But if it give out before the end of the week, we don't git no mo' till the next week."

Thus, the black people, situated somewhat remotely from the main house, got their food supply only once a week. This necessitated no small amount of borrowing and repaying among them.

This was no hardship, but its melancholy aspect was the inequality with which whites and blacks were treated. They were not served food equally, and much less did they have meals together. In this last quarter of the Nineteenth Century, almost no one supposed that the two races should stand on equal ground.

The reporters managed to interview five other African-Americans. The newspaper faithfully printed what was said in the interviews. Four of the five included two crippled men, a blind man, and a woman sick a-bed. They had none but the pettiest complaints, more or less of the "you asked me, so I'll think of something," variety. Even so, one of the cripples was careful to say that the superintendent was kind enough in his speech, using no harsh language to anybody.

The fifth person, the peg-leg, was a different story. He seemed to have a pronounced dementia, and was very bitter in his remarks against the superintendent. Such complaining was nothing new with him, for he said that Dr. Hope had warned him about it. The superintendent, he said, had told him that he would "burn me out," if he did not quit complaining! His poor hearing had mistaken the word "turn" for "burn."

This peg-legged man was obviously a pain to live with, both for Dr. Hope, and also for his fellow inmates. But the superintendent's plain speaking was not confined to this man. He was quite direct to others, when he felt it necessary. Indeed, the harshest thing that the black inmates had been able to say, in the <u>Atlanta</u> <u>Constitution</u> inquiry days earlier, was about words. They testified that Dr. Hope sometimes snapped out summary, straight answers.

The infamous Hamp Moss must have talked with the demented man, for he had retailed it over in town that the inmates were frightened to complain. If they did, he said, they would be turned out of the Poor House! When the <u>Constitution</u> had checked out this story with an old African-American man, however, the latter was quoted as saying,

"De doctor say dis: Dem dat don't like what dey got kin get fudder!"

This statement tallies with the answer attributed to Dr. Hope about ninety days later by a weak-minded white man named Johnson. He was a person who had, in fact, "gotten further," by leaving the Poor House. Interviewed by the Atlanta Evening Capitol, he said that he had made complaints to the superintendent, but that whenever anyone did that, Dr. Hope used to say,

"If you don't like what I give you, take to the road!"

Obviously, the doctor weighed each complaint, and did not answer every one in that gruff manner. However, the reports of short replies are patently true. The superintendent was confronted daily with minor complaints. They amounted only to carping of a Poor House population with nothing but idle time on their hands. Unable to satisfy every whim, the doctor had a stock answer, and frequently voiced it. But the record showed that he never actually turned anyone out of the Poor House.

As a matter of fact, the superintendent had rather have heard the complaints than to have inmates going with them to outside persons. A couple of reports of record state that he had cautioned the inmates not to go out and spread rumors, but to come directly to him. In this, he was asking for no more than his due.

*   *   *   *   *

The reporters ended their day-long Sunday's task in the late afternoon. They set their notes in order, left the Poor House, and drove back to Atlanta. They knew, however, that their job was not finished. It was expected that they see the Poor House, and they had done it. They had, in effect, put their readers on the scene. The interviews with inmates would bring an intimacy to their reports.

But much more waited to be done. At the very least, the newsmen would have to top off their investigation by talking with the men-in-the-know, who had the ultimate oversight of the Poor House. These men, members of the County Commission, could seal the investigation with their authoritative testimony. The election was coming on very soon, and the newspaper's conclusions must be stated, and then tied up with a neat bow of endorsement.

CHAPTER EIGHTEEN

TRIUMPH AND TRAGEDY

"I form the light and create darkness."
- Isaiah 45:7

In view of the impending election, one <u>Capitol</u> reporter was immediately dispatched to follow up on the paper's Poor House survey.[124] He went to talk with men known to be both knowledgeable and responsible. One was John Tyler Cooper, clerk of the county commissioners' court. The other was C. W. Hunnicutt, a county commissioner who was a member of the commission's Poor House committee. If these men gave favorable evidence about the operation of the facility, the editors would throw the <u>Capitol's</u> support to Dr. Hope.

Cooper gave the vital statistics of the Poor House. He said that the average number of inmates at the institution at any one time in the past year had been 48, with a steady turnover. Dr. Hope's salary was $ 75.00 per month. As for the support of the paupers, it was paid by the county directly. The superintendent sent the commission the bills for everything bought. The average daily cost to the county for each inmate was running at about 10 ¼ cents per day. The rest of their necessary food was raised on the Poor Farm itself. Cooper's remarks were very positive in support of the re-election of Dr. Hope.

Moving over to Hunnicutt's office, the newsman found that he was even more fulsome in his praise of the Poor House management:

"I know all about the alms house and the treatment of its inmates. They are well fed and clothed. And I can tell why all this stir has been made. It is only a few days before an election will be held for Dr. Hope's successor, and there is more than one aspirant for the position. It is certainly strange that Dr. Hope should have held his position for five years and nothing be said against him until now."

This last assertion, though well-intended, was not accurate. There *had* been the trumped-up complaints of three years before, which had proved as groundless as the current ones. Hunnicutt continued,

"Besides, what benefit could Dr. Hope receive from not feeding the paupers? The commissioners pay all the expense and Dr. Hope has nothing to do with it. He couldn't take the goods purchased and sell them for he would soon be detected."

Hunnicutt, like everyone else, was well aware that the Hamp Moss accusations had been based on alleged racial discrimination:

"I tell you there are hundreds of families in Atlanta who are not as well taken care of as the county's paupers, and such is the case especially among the colored people. I can convince any newspaper man of the fact (of African-American poverty) by simply driving him around the city for half a day. Dr. Hope has done his duty. I visited the poor house about three weeks ago, with other commissioners, and Dr. Hope did not know we were coming. I had the opportunity of fully investigating management of the institution and was satisfied."

The reporter pressed a point learned the day before: "What about the short rations on coffee?"

"We (the Commission) ordered the paupers given only one cup a day. That is as much as I get."

"What about food (that would be considered) wholesome for the sick?"

"They get it, for I have seen it given to them."

"So you are fully satisfied that Dr. Hope has done his duty by the paupers?"

"Yes, I am. If everybody in Atlanta was as well taken care of, the city would be much better off, and hundreds of families be made much happier."

Concluding their investigation on this positive note, the <u>Capitol</u> came out very strongly for the re-election of Robert Hope.

*   *   *   *   *

Well before this endorsement, the <u>Atlanta</u> <u>Journal</u> had also been supporting Dr. Hope.[125] A special article had appeared in the paper, headed, simply, "Fulton County Alms House." This piece, although it repeats some information earlier given, is worth quoting. It contains an abundance of precise description not shown elsewhere.

"The Fulton County alms house is situated on a commanding eminence, eight miles from this city, in Buckhead district, between the Roswell and Norcross (that is, Peachtree) roads, and reflects the highest credit on the county commissioners."

The "commanding eminence" which was crowned by the alms house, must have looked very commanding indeed, if the <u>Journal</u> reporter, coming from the paper's offices at 14 Alabama Street, approached it along Piedmont Road. Today, even with the grading and paving done since 1886, Piedmont climbs up, and up, for a third of a mile, before it reaches the old alms house property at the crossing of Peachtree. A good horse pulling a buggy or carriage, would have had to work for its oats.

"The county owns 320 acres of choice land, and the site of the building was specially selected for its eligibility. The ground gently slopes away on all sides, affording a rapid outlet for all water falling on the surface of the ground. The site was selected in the woods, and the grounds have been so arranged as to leave a grove in front, which will be sowed down in grass and beautified. The building in front is two stories high, with 84 feet front. Two wings, 152 feet long, run back, leaving a beautiful court between. In this court is a well of excellent water.

"There are thirty rooms in the building, excellently arranged for comfort and convenience, and well ventilated. The edifice is of brick – good brick made on the place – and covered with slate. The building is symmetrical, without useless ornamentation, and well suited for its purposes. A marble slab near the main entrance contains the names of the commissioners."

The Journal next revealed that the new main house was a $30,000 structure – a huge sum in 1886. Money had been saved on it, however, to the great credit of the commissioners, and of the superintendent.

"The cost of the building was $ 9,000, about one-third of what it would have cost to build it by contract. A six-foot well is to be supplied with horse power to pump water into the alms house and supply the laundry.

The Journal waxed just as enthusiastic about the inmates served in the Poor House, and the way in which they were served:

"There are thirty whites and twenty-one colored inmates on the farm. The colored people inhabit the old quarters at the alms house. There remain on hand 125,000 brick, which will be used in building brick houses for them. Everything is neat and clean about the alms house. The dining room is supplied with a long table, crockery in abundance, and all the white inmates sit down to the same table, supplied with plain but substantial food. The beds are all that could be desired.

"In a majority of the alms houses the inmates have a list-less, indifferent, hopeless expression on their countenances. In this one there is a noticeable exception. All look cheerful and express themselves as receiving the kindest treatment and best of care.

"Dr. R.L. Hope, the superintendent, is a practicing physician, and looks after their health as well as their other wants.

"Mr. Hope is a kind hearted, wide awake, thorough going, common sense man, the right kind of a man for the position.

"He has thirty-three acres in cultivation and expects to get twelve acres of bottom land in cultivation for vegetables."

"The alms house is in a healthy section and free from contagion.

"Fulton county may well feel proud of this institution. In a few years it will be an attractive feature in Buckhead district, and a lasting monument to the present commissioners."

*   *   *   *   *

It was quite clear, as the election was almost upon the voters, that Robert Hope had slain his dragons. When the balloting did take place, he was resoundingly re-elected.

The superintendent had finished five years at the helm of the Poor House, and in the secret will of God, he had almost a quarter-century yet to go. There would be other elections ahead, but none quite so difficult to get through as this one had been. As the Poor House kept steadily improving, he would never again be so severely under the gun of criticism.

*   *   *   *   *

In the summer of 1886, just following the major hurdles that had been passed, leading to the superintendent's exoneration, tragedy struck. Della, the doctor's wife, contracted poliomyelitis. That crippling disease, which permanently disabled so many, was finally overcome by Dr. Jonas Salk's 1954 development of a vaccine. Polio usually attacked children, so that it was dubbed, "infantile paralysis." But the disease was not always so selective – a fact especially dramatized by its assault on Franklin Delano Roosevelt in 1921. Like Roosevelt much later, Della gradually responded to treatment. The virulence of the disease subsided, but it left her, at twenty-three, crippled for life. Ever afterward, she got about in metal braces, and on crutches.

From this cruel blow, this discipline of life, Della rebounded, conscious that she was the mistress of the Poor House. The disability did severely limit her, however, and it imposed a hardship on Robert Hope. What she could no longer do, he must. It was he who was responsible for meeting the children's needs in many areas which ordinarily would have fallen to the mother.

CHAPTER NINETEEN

CONVICT CAMP

"Give us, in mercy, better homes when we're a-lying in our cradles; give us better food when we're a-working for our lives; give us kinder laws to bring us back when we're a-going wrong; and don't set Jail, Jail, Jail afore us, everywhere we turn."

> *- The Chimes*, Third Quarter
> Charles Dickens

The Poor House had originally consisted only of the two principal sections, one for whites, the other for blacks. Then a third element had been introduced in 1882, just the year after Dr. Hope became the superintendent. Female convicts were added to the Poor House population, and rooms were found in which to house them. In 1882, the females actually made some bricks, which were used for patchwork needs around the place, but this work was never a large operation, although one newspaper asserted that it was.

Two years later, male convicts were brought in as a temporary work force, for the Poor House expansion. The presence of male convicts on the Poor House grounds proved to be more than temporary. Initially, however, they were lodged in makeshift housing. There were tents, and also lean-to wooden constructs.

These men, prisoners from the North Atlanta convict camp, were joined in their work by a few more from the camp that had been established at the Chattahoochee brick company. The latter were the more knowledgeable brick makers, and they sped the work along.

Since the Poor House farm was quite spacious, at 330 acres, it seemed a safe idea to lodge the lawbreakers there. When not working, they could be isolated under guard, well away from the other inmates. Thus, no time would be lost in transporting them daily to and fro.

As previously related (see Chap. 15), the new main house was completed, December, 1885. But this main building was only the beginning. The rest of their labors were still unfinished as the cold winter of 1885-86 loomed. It became clear that the convicts were either going to have to return to their respective camps, or that warmer, more substantial houses must be put up for them on the Poor Farm.

Someone on the county commission decided that the men should be kept on the Poor House property permanently. This idea was successfully sold to the entire commission. The convicts could complete the Poor House construction, and later till the farm, when not working on improving the county's roads. So it was that the "chain-gang" was made a semi-permanent adjunct to the Poor House. It was periodically reported on to the public by the commission.

Superintendent Hope had won the 1886 election, and he was sympathetic towards the African-Americans. Yet, now, the permanent settlement of the convicts, black and white, was bad news for the Poor House blacks. Already forced to wait until last for their new accommodations, they suddenly found themselves even lower on the list of priorities. Their housing had been improved, but the process was incomplete. It would remain incomplete until the convicts' permanent housing could be taken care of.

When 1887 rolled in, the blacks were put off again, as yet another group were added to the Poor House complex. The state legislature enacted a general law that individual Georgia counties, rather than the state asylum, should take care of their "harmless lunatics." Many such people would be transferred from Milledgeville to Buckhead's now famous Poor House, where provision must be made for them. Meanwhile, the mentally sound blacks would again be obliged to remain in inadequate homes, places with cracks and holes in them.

*   *   *   *   *

Promises, promises! The superintendent was not happy about the long delay in finishing the housing for his black inmates. He could do little, however, except to lose sleep over it. He prowled about the house, fretting in the night. Child of his time, man of the 1880's, he was not questioning the permanent position of the black race as the underclass. Yet neither was he anything like a slave overseer. He was a *doctor,* and one with a Calvinistic conscience at that:

"The colored people *must* be helped. Their cabins were bad two years ago, and now are wholly unfitted to protect them against the cruel blasts of what must be a severe winter."[126]

Another winter was coming on like the clap of doom. Like those before it, the winter of 1887-88 would slow or halt the progress that the young doctor so desperately wanted to make. Boiling with impatience, not sleeping, not able to sleep, Robert repeated his midnight rambles over Poor House property, just as in 1885. And, as two years before, Della glimpsed him through the window from time to time. One moonlit night, he looked ghostlike, capped, and with overcoat on over his nightshirt. His weary figure was trudging through the alternating shadows and silvery light, up the path to the spot where the new Negro homes would be built.

"There he prayed."[127]

Given the insomnia problem, he might have been excused for any daytime irritability. Yet he maintained his equilibrium pretty well. Still, on the day that he gave orders that work on the "lunatics' quarters" would cease for an entire week, two, if necessary, it was confusing. He was looked on by some as a lunatic himself!

However, he would fool such critics, because he had a plan. He had noticed the ways in which opportunity was being squandered, through inefficient use of materials, through overlapping work assignments, and the like. By straightening out these things, by working double shifts (with incentives of food treats, and promises of future time off from farm work), and by taking every spare piece of lumber available, he would correct the problem. On his plan, both the blacks and the weak-minded folk could be properly housed, he was convinced. He strongly wished to pursue his original intention to give the blacks proper lodging before he did anything else.

Amazing as it must have seemed to the gainsayers, it worked! The convicts shored up the negroes' lodgings, giving priority to those of the elderly. All the apertures were plugged. In some places, the wooden structures were so old and rotted that the patching was rather akin to sewing a new piece of cloth on an old garment. Robert reported,

> "I was afraid that we would knock down the existing shacks in the process. We were like to hurt the negroes more than help them."[128]

This work on the African-American quarters was accomplished before the doctor's troops turned themselves again to work on the lodgings for the weak-minded people. The winter arrived on schedule, and this time the black inmates found it much more to their liking. The repairs, hastily arranged, had been effective.

* * * * *

As 1888 dawned, the names of more convicts had to be added to the roll at the Poor House. The Fulton County Grand Jury desired it to be done because of the sorry conditions existing at other places where convicts were incarcerated. The contrast between their miseries and the Poor House's comforts were glaring.

On January 6, the grand jury presented a lengthy paper to the Superior Court, stating their full satisfaction with the Poor House. The inmates were well fed, and seemed contented, the report said. It concluded,

> "Taking the establishment as a whole we think it is one of the best institutions of its kind in the South and reflects great

credit on the county officials and on Dr. Hope, the superintendent in charge."[129]

When salary decision time rolled around in the autumn, the grand jury gave tangible proof of their confidence in Dr. Hope, by recommending a salary increase. The full recommendation called for his services to be retained for the new term, and also for the increase, which was from $ 75 per month to $ 100 per month.[130]

* * * * *

Very different from the model Poor House, were the Fulton County Jail, and the convict confinement camps. Grand Jury reports throughout 1888 lamented the woeful physical conditions of these places, and also scored the jailers. According to one published news report, the grand jury regarded the jail as "a blot upon the good name of Fulton County."[131]

The newspaper detailed the grand jury's complaints about the jail. It was overcrowded, the women's section was a firetrap, and open water closets constantly wafted sewer gases into the jail. There were no spittoons, so the hot air floor through which all the jail's heat came up from the furnace below was used by tobacco-chewing convicts as one grand spittoon. The floor was "filthy beyond expression."

Moreover, physical discomfort for the prisoners was their daily way of life. Ventilation in the jail was far from perfect. There was also no way for the prisoners to keep decently clean, and free from vermin. They were frequently compelled to sleep on the wet or damp floor without sufficient covering. To name the discomfort, was to discover that the jail had it. In 1888, Europe's medieval past was alive in Atlanta, in its jail.

A further key shortcoming was that the jail's food was shameful. Robert Hope had been through the round of food complaints, too, at the Poor House. The jail's food, though, was not alleged to be merely too plain, or short-rationed. It was hardly fit for human consumption. Meat was half-cooked, and bread was stale, and often sour. Vegetable food was provided infrequently.

Topping off the whole shocking scene at the jail was the regular practice of outright cruelty. Stronger prisoners were allowed to whip weaker ones with straps, as punishment. Mere babes were confined in the jail along with parents.

The county's convict camps away from the jail were in better case, but only comparatively. The one which was kept at the Chattahoochee brick company was found to be in "admirable condition," so the picture was not all bad.

On the other hand, the convict camp near the East Tennessee shops, as they were called, was considered to be only in "fair condition," except for the cooking utensils, which were disgustingly filthy." From the same camp drainage ran from its stables, kennels, and pig pens into Todd's Branch, and thence into the Atlanta Water Works.

The third of the county's camps, the one near North Atlanta, was probably the worst of the lot. The grand jury thought it was "a disgrace to any civilized community." Its prison was too small, and only a few feet from its windows was a pig pen and swill tubs.

Amid these horrors, Atlanta's jails had one thing going for them that those of the Middle Ages had not: an enlightened public sensitivity to their problems. Thus the grand jury strongly recommended reforms in all these jails and camps. Until these could be made effective, however, the grand jury thought that a partial solution was possible. That solution was to move some of the convicts to the better surroundings of the Poor House convict camp, and so it was done.

*   *   *   *   *

Robert Hope was learning that success brings problems as surely as does failure. The increased population at the Poor House greatly added to the demands on him. He had no responsibility for guarding the prisoners, but he did have to examine and treat them for illnesses, with a chain gang guard nearby. It was about this time that a newspaper published the remark of another public servant, calling Dr. Hope "one of the busiest men in the county."[132] The title was justly his. He was "doctor, lawyer, Indian chief," and now, keeper of the gaol besides.

To the doctor's great relief, the larger, more recent part of the convict responsibility did not continue for long. The county convict camps were improved as demanded, so that the men could return there. Besides this, even the men whose residence at the Poor Farm camp dated back to 1885 could be transferred out. The brick-making was done, the Poor House buildings were completed and there was no further need for convict workers to live on the place. The female convict section remained part of the Poor House complex for years, but male convicts were brought in only periodically, to farm.

*   *   *   *   *

During the period that the male convicts were living on Poor House property, one of them made a lasting memory. He was a black man with the stamp of evil permanently impressed on his face. He owned a spoon which he took care to sharpen every day at lunch time. It was never taken from him, and nothing ever came of it. But the guard in the wooden barracks where this man was quartered told Dr. Hope that at whatever time of night he might awaken, he heard the same sound. It was this prisoner's soft, but continual, jingling of his chain: Tink, tink, tinka-tink. All night long, every night, it went on, yet there was never any evidence that the man had tried to saw the chain links with the spoon, or with any other tool. The phenomenon made the guard nervous, but the doctor laughed.

"He just has insomnia. I have had it myself, but for a different reason than his!"[133]

CHAPTER TWENTY

IMBECILES

"Lord, have mercy on my son, for he is a lunatic, and is very ill; for he often falls into the fire, and and often into the water."

- St. Matthew 17.15

Inevitably, a certain percentage of the Poor House inmates were persons of weak mind. These were sometimes aged people who had lost their reason as the years piled up. Almost as often they were retarded younger inmates who were at the Poor House because they had been incapable of earning a living, and would surely never be able to do so. The departments for the whites, for the blacks, and for the convicts, were none of them a fit place for the insane. Consequently, the Poor House soon added yet another section. The need for it became especially apparent when, as previously told, an influx of more of the weak-minded came from Milledgeville.

Already, by 1886, Doctor Hope had come to realize that the "lunatics," or "imbeciles," as they were variously, and crassly, called, must have a separate place. To segregate them from the other inmates, he initially placed them in the large hospital room of the main house. Other inmates kept to their private rooms in the same structure.

This expedient was only partly successful. The superintendent had most of the burden of caring for the insane, and the work was exhausting. Moreover, this year of 1886 was the year that Robert's political foes made their second assault on him.

The weapon that the assailants used was an ugly story briefly mentioned earlier (see Chapter 16, pages 117-118). Former inmate C.S. Bailey had accused the superintendent of the cruelty of whipping a female inmate. This story is worth some closer scrutiny.

Initially, one of the newspapers carried the story under the headline, "A Woman Whipped."[134] Fortunately, the truth about the whipping story was promptly ferreted out. The "woman whipped" was Jane Woods, one of the so-called imbeciles. Efforts had been made to get her into the state asylum at Milledgeville. Not only was Jane retarded, but she was further burdened with a bad spirit. This negative attitude of hers customarily erupted about once a month in some sort of naughtiness or violence.

On one occasion, Jane had physically attacked another inmate, beating her in the face.

Dr. Hope had had her tied, and he was escorting her up the hall towards the cooking room, when she begged, and promised to behave. He let her off.

A few days later, she had a difficulty with a woman named Greenway. The doctor was summoned, and found Jane in the other woman's room, "mad as hops" about something or other. When she saw the superintendent, Jane ran from the room, throwing a stick of firewood at him as she went. He had her caught, and she was tied up in one of the rooms. He then administered the whipping himself, but as a "whipping" it was a non-event.

Under close questioning by the reporter, C. S. Bailey changed his story somewhat – changed it enough that his charge of cruelty disappeared. The revision went like this: After Jane had been tied, Dr. Hope took a deep breath, and wielding a limber willow rod "about the size of your little finger," he began to lay it on her backside. Again she begged, and after half a dozen half-hearted strikes, he let her off.

This was the only corporal punishment of record at the Poor House during Robert Hope's twenty-nine-year administration. He shrank from this kind of disciplinary duty, just as later he spared the rod with his own children. According to his daughter Martha, he preferred talking instead. At home, the woodshed was seldom used. On the rare occasions when it was, it was the scene of a thirty-second switching, after "Dad" had inflicted an hour's lecture on the errant child.

* * * * *

By 1887, twenty-eight-year-old Dr. Robert Hope was barely hanging on, because of the greatly increased work. Since the rooms in the new Poor House were now more numerous than formerly, he had been able to assign some in a block, and designate them "the insane ward." The insane ward was not yet, in itself, overwhelming, because the number of mentally deficient was small. That year there were but seven of them regularly at the Poor House - five whites, and two blacks. Mercifully, only one was so seriously impaired as to have to be locked up.

Locked up in a plain, and somewhat cheerless room at all times! This was the only cruelty at the Poor House – a cruelty unintended. The lock-up was a horror for the victim, no doubt, but it was virtually the only answer for the violent. Psychiatry was in its infancy, so that knowledge of treatment and sedation through proper use of drugs was lacking. To have visited the inside of a mental institution of the 1940's or even later, was to have seen hospital personnel helpless to aid some miserable afflicted inmate. The latter inhabited a padded cell. To the howling, head-wagging, hair-tearing, self-inflicted hurts, there was no solution other than the straitjacket. It was indeed a mercy that only one was in such extreme shape in the Poor House.

It was in that same year of 1887, of course, and with winter coming on, that the legislature shifted the "harmless lunatics" from Milledgeville to the care of their parent counties.[135] Four more were added to the seven already at the Poor House, and before long, the number grew to sixteen. Now all of them were housed in a good, solid building erected for their occupancy at this time, and situated just off the Peachtree Road.

Having this special place to house the mentally defective was helpful, but it did not lighten the load of the superintendent. It became obvious, when the number of the "imbeciles" grew from seven to eleven, that the time had come to hire more help.

By the permission of the county commissioners, Robert engaged one Mrs. D. Gallagher, and the weak-minded inmates were placed under her immediate care. Mrs. Gallagher was an Irish lady of great energy and discipline. Throughout the years that she held forth in the Poor House imbecile ward, she was lauded repeatedly by the Atlanta press, and was loved by the mentally defective whom she served. Always kind, she nevertheless kept things moving with snap, and the inmates were clean, healthy, and satisfied. They did love this woman whom they could depend on. And the doctor was observed to be going around with a relaxed grin!

Just as other sections of the Poor House complex had been outgrown, so also the original building put up for the insane proved in the long run to be inadequate. In 1893, with twenty-five mentally deficient folk aboard, the superintendent would be telling the county commissioners,

"We face an absolute necessity. There has to be a new, separate building in which the imbeciles can be cared for."[136]

The 1887 imbecile building was full to overflowing, and the overflow people had been relocated back where the imbecile ward had begun, in the Poor House main building.

The doctor was used to living with makeshift, but he never supinely accepted it. Enough was enough, he thought, and he was determined to get a larger place for these people. For the purpose of getting his point across, he assiduously cultivated W. R. Brown, the chairman of the county commissioners board. He popped into Brown's Victorian baroque office on his every trip to the Five Points vicinity in downtown Atlanta. This would go on through 1894.

Yet, when he made his annual report to the board itself, in January, 1895, he made no mention of the need for a new unit for the insane.[137] He simply said,

"The women convicts are doing a lot of work that seems to agree with them, as only one of them has been sick during the year."

He continued,

"On the 25th of December, 1893, there were in the alms house 84 inmates, and during the year 156 have been admitted, 94 have been discharged or died, leaving on the 25th of December, 1894, 155 inmates in the place."

* * * * *

Instead of simply telling the commissioners the need, Robert would have them come and see for themselves. A few days after the annual report, he had the commissioners out to the alms house for a country style meal, in the rustic grand manner. Della and one Poor House cook worked their fingers to the bone, preparing five kinds of meat, half a dozen different vegetable dishes, and other assorted delicacies. The city's newspapers had it all, next day:

"FEAST AT THE ALMSHOUSE – County Commissioners Partake of a Royal Meal in the Home of the Poor."

The reporter evidently attended the meal as an extra guest, as shown by his intimate knowledge of the fare, and the way that the visit proceeded. His story ran,

"There was a regular love feast and 'hog killing time' at the county almshouse yesterday afternoon. It was attended by members of the board of county commissioners and a few friends invited to partake of the feast by Dr. Hope, the superintendent.

"The commissioners had set aside yesterday as a time for making an inspection of the place and Dr. Hope prepared a dinner for them. He had the old time, long-legged, blue stem collards, baked turkey, roast peacock, spare ribs, backbone, sausage, crackling bread, biscuits and cake 'like your mother used to make,' sure enough 'simmon beer and many other things on that line.

"Those present were Charles Collier, Joseph Thompson, Jack J. Spalding, Walter R. Brown, commission chairman, Forrest Adair, commission clerk Kontz, and Mssrs. George Hope, Thomas Dunlop, A.B. Steele, Hugh McKeldin, and (initials lost) Johnson."[138] It will be noted that Dr. Hope's brother was among the guests. Each Commission non-member present, the superintendent knew, would only strengthen his hand, as they influenced the members.

Dr. and Mrs. Hope made a total of thirteen around the big table. There was good fellowship, and good-natured banter, and the meal was finished in high good humor. The commissioners were then shown the sorry state of the provision for the insane, its now crowded situation being dramatically contrasted with the excellent condition of the rest of the Poor House. Robert of course made this presentation the main event of the afternoon. There was general nodding and tsk-tsking on the part of the commissioners. To a man, they agreed that something certainly should be done. Robert had made his point.

That evening, after all the men had gone home, Robert and Della strolled back up to the imbeciles' quarters, the focus of the day's doing. Della wanted to know whether her husband thought the commissioners really would do anything about this "insane department." He admitted that it was hard to say. The men evidently had been impressed with the need, but sometimes mills grind slowly. Money was the problem. The commissioners did not have it, and did not want to raise taxes to get it.

*   *   *   *   *

The commissioners were skittish about any additional monetary commitments because the Panic of 1893, followed by a severe depression, had shaken everyone's confidence.

That confidence was restored, however, by the greatest public event that the City of Atlanta had ever hosted, the Cotton States and International Exposition of 1895.[139]

The bankers and business leaders reasoned, after the fact, that if a city of 75,000 could put on this money-making event, it could do anything. Their thinking was sound. The Exposition had cost two-and-half, to three million dollars, in a year when only $ 64 million cleared Atlanta banks. The city had been willing to take the risk, and had come out a big winner, financially, and in publicity for the city. Now, surely, these captains of business, finance, and politics could do whatever they chose!

That was the optimism and rejoicing *after* the Exposition was over and done. *Before* the Exposition, there was nervousness, and mixed feelings and actions. Exploding across Atlanta's New South history like fireworks in the night sky, were the fair's events and statistics before the Event: Former mayor W.A. Hemphill suggesting the Exposition; Hemphill and Howard E.W. Palmer being elected the president and director-general of the organizing committee, then both of them suddenly retiring "for business and health reasons, respectively"; Charles Collier, the new Exposition president, leading a delegation to Washington, D.C., to get money for the project, where Tuskegee Institute's Booker T. Washington speaks in its behalf; Atlanta congressman L.F. Livingstone, stung by opposition from those who call the Exposition a mere money-making scheme for the cotton interests; Livingstone carrying the day by rebutting, "This Exposition is for all those who grow cotton and all those who *wear* cotton."

The dance went on, with President Grover Cleveland approving a $200,000 grant for a U.S. Government exhibit at the Exposition; later opening the fair itself by remote control telegraph key from his study at Gray Gables; still later, coming in person to Atlanta to deliver a speech at the Exposition.

The fair drew 800,000 people to its 6,000 exhibits in its first one hundred days, at beautiful, new, Piedmont Park, built for the occasion. On opening day, there had been Victor Herbert and orchestra, playing his grand, new, "Salute to Atlanta." Then came the long run of "Buffalo Bill" Cody, and his Wild West Show, entertaining thousands daily.

There were the governors of various states, present at the fair to speak on the days which had been designated as specially honoring their respective states. A "Blue and Gray Day" was declared, and former generals, Longstreet of the Confederacy, and Schofield of the Union, appeared, to hear Ohio governor William McKinley's speech.

One excitement followed another. W.A. Hemphill resurfaced, to pin a Confederate Veterans badge on General Fairchild, the retired Yankee general who was the ex-commander of the Grand Army of the Republic. President Cleveland lunched at the Piedmont Driving Club. A Southern Railways spur line was built directly into the fair. John Philip Sousa and his band played the fair's theme, Sousa's new, "King Cotton" march.

In the Mexican Village, the toreros wanted to present live bull fights; Atlanta authorities prevented it. Meanwhile, the multitudes gaped at Lake Clara Meer's marvelous electrical fountain.

There was much to learn from the wealth of exhibit buildings! The structures were named for the subjects they housed, of course. They were: the Manufacturer's, the Fire, Alabama, California, Georgia, Illinois, Massachusetts, New York, Pennsylvania, U.S. Government, Fine Arts, Plant System, Agricultural, Machinery, Minerals and Forestry, Negro, Southern Railway, Transportation, Women's, U.S. Army Encampment, 1849 Mining Camp, and the Japanese Village.

The fun-and-games section, of course, was the midway. It ran along beside Tenth Street, from Argonne to Parkway Drive (now called "Charles Allen Drive") – a distance of about 1,300 feet. The midway offered "Rocky Mountain Ponies," "Monkey Paradise," "Ostrich Farm," "Indian Village," "Rolstair's Illusions," "Living Pictures"(a primitive movie), "Chinese Village," "Beauty Show," "German Village," "Vaudeville," "Animal Arena," "Water Chutes," "Exhibit Train Shed," "Phoenix Wheel" (a ferris wheel named for Atlanta's resurgent spirit – as the wheel turns, the seats go down, but they rise again), "Mystic Maze," "Streets of Cairo," "Moorish Palace," and a dozen more.

It was fun, and wild, pushing the envelope on some Victorian limits. It was the Gay 'Nineties. Onward-and-upward-forever Darwinian optimism scoffed at the dragging economy, which would drag on for another couple of years. The commissioners caught the general spirit, saying to themselves, "don't be afraid." Somehow, the fair fulfilled its intended mission, and more. Boosted monetarily and psychologically, boldness replacing their former timidity, the commissioners were ready to help the Poor House.

*   *   *   *   *

At the Fulton County Commission's meeting on December 27, 1895, Chairman W. R. Brown was primed to carry the ball on the issue of improving facilities for the mentally deficient.[140] He told the commissioners,

> "My idea is to have the commissioners erect a new building for this particular class of inmates and have the building so constructed that there will be no possibility of the unfortunates injuring themselves. The building should have every modern convenience; the walls should be so arranged and constructed that they could not fall or hurt themselves against sharp corners or hard places; the stoves should be so protected that if one of the inmates should fall he would not be burned."

And Brown, having personally re-visited the Poor House just the day before, on the 26th, now took the opportunity to boost the superintendent:

> "I have found the farm to be in the very best condition and am gratified at what I saw yesterday. Dr. Hope has made many needed improvements and he is conducting everything in an excellent manner. If the new building can be placed on the grounds, then all will be in the very best possible shape.
> "There are at present about seventy-five inmates of the farm (he was not counting the insane and the convicts). They

151

are all well and are being cared for in an exceedingly satis-factory way. The farm has been practically self-sustaining this year, and much money has been saved in the conduct of affairs. We have had about 150 acres in cultivation and the crops were good and the harvests large. Everything was found in good shape and I am pleased with the way things are conducted."

He sat down. Someone made a motion that the commissioners authorize a new building for the mental patients. The commissioners went for it, and Brown's gavel fell - "Done!" The work would begin in the new year, 1896.

The Cotton States and International Exposition closed, December 31, 1895.

CHAPTER TWENTY-ONE

INMATE OF CONSEQUENCE

"Remember me, not for what I may become in the future, but for what I have been."

> *- Words spoken in his resig-*
> *nation speech to his congre-*
> *gation by a Miami minister*
> *afflicted with Alzheimer's*
> *disease.*

Robert Hope's persistence had paid off, towards the building of a new insane ward, as had chairman W.R. Brown's clout. The Cotton States and International Exposition, with its gaiety and euphoria had helped, too. In the newspapers, the fair's brilliance and the insane ward's inadequacy appeared side by side, in great contrast. But perhaps most tellingly of all, to give the building plan a lift, was the day when Major Robert N. Ely was called beyond this life.

On January 22, 1895, a reporter for the Atlanta Constitution had taken note of Ely's presence at the Poor House. He had lamented,

"It is a reproach to the State of Georgia that among the inmates of the county lunatic asylum is one of the most distinguished men that ever illustrated Georgia's public service. This man is Attorney-General Robert N. Ely."[141]

The former attorney-general had ranked among the leading lawyers of the South, prior to the mental troubles that landed him in the imbecile ward of the Poor House. He was described as "a man of broad proportions - - his body cast in the same gigantic mold as the one of in which his mind was fashioned." Ely tipped the scales at considerably more than two hundred pounds, possibly approaching two hundred fifty. His big frame and commanding bearing always drew attention in a crowd.

Ely had the manners of a gentleman of the old school, and it was said that he was never so preoccupied as to forget the rules of social courtesy. Kind, obliging, charming, he had many friends.

As a lawyer, his reputation was that he had no peer in this state. His record during his term of office as attorney-general was superlative. He collected a vast sum of money for the state, and put it into the treasury.

Ely lived an interesting life, and by the world's standard a very successful one. Born in Columbus, Georgia in 1835, he was the grandson of able state senator Major Robert Newsome, a man proverbial for his integrity. He graduated with highest honors from Mercer University, which was at that time located at Penfield, Georgia. He studied law under Judge D. A. Vason, was admitted to the bar, and began his practice at Albany, Georgia. He organized a law partnership, Ely and Slaughter.

In 1861, Ely enlisted in the Confederate Army, and served throughout the entire four-year struggle. He distinguished himself as a gallant soldier, and as quartermaster and major in Alfred H. Colquitt's brigade. His link with Colquitt paid off for him after the war, for in 1876, with the close of Reconstruction in Georgia, he ardently supported his former commander in his race for the governorship. When Colquitt won, he assigned Ely to the position of attorney-general.

As attorney-general, Ely joined the famous General Robert Toombs in bringing suit against the railroads for collection of back taxes. These actions brought an immense sum into the state's coffers. Ely's own legitimate fees from the litigation amounted to $ 60,000 - a fortune in those days. Toombs said of him,

"I consider Major Ely one of the ablest lawyers in the state. He understands the railroad situation much better than I do."

After his term in office expired, Ely opened a law office in Atlanta. He was a consistent member of the First Baptist Church. He was very liberal with his means, dispensing charity with a lavish hand.

Ely's kindnesses were extended to his family. He educated a number of his younger kinsmen as attorneys. And, family-wise, he was well-connected. He was nephew to Judge D.A. Newsome, who had served as his secretary during his years as attorney-general. Ely was also brother to Mrs. Abner R. Calloway, of LaGrange, Georgia, and a cousin of Mr. Willis Reagan, of Atlanta.

Ely did not have an immediate family, but otherwise, he was a man wealthy, good-looking, mature, at the height of his powers at age 45. He was a man at whom one might look and say, "He has everything going for him."

Not quite everything. Following his term as attorney-general, he remained in Atlanta in the practice of law only a relatively few years. He had purchased a large plantation in southwest Georgia, and he left Atlanta to devote himself to agricultural pursuits. This retirement to the plantation proved to be a terrible career change. Ely did not know experimental farming. Over the ensuing years, he made mistakes which he attempted to correct with more money. Ultimately, he lost his entire fortune.

Depressed by this sour turn of fate, he never regained his former buoyancy of spirit.

He mourned his losses, and seemingly did so until his mind became unbalanced. At least, that is the way it looked to those who knew him. Wise as he was in the legal profession, he was simply not able to overcome the "vain regrets." He did not know how to handle adversity, and apparently, it cost him his sanity.

Ely was examined by the county ordinary, and was sent to the state asylum at Milledgeville. Being crazy, but not stupid, he escaped from that institution, and got back to Atlanta. There, however, he was apprehended, and sent back to Milledgeville by Ordinary Calhoun.

The authorities there refused to receive him, and thus he came to Dr. Robert Hope at the Fulton County Poor House.

In his time at the Poor House "lunatic asylum," Ely was a sad figure. He raved about soon coming into forty million dollars, after which he would devote himself to the Christian ministry! Former acquaintances could hardly believe that this was the same man they had known.

After two years in the Poor House lunatic asylum, Ely died of a paralytic stroke at age sixty. Dr. Hope went over to Atlanta to purchase a simple casket for the major's body. In talking to reporters, he said that Ely's complaints had begun a month earlier, and thorough medical examination had revealed partial paralysis.

"He received careful nursing," the doctor said, "and everything that medical skill could do for him, in the way of relieving his sufferings, was freely prescribed. I had no trouble with him as a patient, and he gave me very little uneasiness or concern during his stay on the farm. I knew his antecedents, and was familiar with his distinguished record as the attorney-general of the state. A more pathetic story I have never known, and his sad death is one that touches me profoundly."[142]

Dr. Hope bought the coffin, and spent the greater part of the day in the city, probing what was to be done, and informing notable citizens of the death. Telegrams were dispatched to the relatives at Leesburg, and LaGrange, Georgia. Dr. Hope told a funeral director to hold the remains until further notice. In the meantime, Atlanta relatives and friends of the major conferred by telephone. They decided that the body was to be cremated, and the ashes were to be buried in Westview Cemetery. This open field was the same one where Ely had faced Yankee shell and shot in the Battle of Ezra Church, 1864.

On the day of the memorial service, the Georgia Confederate Veterans were turned out, to take part in the ceremony. Some were in grey uniforms and regalia. The service and eulogy were conducted in keeping with the attorney-general's distinguished public record.

*   *   *   *   *

Robert Hope's work in behalf of Major Ely did not go unrecognized. A day after the funeral he received a handwritten, four-page letter from Ely's sister, Mrs. Calloway, of LaGrange.[143] She thanked him for his many kindnesses to her "dear brother." She pleadingly asked if Ely knew that he was near death. Had he been ready to meet his Maker? During the time that he had spent with her, she said, he had read his Bible and had taken great interest in attending church. He had also been a generous giver, as long as "he had money to throw in when the basket came round."

But, tragically, as often happens with schizoid paranoia, he had turned against his beloved sister. It was, she went on,

> "- - when he found out that I thought he had best be sent to the asylum, and from that time I lost all influence with him and he seemed lose all the love he had for me, because he said I was not any friend to him, and after that I could not keep him with me - -."

But it is ever true that there is a destiny that shapes our ends, bringing good out of evil. From the time of Ely's funeral, many Atlantans were convinced that the Poor House facilities for the insane should be the best available. The untimely death of this lonely, riches-to-rags leader proved most timely to spearhead improvement of the Poor House lunatic asylum.

* * * * *

Robert's and Della's first child to survive into adulthood had been born by this time.

He was Hollis Frank, who followed his father's footsteps into the medical profession, graduating from the medical school at Emory in 1913. After serving in the U.S. Army in the First World War, Hollis became, like his father, an Atlanta civil servant. He was for many years the physician of the Atlanta City Jail.[144]

Robert was a man of affairs, seemingly over his head in work responsibilities at all times. Nonetheless, he was also obliged to take on much of the care of his children. He had little choice, since Della was so crippled with polio, that she needed whatever help he could give. His pattern was to visit his children at mealtimes and bedtimes. He thus showed his love for them. His manner with his children was complex, and in step with that of the Victorian and Edwardian eras. He was loving, able to be entreated, but also moral, didactic, and dominating.

Perhaps he had learned, years earlier, how to run the lives of his children, and of the Poor House inmates. His own life had been run by the orphanage matron and master.

Eventually, as Della became able again to bear children, following her crippling illness, more came along. Five little ones who lived to adulthood were born in the last decade of the Nineteenth Century, and the first decade of the Twentieth. Hollis, Lucien, Martha, Henry, and Betty, all gave Robert and Della grandchildren.

CHAPTER TWENTY-TWO

INTERESTING INMATES

"Give me your poor, your tired, your huddled masses - -"
- Statue of Liberty inscription

The Poor House at this time had the unenviable assignment of taking virtually whomever was sent to it. Robert N. Ely was a memorable case, but was only one of many seen at the Poor House through the years. Individuals continued to come and go. The doctor treated some real characters!

Back in the 'Eighties, a couple of <u>Constitution</u> reporters had toured the Poor House for the express purpose of gathering human interest material for the newspaper.[145] They were not disappointed. This was in 1884, when Dr. Hope had been the resident physician for only two and a half years. The reporters met two very elderly matriarchs whose life histories were far, far out of the ordinary.

The first old woman was sitting in a chair near the entrance to one of the wooden cabins of the "colored" quarters. She said that her name was "Aunt Judy," and the poor old thing claimed that her bent form bore the weight of one hundred and nine years! It was easy to believe. Aunt Judy's hearing was gone, and her sight nearly so. She had no teeth, and her mouth was deep-sunken.

Aunt Judy was unable to understand either words or signs clearly, yet she seemed generally happy and contented. The reporters somehow got across to her the idea that they had come to find out something about her. She obliged, since, though she could not hear, she could talk. She said that she had but two desires: to go to Macon to see her grandchildren, and to go to Glory.

Aunt Judy said that she had come from "ole Ferginny," but, at a hundred and nine years, she had no doubt seen many a year in Georgia. The reporters knew that Eli Whitney had invented the cotton gin in 1793. The availability of that machine had enormously expanded the Deep South's rate of combing out the seeds from the cotton bolls. As a result, cotton lands increased all across the South. The Deep South needed more and more field hands to pick the cotton, and the Upper South was where they were obtained.

Given that background, it was not hard to see Aunt Judy as a 25-year-old in 1800, being taken south as a living embodiment of the long-forgotten old song,

"Carry me back to old Virginny,
Dere's whar de cotton and de cawn and taters grow!
Dere's whar de birds sing so sweet in de springtime,
Dere's whar dis ole darky's heart am eber long to go."

When one of the news scribes dropped a nickel into her withered old palm, Aunt Judy uttered an ejaculation of thanks: "Thanks, massa, thanks; honor to God! Glory!"

She related that she had been deserted by her daughter, then had been sent to the Poor House by another woman. After telling the men again that she yearned to go to Macon to visit her grandchildren, she lapsed into a muttering trance, during which the reporter picked up the words, "The Bible says, 'Lean upon Me and ye shall not perish.' My children! How I gwine ter got there?"

*　*　*　*　*

At the very moment that Aunt Judy was in her trance, up lurched an old woman whose age was reputed to be even greater than Aunt Judy's. Old Aunt Mason McMasters, *one hundred and fifteen years old,* glared with apparent good humor at Aunt Judy, who glared good-humoredly back. Yet to the practiced eye of the reporter, the look of both women was one of unmistakable jealousy. Plainly, they were rivals for the honorary office of "queen mother" of the village.

Aunt Mason McMasters, although older than Aunt Judy, had escaped the stone-deafness that limited the other. Her story, for interest, was matched by her ability to tell it. "Chipper as a bird and talked glibly as a high school girl," the reporter said of her. She had apparently originated in the same Upper South part of the country as Aunt Judy, for she said, Oh, yes, she had seen General Washington and the army of the Revolution.

"What sort of clothes did they wear?" one of the reporters wanted to know.

"Leather britches, short knees, long stockings, funny hats, and big buckles right here," she said, putting her hands on her knees.

It sounded authentic. At 115, she might have seen the Continentals on the march at any time during the 1776-83 war, and would have been well able to recall details.

Both women said that they had used tobacco for as long as they could remember.

They either chewed it, or "dipped" it. If they had smoked, dragging the noxious fumes into their lungs, they could scarcely have survived to be centenarians-plus. In more recent times, British prime minister Winston Churchill, and American entertainer George Burns both lived long, as notable cigar-smokers. Cigar smoke is not inhaled, however, and the cigars of those men may have become more their signature props than objects of addiction.

Aunt Mason had been a slave of a man by the name of McMasters. She related to the reporters a little story of how the announcement of Emancipation had stricken her with apprehension. Like many slaves, she was wary of going out on her own for the first time in her life. Familial attachments made many slaves in Old Testament times feel the same way. Thus, the Law of God graciously allowed for them to remain in slavery under their kindly master (Exod 21.6; Deut 17.15).

Aunt Mason timidly asked Mr. McMasters if he wanted her to work for him still. Work! at age 96! For this had been nineteen years ago, in 1865.

"No," McMasters replied. "I don't want you anymore, Aunt Macey."

"Can't I take up ashes, like I used to?"

"No."

"And he would not let me touch them," she mournfully recounted.

Sad though Aunt Macey's experience was, the former slave owner had had a hard choice. If he had continued to own an aged slave, he would have had to care for her, in keeping with his obligation. But the legal situation had changed. In the Emancipation Proclamation, there was no Old Testament provision for continued slavery. McMasters had no slave, and was faced with either hiring or not hiring a 96-year-old free woman. He chose to put her into the care of the Poor House. It may appear selfish on his part, but it was doubtless the right thing to do. The Poor House could do a much better job of caring for Aunt Macey than he could.

And how did Aunt Mason spend her time now? "I sew a little bit, I eat a little bit, I work a little bit." She was all good cheer, and even made an attempt to dance a jig for the reporters.

Three oddities about Aunt Mason's life were revealed, as the men continued interviewing her. The first, her father was an American Indian. The second, she had never been sick, she said, a day in her life. The third, she had borne *twenty-three children*!

Aunt Macey did not say how many of her children had died – perhaps *all* of them, by that time? The oldest of them could have been a hundred years old. But if any were living, it was a shame that none of them either cared enough, or were able, to bring her out of the Poor House.

* * * * *

The Poor House! The very name bespeaks failure or tragedy. Many of the inmates' stories *were* tragic, or comic-tragic, like that of the earlier mentioned little dwarf, Jim Hill (see Chapter 12, Page 84).

Hill was the ill-favored but generally good-natured fellow who fell in love with one of the female convicts, in the 1880's. Moving forward again, into the 1890's, we find Hill again on the pages of the newspapers in 1894. The paper featured him in a story because, it said, he was then the oldest inmate in the Poor House, in point of residence. He had been there since 1882.

Little better than half-witted, and partially hunchbacked, he managed to be helpful around the Poor House. He was visibly delighted to bring in the wood needed in the stoves and fireplaces. To say that he was "helpful," badly understates the reality. Jim Hill was an incessant worker, always asking to relieve everyone else of his labors, no matter what they were. "His inclinations in this respect are generously indulged," the newspaper slyly commented.

Hill's story is sorrowful, though predictable, given his deficient mentality.[146] Early in the 'Eighties, it must have been 1881, or 1882, he inherited from his brother a substantial sum of money. The peculiar little man naively placed it in his pockets, and left his home state of Michigan, bitten by the bug of wanderlust. He got to South Georgia, and toured the area with a hand-organ and a monkey.

Ever with an eye for the ladies, Jim soon fell prey to an adventuress. Women! They were Jim's ruin. He was desperately smitten with this one, and she traveled with him for a short time. They lived the life of vagabondage, sleeping in hay lofts, and such. One night, the two sought shelter until morning in a barn. When Hill awoke, at first light, his money, the hand-organ, and the monkey were gone, as was his erstwhile lover! Never again did he hear anything of her, or of his property.

Poor, victimized Jim Hill made his way to Atlanta, found himself unable to make a living, and drifted out to the Poor House. Victor Hugo wrote of the hunchback of Notre Dame, and his hopeless love of the gypsy, Esmeralda. He might have done wonders, instead, with the life's story of tender, ugly, mistreated, little dwarf Jim.

*   *   *   *   *

Irish whiskey!

Irish whiskey was the undoing of another inmate, a man who had gained Atlanta street notoriety before his almshouse days. This man was nicknamed "Limerick." Actually, his true name was

William Powers, and he was a son of Ireland who had emigrated to the United States. The <u>Atlanta</u> <u>Constitution</u> in 1886 characterized "Old Limerick" as "Atlanta's most famous vagabond."[147]

After Limerick had come to the United States, he lived in Virginia for twenty-two years. He then moved to Atlanta. He followed the tailoring trade, and fitted many of the city's residents with clothing. He served in the Confederate army.

Limerick's reputation was that of an alcoholic. He had most likely become addicted to strong drink even before he left Ireland. He continued to drink in Virginia, and in Atlanta, he lost his fortune, his friends' respect, and his self-respect.

Poor Limerick was sober only when in jail. By 1886, his name had appeared on the Atlanta police docket 420 times, and fines totaled $1,950. Since he never paid the fines, he had spent an accumulated total of five years in the Atlanta stockade, during the thirty-two years that he had lived in the city.

Limerick's peculiarities were manifold. Among them: He was somewhat of an orator, or loudmouth, but usually got quite mixed up. For example, he claimed to have been born in 1800, and to have emigrated to America in 1832. He may indeed have *looked* 86, in 1886, but it is almost certain that he was not that old.

Another oddity about him: When drunk, like many other inebriates, he would become noisy and disorderly. When an officer attempted to arrest him, he would fall on his back and kick at the man until he exhausted himself!

Limerick carried all kinds of trash in his pockets – string, spools, broken combs, pins, pencils, pieces of ribbon. Whenever he was put in the pokey, he would haul out all these items, put them in a pile in his cell, and solemnly march round and round it.

In 1890, being, as the papers later reported, "over 70," he went off on one of his occasional tramping expeditions to neighboring towns. This time, his absence from Atlanta was the longest ever – four years. When he came back in June, 1894, it took him only a few weeks to be arraigned before Recorder Calhoun. The charge: drunk on the street.

"Old Limerick" promised Calhoun the same thing he had promised him before, that he would leave Atlanta. This time, however, having been overtaken by feebleness, he was unable to leave. Instead, he was picked up, and sent to Dr. Robert Hope at the Poor House.

Dr. Hope assigned him a room. The day after his arrival, Limerick, or Powers, sat in a corner of the front porch of the main building, looking emaciated. The Poor House had gained considerable popularity with the newspapers, as a fertile field for interesting stories. One of the papers had a man on the spot that day. His eye lighted on Powers, and he approached, and met him.

Powers gave out his name as "Powell Brown," and though several other inmates were sitting nearby, none corrected the name. The gullible reporter duly called him by that fictitious name in the published news article the next day.

The reporter heard Powers' story, and sized him up as "loquacious, if confused."

He asked him, "What do you intend to do now?"

"I'm going to stay here until November, so I can have time to decide where to go."

But Powers instantly changed his mind, for in just a few moments he got out of his chair, and walked unsteadily over to the front steps. He announced to one and all,

"I'm going to Ireland. Yes, I'm going back."

This brought guffaws from the other old folks, and Limerick winced, realizing why they laughed. But he retorted,

"Get transportation in New York. Have relatives there."

Such a sweeping plan was plainly beyond the capability of the old fellow to carry it out. He was physically weak and also failing in mind. A few moments later, he had resumed his seat. Being asked his age, he wandered:

"You begin at the Babylonian Captivity. You see, Washington was born, April 22, 1831."

"February," someone corrected him. No mention that he was also a century off, on the year of Washington's birth, too: 1732.

"No," Limerick insisted, "April – old calendar. I was twenty-nine years of age then. I'm afraid I'm getting old."

Yes, he was. No doubt, Limerick would never leave the Poor House.

* * * * *

Often, when parents' fortunes changed, and they were obliged to go into the Poor House, they begged Robert Hope to allow them to bring in their whole family. He invariably accommodated them. This practice started as far back as 1883 or 1884, for the superintendent believed that keeping families together was of supreme importance.

Three reporters from the <u>Atlanta</u> <u>Constitution</u> had been charmed with what they saw in 1883, on the Poor House grounds.[148] Dr. Hope had been superintendent for two years. As the reporters passed the small wooden structures which still housed the white inmates at that time, they glimpsed two blue eyes, deep, clear, and bright, staring at them. The eyes, wide and wondering, continued to stare, until the baby's face broke into smiles.

Smiling back, and peering closer, they saw a muscular and energetic female standing over the child, industriously trying to give it a Turkish bath in about a pint of cold water and soap suds. If she lacked anything in amount of water, she made up for it in furious scrubbing. The reporters wondered that the young 'un's head did not cave in under the pressure! The plump little arms and legs, the cute little shoulders and neck, all stood in sore need of water, but the happy face was the first thing to be cleared of dirt. The little eyelids, dewy after a dousing, popped open to reveal eyes shining like patches of blue sky after a spring shower.

The reporters who witnessed this scene met the woman who had been scrubbing the baby so hard. She was Mrs. Gallagher, who would be a Poor House full-time employee in three or four years (see Chapter Twenty, page 146). She was only filling in, today. Was the child hers, one of the men wanted to know? The newspaper printed her reply verbatim. It was spoken in Emerald Isle cadences so Irish that they might have been printed in green ink:

"No, this baby belongs to the cook. Pity it is, too, that such a likely young one should bring up in such a place. Be yez the commissioners?"

No, the commissioners had come, they said, but they were meeting over in the superintendent's home. And, to the reporters, it seemed somewhat incongruous that this was wash day for the cook's baby, on the very day that the cook herself had to prepare a big meal for the commissioners. Mrs. Gallagher replied,

"Blessed little time does its mother have to tend it! It's the commissioners are out here today, and where's the harm o' seein' that the child is decent-lookin', to be shore?"

$$* \quad * \quad * \quad * \quad *$$

Among the many Poor House episodes concerning children, some were heart-wrenching.[149] A few years after the reporters were charmed by the conversation with Mrs. Gallagher, came Wenston Kohut, from the port city of Charleston. He came, not to the Poor House, but to Atlanta, bringing his wife and five children with him. He needed work, but after two weeks in the Gate City, he had found none.

Bidding his family goodbye, one morning, at the door of their cottage in Bellwood, Kohut set out to try to find a job in another town. For a few days after that, no word was heard from him. Then came the message that he was dead. Only that – "dead." No time or place of the death was shown, nor any circumstances. Just,"dead."

Newspaper accounts are lacking concerning what, or how much, investigation Mrs. Kohut was able to do. It was reported that, grieving, she became ill and almost died. She and her children, half-starved, were brought to the Poor House.

Dr. Hope began to minister to the wispy little woman with the drawn face. He cared for her as she lay convalescent for a couple of days. At times her mind wandered. She babbled, dreaming of the happy days. Then she would awake with a start, and the horrible realization would burst upon her: *"This* is where I *really* am! *This* is what has really happened!"

Meanwhile, outside, the five children, aged eight and under, played, oblivious to it all.

They were pouring water in the sand, and shaping the mud into various objects, to represent wares in a miniature store. They could hardly have been more content, laughing and playing with their siblings. Robert Hope gazed, and slowly shook his head, saying nothing. But, having come out of the orphanage himself, he had good hopes that these little ones would emerge from the Poor House to become useful citizens.

*   *   *   *   *

Poor House feature articles appeared in the Atlanta newspapers of the 1880's and 1890's, concerning at least two "famous" (or infamous) Atlanta prostitutes.[150] These women wound up in the Poor House after their beauty had vanished. One of them was a pitiful case with tuberculosis, from which she eventually died.

The other prostitute, Myrtle Blake, was the subject of more interesting story. Myrtle had been apprehended on a criminal charge of larceny. She had been living at a disreputable local resort, where she had robbed a farmer of $25, and had relieved another man of his watch. A rash of sensational news articles appeared about her in the newspapers in 1897.

There was no doubt of Myrtle Blake's guilt. She was as guilty as sin, besides being a young woman of generally dissolute character. She was sentenced to serve nine months for the larceny, and was to serve it at the Poor Farm's convict section. There it happened that in that year she was the only white woman among a score of female convicts.

Victorian sensibilities concerning the fair sex came to the surface in her behalf, because she was forced to wear stripes at the Poor House. This kind of clothing did not match the era's exalted image of womanhood, prostitute or no.

Race prejudice was also aroused, because this white woman had to eat, sleep, and work with her black sisters, who outnumbered her twenty to one. It was perfectly all right for black women to have to wear the striped uniforms, but a shame for a white woman to have to do so. Indeed, many cried out that it was "quite unusual" for a white woman to have to serve as a convict, anyway. Myrtle's pitying partisans got busy to try to shorten her sentence, and also to raise the money for her fine.

Robert Hope thought that he ought to be even-handed in his treatment of the prisoners,

but he compromised with the widespread protest. He decided to give her no heavy work, setting her instead to the task of sewing for the others. On the other hand, she must continue to wear the stripes.

Now the episode took a fascinating turn, as Judge John D. Berry, judge of the criminal court, intervened. Judge Berry's ideas were more in tune with the thinking of the Nineteenth Century. He issued an order that Myrtle Blake *not* be forced to wear the black-and-white striped garb. A chivalrous rescue!

When interviewed by newsmen, Berry's only explanation was racist: Since Myrtle Blake was the only white woman in the convict camp, he wished her to be allowed to wear her own clothing, so as not to suffer "unnecessary humiliation." Earlier, the wording of his order to Dr. Hope had included the opinion that if the woman had to wear stripes, her disgrace and humiliation would be greater than her offense.

The Poor House superintendent was forced to wrestle with his conscience. He felt that he was right, and thus was stung by the judge's order. Instead of answering the order personally, he took it immediately to the county commissioners for advice. Would his own fair judgment be maintained, or not? Could the Poor House superintendent be master in his own house?

The commissioners' answer was "yes." They reacted negatively to what they saw as the judge's high-handedness. Chairman Forrest Adair said that Myrtle must wear the stripes. Commissioner Walter Brown backed up that opinion, saying, "We have no star boarders, and must treat all alike."

County Attorney Rosser was asked to give his opinion, which proved to be in agreement with that of the commissioners. Adair then sent Judge Berry a formal note protesting that such an order as his, showing such obvious favoritism to one inmate, would subvert the whole discipline of the convict camp. Further, he said, exertion of outside influences such as the judge's undermined the lawful authority of the board of county commissioners.

So it was that Berry's order was overturned. Since he had thrust his oar in without much legal authority, he now backed off. The commission's judgment, and that of Robert Hope, prevailed.

Myrtle Blake must don stripes, and she must serve the full nine months. Maybe white women were still regarded as special, and intrinsically different from black women. But with this incident, equal rights of a sort won out, in Georgia, even if only in the convict camp.

CHAPTER TWENTY-THREE

OLD SOLDIERS

"Old soldiers never die, they just fade away."
>   - *An old barrack ballad*,
>   quoted by Gen. Douglas
>   McArthur, to the U.S.
>   Congress

The annals of the Poor House abound with inmates who were Confederate veterans. At one point in the 'Nineties there were ten of them residing there under Dr. Hope's watchful eye.[151] Two of the ex-soldiers were minus a leg.

Unlike many inmates who were older, the veterans were mentally sharp, conscious of their surroundings, and desirous of better. The "better" that was particularly in view was the Confederate Veterans' Home, where they could be with more men of their kind. Most of this Confederate squad lived for a year in the hope that they would be accepted into that haven.

The Confederate Veterans' Home had been constructed for men like these. It was located in the woods just beyond Grant Park, in East Atlanta, on a road which became known as Confederate Avenue. Unfortunately, the hopes of the men at the Poor House were dashed. All ten were rejected, and they settled into apathy, with no hope of ever getting away from the Poor House. They had thought that the atmosphere would have been more congenial at the Veterans' Home.

It no doubt would have been, for at the Veterans' Home everything was oriented towards them. At the Poor House, they were only ten men among the 155 inmates whom the institution now had under its care.

* * * * *

One of the veterans, J. H. Henson, had marched in Virginia under Stonewall Jackson, and had been wounded. His eyes blazed with pride as he told Robert Hope of serving in Virginia with Jackson's "foot cavalry," as the general's fast-moving infantry were nicknamed. But Henson spoke reproachfully of the Veterans' Home which had turned him down. Why would they do that? He did not understand.

* * * * *

Another of these former Rebels, one of Longstreet's men, busied himself as "the statesman of the Poor House." He forgot his severe rheumatism by plunging into the study of financial problems. He was intensely interested in national issues, and eagerly soaked up the contents of any daily newspaper that he could get his hands on.

"I see that Mr. Cleveland (President Grover Cleveland) has called an extra session," he announced one day. "I hope he'll do something for the poor. Then maybe I can get to my relatives in Resaca."

He asserted that just before the Civil War he had lost twenty-three slaves by drowning! Since no printed explanation survives, one wonders what may have been the circumstances of that long ago mass tragedy. Since that time of the drowning, he insisted, he had been followed by ill luck. Now confined to the Poor House, he said that the only property he possessed in the world was some land in Missouri. He was unable to sell it because of hard times.

* * * * *

A real profile of courage and honor was that of fifty-eight-year-old Civil War veteran J. W. Higgins. He was not one of the aforementioned ten. Rather, he was an old soldier who lived at the Poor House for just a period of weeks in the winter of 1895-96.

Higgins had dwelt for a number of years in a miserable little house, a shanty near the Chattahoochee River. It was located northwest of Atlanta, in a place that today would be fixed as "inside the Perimeter." He did odd jobs of work around the lower end of Marietta Street, in what had become part of downtown Atlanta. He also did the same just at Five Points, the very center of the city. He walked to these jobs each and every day, and back home again.

It was a severe strain on his fast-failing body to plod a distance of six miles each way daily, except Sundays. Yet, by this twelve-mile round-trip trek he got to his work, and was able to make enough money to keep himself alive. That was the limit of what he could do.

In 1895, however, the Georgia state legislature made a decision in behalf of old soldiers. Those who could show that they were aged, poor, or diseased to the point of inability to make a living, should receive a pension. That ruling perfectly suited Higgins' case, for he had many aches and pains. Most serious of all was his dropsy (weak heart condition), that was severely damaging his whole constitution. He therefore applied for a pension, and went around as happy as could be for a period of weeks, believing that he would soon be able to go to the state treasurer and pick up a much-needed $60.00.

Cruel fate! The news came through that there so many veterans in the same plight as he, that there would be a delay. The money was short, and no claims would be paid until the legislature met again to make another appropriation. Higgins wearily took up his hard life again, and waited for the promised relief.

After months more, the legislative session finally rolled around. But by that time, as his disease had advanced, the poor fellow was in such sorry condition that he needed physical help. He sought and obtained permission to enter the Poor House.

Dr. Hope gave Higgins the very kindest treatment, especially since he saw that the veteran was not long for this world. When the payment of his pension began, Higgins had only one more week to live, as it proved. He could not know this, but he was certainly aware of the parlous state of his health, and knew that the end could not be far off.

He professed himself gratified to know that the money would give him a decent burial.

He wanted to rest among the Confederate dead in Westview Cemetery – would Dr. Hope find out for him how much that would cost? Away went the superintendent, returning after some time to say that the burial in Westview would cost Higgins $43.00.

Saturday dawned, and Higgins was feeling quite poorly. He said that he was much afraid that the end for him would come before the pension could be drawn. In that case, he would not have enough money to pay for his burial. His body would surely go to the potter's field!

To gratify this inmate, Dr. Hope again slapped the reins, and clucked his horse into motion. His buggy wheeled down the rutted driveway, out onto Piedmont, thence to Roswell Road, on through Buckhead, and straight down Peachtree Road to Atlanta and the treasurer's office. He drew out Higgins' $60.00, brought it back to the Poor House, and put it into Higgins' hands. The old veteran fingered it, caressed it, as if it were some living pet. He felt so proud and thankful!

Dr. Hope reminded him that he had confided that there were individuals to whom he owed money. Now he had the means to pay them off, did he not? Higgins acknowledged it, and made out a list of his creditors. All the debts were small ones, and he made the doctor promise to pay them off for him. The total of these debts was $17.00, just enough to completely absorb the remainder of Higgins' money, once the funeral was financed.

The honest old man then calmly awaited the end of his life, which came on the following Friday. His body was laid away among those of his wartime comrades at Westview, and there it rests today.

CHAPTER TWENTY-FOUR

ONE WHO LOST A FORTUNE

"Heaven's help is better than early rising."
Don Quixote
Miguel de Cervantes

It is discouraging for men to give their utmost effort in a great war, and wind up on the losing side. So it was for the Confederate veterans who survived their huge conflict. Add to that military loss the further inability to win in the postwar world, and the discouragement must have been crushing. For some did fail, and ended up living in the Poor House.

Of all the tales of bitterness and loss brought to the Poor House by veterans in the 'Eighties and 'Nineties, none could top that of Major Alexander Ratteree, for unrelieved woe.[152]

Robert Hope received Major Ratteree into the Poor House, July 22, 1897. Ratteree was interviewed at length by news reporters the following December. At that time he was the oldest and most interesting person in the establishment.

Ninety-three years old, Alexander Ratteree had been born in Clayton County in 1804. He had lived for most of his life in the area south-southwest of Atlanta. In this section, in the 1850's, the eastern terminus of the new Atlanta and West Point Railroad was built. A little town grew up there, named, appropriately, East Point. From the 1830's, and for many years thereafter, Ratteree was an extensive landowner in the sections of the county which eventually became East Point and College Park.

The news articles did not mention a fact revealed to the author in personal conversation by the late curator of the Atlanta Historical Society, Franklin Garrett. Major Ratteree's constant activity was that of suing people in the law courts. Garrett had checked the facts, and had written of them in his massive <u>Atlanta</u> and <u>Its</u> <u>Environs</u>.[153]

Besides owning a lot of property, Ratteree was, indeed, for nearly six decades one of the most litigious citizens of DeKalb, later, Fulton County. His name appears frequently, sometimes as plaintiff, sometimes as defendant, in the pages of the Georgia Supreme Court Reports, down to the early 'Nineties. Almost all of the cases concerned a dispute over some piece of property.

When he entered the Poor House, in '97, Ratteree had a wife and three quite mature children living south of East Point, but they were not able to support him. Why in the world was he in the Poor House, if he had owned so much, and had battled so often and hard for it in court? His tale was amazing.

The major was far gone in deafness and blindness, but his mind was sharp, and he was well able to relate this – the story of his life as he saw it.

He said that he was at one time worth $250,000, which, for purchasing power, would be equal to millions today. His Achilles heel, he claimed, was his excessive trust in human nature. This cost him all his fortune, and he had told Dr. Hope that he was now happy to live anywhere at all, including the Poor House.

Ratteree was not always a loser. For example, at one time before the War Between the States, he sold a single lot in East Point to J. G. Blount, for $6,000. That was an extremely high price in those days for a piece of land that size.

It was in those prewar days, however, that his losing ways set in. He lent $3,000 to his brother-in-law. It was never returned. Wisdom teaches that the lender must be prepared for the total loss of a "casual" loan, i.e., a loan to family, or one without written contract. Ratteree, however, was not emotionally ready for the loss. He remembered well, until his dying day, how his trusted relative had treated him.

This reverse did not cure Ratteree. He soon proved that he was still vulnerable, when another relative forged an order on him for five of his favorite horses, and sold them!

During that same peacetime period, Ratteree was running the first steam driven sawmill ever seen in this part of the country. In some undisclosed way, he was cheated out of it, and never got back a cent.

Ratteree repeated his lament, as he told his stories: "Overconfidence in mankind is the only reason I can give for my downfall."

Illustrative of that weakness of too much trust, was his trip to Alabama. There Ratteree gave a man the deeds to about 5,000 acres of Alabama land to sell for him. The chap did sell the land, and sent Ratteree a post office order for $7.25, saying that this was Ratteree's share of the money for which the property was sold!

No doubt, his self-confessed naiveté about the dark side of human nature was not the only cause of Ratteree's misfortunes. To a certain extent, the man was just snake-bit. It was as if the stars in their courses fought against him. Witness the time that he fell sick at the wrong moment. He had been hard-pressed for ready cash, and so mortgaged 2,000 of his acres for $325. Having done that, he promptly, and inopportunely, became ill. While he lay flat on his back, the mortgage was foreclosed, and he forfeited the land. The $325 paid his doctor's bill.

He had suffered the slings and arrows of unrighteous fortune, but Ratteree was still a rich man, *very* rich. About that time, the Confederate cannon boomed out, in Charleston harbor, and the Civil War was beginning. Ratteree had $60,000 in cold cash, plus 40 head of cattle, 75 Negro slaves, and approximately 150,000 acres of land. Leaving his worldly goods behind, he went off to war with a commission in the Confederate army.

All was well with Ratteree's material assets for a few years, but as the fighting neared Atlanta, in 1864, anyone owning anything was nervous. Its destruction would be assured by Sherman's presence!

Ratteree's goods were not directly destroyed by Sherman, but a real Job's calamity befell him. Jim Fulton, cashier of the old Fulton bank, left the city with all the bank's money. He intended to safeguard it from the invaders, and from local looters. Alas, he returned after the Yankees had captured Atlanta, and had departed. But Jim Fulton did not have the money. The Yankee soldiers had captured him, and had unburdened him of all that he was carrying. At this one stroke, Ratteree was out a cool $47,000 of his fortune.

Yet, prior to that loss he had other valuable resources. There was $9,500 in gold, and $1,000 in silver, buried in an old tin box in a peach orchard on his property. The major was with Hood's Army of Tennessee, and from wherever around Atlanta his unit was, at the time, Ratteree sent his wife a letter. In it, he told her exactly where the money was. Risky correspondence! The Yankees intercepted the postal rider, relieved him of his post bag, read the letter, went to the orchard, and dug up the money.

After these blows, Ratteree was left penniless, except for his slaves and livestock. He said that, once, before the war, he had made $15,000 in eight days, trading in slaves. But now, with the war having come to Atlanta, both his slaves and his livestock were precarious possessions. The Confederates were defending the city from behind immensely strong fortifications. The Federals were opposite them in their own trench lines, which were not extended far enough to block off access to the south. Ratteree was thus able to ride down to East Point to visit his holdings. He found the blacks gone, and his animals gone, as well.

As the fighting continued around Atlanta, Ratteree had the notion that Yankee losses had been considerably higher than those of the Confederates, which up to this time they assuredly had been. With Hood having taken over command of the army from Johnston, that would change, but Ratteree at this point was optimistic. He knew that he still had his land, at least. He also hoped to get back his money, which was off in the blue with Jim Fulton. So he battled to hang onto his diminished resources.

Although the army had been repeatedly outflanked and forced back by Sherman, all the way from Dalton, the Confederate soldiers' morale was still high. As for Ratteree, it was at this time that he performed acts of battlefield bravery, and received his promotion from captain to the rank of major.

One of his private battles was for his bees and honey. Ratteree originally had about fifty "bee gums" – beehives made of hollow log sections of gum trees. However, soldiers, of which army he did not say, were continually stealing them. Their procedure was to smoke the bees out, then carry off the entire hive, to separate the comb and honey from it at their leisure.

Finally, soldiers had stolen all but nine. Ratteree came along and robbed the nine himself, leaving the bee gums standing in place, as if they had not been touched. The following night, the soldiers returned, and confiscated the nine. Carrying them up the road, they noticed that they felt a bit light. They discovered to their disgust that the hives were empty, except for some deceased bees. The men threw them beside the road, where Ratteree delightedly found them the next day. The soldiers never raided his East Point home after that, and the oldster chuckled in remembrance of the joke he had played on them.

Ratteree was only one of many thousands ruined by the war, but after the Lost Cause, he continued his losing ways. Owning about 50,000 acres in south Georgia, he again fell ill. While he was sick abed, his children got hold of the deeds to the land. Not realizing what they were, they tore them up. It is possible that they imagined them worthless, like so many other official documents, following the Confederacy's demise. Or, more likely, they simply did not look official, being handwritten. The deeds had not been recorded, so Ratteree was prevented from getting copies to replace the ones destroyed. Thus he lost all his property in south Georgia.

He had been a major in Reed's famous regiment. He told Dr. Hope that he was due to receive a pension from the State of Georgia. He could not get it, because he was the last surviving soldier of that regiment. Unfortunate consequence of living so long! With the others all dead, he was unable to prove that he had served in the army. This may seem to have been a curious reason, in view of the existence of the Confederate army's muster-rolls. Those who have sought records of other Confederate soldiers, however, know that the information is sometimes hard to come by.

For all his hopeless fixation on the empty half of life's cup, Ratteree may be forgiven, when one ponders his complete loss of everything. He really had nothing left, by the time that the Poor House superintendent came to know him.

Perhaps God wanted to show the major that, "one's life does not consist in the abundance of the things which he possesses" (Luke 12.15). Whatever their purpose, Ratteree's reverses gave him a rich collection of sympathy-evoking yarns, which, like an invalid who "enjoys poor health," he loved to recite.

CHAPTER TWENTY-FIVE

"POOR" HOUSE AND DIRECTOR

"The beauty of the house is order;
The blessing of the house is contentment;
The glory of the house is hospitality;
The crown of the house is godliness."

- Mantlepiece Motto

What a wonderful day to stay in bed!

On Saturday morning, January 5, 1895, a heavy snow mantled the countryside in white. Despite the difficult prospect that travel presented, Constitution reporter L.L. Knight hitched his horses to his buggy.[154] Accompanied by a staff artist, he headed out Peachtree Road, north, towards the Almshouse. Many reporters had visited there over the years, yet, not surprisingly, most Atlantans had never seen the place with their own eyes. Knight was one of them, so he looked forward to the trip.

The drive was painfully slow. The road was so slippery that Knight's usually speedy team struggled to negotiate the steep hills. They passed "Brookwood," the quiet country home of Joseph Thompson. This house at the Peachtree Road and Deering was within a stone's throw of the railroad, where later the Peachtree Station would be built.

The two intrepid newsmen spotted only a few homes dotting the landscape, in the next mile and a half. The horses' hooves slipped and slid, as, carefully, carefully, the buggy descended to Peachtree Creek and drove across. From there it was uphill, to see the home of Samuel Pharr, and then a level road onward, to sloppity-slop into Buckhead. In the next day's newspaper, they would remark on "the old village of Buckhead, now designated by the more stylish name of Atlanta Heights."[155]

It had been a six-mile drive from Atlanta. In the middle of Buckhead they saw a dilapidated, weather-beaten old blacksmith shop, which faced the angle where the Roswell Road forked off to the left. Again, carefully delineating their route, the newspapermen noted that they could have followed Roswell Road, for it would touch "the rear extremity of the pauper farm." However, Knight stuck to the right, and continued on Peachtree Road for "a few hundred yards," to the intersection with Piedmont Road. There he turned left, and followed Piedmont to the front entrance of the almshouse.

Knight's initial view of the Poor House surprised him:

"It presented a much more inviting figure than the imagination had given to it in advance. The word 'poorhouse' carried with it a suggestion that divorces it completely from all ideas of comfort or beauty. It presents to the mind a picture of squalid poverty, indigence, and all those qualities which belong to misfortune and misery. The sight of the building put an end to these visions and clearly exposed them as utter misconception."

What did Knight see, instead of the poor visions he expected?[156]

"A long fence neatly enameled with a fresh coat of white paint lined the roadside in front of the building and gave the buggy an entrance into the grounds through a large open gate. A winding path extended from the gate, a distance of 200 feet, to the front of the building and then curved off to a corresponding gate further (sic) up the road. The ample grounds created a pleasing prospect and suggested the beauty they would shortly assume when the snows of winter should yield to the refreshing verdure of spring and the overshadowing trees should begin to display their full opulence of bloom and foliage."

The reporter then focused on the Poor House main building itself, describing it as "a handsome two-storey structure, built entirely of brick." Just to the left of the entrance was an inscription showing the date that the building was erected, "A.D. 1885," with the names of the county commissioners, and of the architects, Bruce and Morgan.

The two men, Knight, and his staff artist, entered the building, and discovered the following:

"Dr. Hope, with his wife and two little children, occupies two of the front rooms on the lower floor of the building and others in the rear on the second floor. The front room to the left of the main hall is used as a visitors' parlor and in the rear of this is Dr. Hope's private office with a little drug shop opening into it. On the opposite side of the hallway is a cozy sitting room neatly furnished. Into this apartment Dr. Hope ushered his two visitors and gave them a full account of the past record and practical operations of the farm."

* * * * *

Robert Hope was not yet thirty-six years of age. Knight described him:[157]

"In his personal appearance Dr. Hope is rather above the medium height, slenderly built and wears a well-kept beard, which gives to him a dignified countenance that is both professional and prepossessing. His manner is quiet and unassuming and his conversation rich, animated and interesting. He prefers, however, to adopt the subject of discussion introduced by his visitor and rarely obtrudes one of his own suggestions unless it naturally springs from the previous subject matter of conversation. In going over the farm and in looking after the care of the inmates of the poorhouse Dr. Hope is partial to his little sack coat. When he comes to the city, however, he lays aside his little sack coat and puts on his more professional frock. The inmates of the home have a great respect for him and the greater part of them treat him not only with marked deference but with a lavish display of affection."

The Poor House director told all,[158] as Knight interviewed him, scribbling the doctor's remarks as fast as he could, on a large pad. According to Knight, the superintendent passed his hand over his forehead, as if to clear his recollection. Then he said,

"I have been at this place for nearly fourteen years. It hardly seems half as long, for I have been closely occupied, and when we have our hands full of work the flight of time ceases to be observed and years pass in quick succession of days and months. I came here in 1881. Judge W.L. Calhoun, who had just then succeeded Judge Pittman, gave me the appointment. I held my position under this appointment for several months, after which the board of county commissioners was organized and I was elected to the office. The designation of the office was that of superintendent and resident physician and the county almshouse and my duties in addition to the care and treatment of the sick were those of general management and overseeing. The sanitary condition of the farm, the personal habits of the inmates, the records of deaths, admissions and dismissals, the cultivation of the ground in order to make the farm as far as possible self-sustaining – all of these were matters that came within the purview of my office and I so understood them at the time of my installation."

The doctor's questioner had caught the words, "habits of the inmates." So he asked,

"Do you encounter much difficulty in keeping (the inmates) under control?"[159]

"I do," the doctor admitted. "This is one of the most serious difficulties of my work.

I find it a very hard matter to keep the occupants clean; and cleanliness is, of course, a prime consideration at an institution of this kind. There is no telling the diseases that might spring from a disregard of personal attention and for this reason the care of the inmates along this line, is heavily enjoined upon the resident physician. I have found it to be the rule, instead of a mere occasional variation, that a man or woman ceases to be punctilious in regard to personal habits after they get into the poor house and the properties of soap and water seem to lose all fascination for them. I have a man here by the name of Ashley, who moved at one time in the very best society, and was a model, I have no doubt, in his personal neatness and attire. You would be surprised to note the change in his condition. His ideas seem to be reversed and instead of taking a pride in keeping neat he takes a delight in keeping as dirty as possible. It is all I can do to manage him. As the result of this individual care of the inmates and the general superintendence which I have given to the sanitary condition of the farm, no disease of any kind has broken out, and not a single death has occurred during the last ten years except from old age or chronic disabilities. At present we have in the home several old men and women who are over eighty years of age and who have been inmates of the poor house since the war."

*   *   *   *   *

L.L. Knight thought again of how wrong had been his imaginings of the Poor House.

After hearing Dr. Hope's explanation of his operation of the place, Knight was more than merely favorably inclined towards it. He was asking himself what others had asked, is this really a "poor" house? Does it deserve that name? I was expecting something much more humble. This place is not at all lowly or mean. Why, with the free medical care and pleasant surroundings, I might want to spend *my* last days here!

Knight was not finished with his questioning of the doctor, however. He had not seen all of the Poor House that he wanted to see, either. Before he could render the educated opinion that the newspaper's readers deserved, he would have to make a thorough tour. He proceeded to ask more questions, and the most important one concerned whether he might be conducted on a thorough tour. The doctor was most ready to grant him all that he needed.

CHAPTER TWENTY-SIX

POOR PEOPLE ON A RICH FARM

"Christ Jesus, when I come to die
Grant me a clean, sweet summer sky,
Without the mad wind's panther cry.
Send me a little garden breeze
To gossip in magnolia trees;
                    The Priest and the Pirate: A Ballad
                    of Theodosia Burr, Stanza 3 Hervey
                    Allen

<u>A</u>tlanta Constitution newsman L.L. Knight had gotten quite an earful from Dr. Robert Hope, and had seen a lot. He had planned to spend the day at the Poor House, however, and knew that there was much more to see and hear. He pressed the doctor to relate something of the almshouse history of the last fourteen years.[160]

The doctor told Knight the story told before – how there had been only seven or eight wooden structures fronting on Peachtree Road, when he came as superintendent. Then the present facility had at last been built, with the brick made by eighteen women convicts, five men convicts, and two experienced brick molders.

The previously untold "rest of the story" was that, after the convicts had made the brick, they had done their part. They were then put to cultivating the farm and beautifying the grounds. It was a labor in which they were still engaged. The almshouse buildings themselves were finished by hired day labor.

As his words were recorded in the newspaper, Dr. Hope continued,

"It (the almshouse main building) is substantially fireproof, a dead wall constituting the partition between each suite of rooms. In December, 1885, all of the pauper inmates of the Fulton County almshouse were moved into the new building which has since been occupied without interruption. New furniture, bedding, decorative ornaments and wearing apparel were provided and the farm, in a measure, if such a condition may be properly ascribed to an almshouse, began to assume all the outward indications of prosperity."

Dr. Hope was careful to point out that the inmates were expected to pay board, in the form of useful work, for their stay at the Poor House.

"No inmate of the almshouse who is able to work is allowed to remain idle. He must do something, if he only makes a pretence. The impression that when a man goes to the poorhouse he is simply supported without lifting his hand to do a piece of work is a grave misapprehension. There is little idleness on the place except among the old people who are too infirm and weak to perform any great amount of work; and none is expected or required of them. This applies also to the sick and to such as are otherwise disabled. The rule of the almshouse is one of labor and compensation. This, of course, is associated with kind treatment and a humane regard for the unfortunate lot of the individual who belongs to the county's household."

And what were the results of the work done on the place?

"Last year, with the aid of the female convicts, the farm produced 800 bushels of corn, 700 bushels of potatoes, twenty-five two-horse wagon loads of fodder and shucks, 100 bushels of peas, 100 bushels of onions, 2,400 pounds of meat, and such smaller vegetables as the inmates have consumed during the year. We raise on the place chickens, turkeys, guineas, pigeons, hogs, and cows, in addition to such produce as butter, eggs, and milk. The table supply is abundant and the variations are such as to give the inmates a hearty relish for their food. All who are able to come to their meals are required to do so under the rules of the almshouse, and those who are not able to come to the dining room have their meals served to them in their rooms."

Of course the almshouse was not entirely self-sustaining:

"The county supplies all necessary provisions in the way of food and clothing. The expenses last year for running the almshouse were about $6,663. The cost of the asylum was about $850. The number of acres belonging to the farm is about 200 (note: Dr. Hope was figuring the farm acreage separately from that of the other units). Nearly one-fourth of this is under cultivation in the immediate neighborhood of the building. The convict camp is located about a mile from here and the asylum is about a quarter. We have now about 155 inmates in the almshouse, and twenty-five women convicts. Five of these latter are white women, two from Cobb County, one from Polk, and two from Fulton. I keep a record of all statistics and transactions relating to the alms-house and this is ready at any time for inspection."

The reporter had listened, being quite positively affected by Dr. Hope's recitation.

"The quiet life that is spent here on the farm is relieved only by the odd and unique characters who give it a rather comical variety," the doctor went on. He told Knight about the dwarf, little Jim Hill. He also told of an old lady who scorned Christmas dainties at the dinner table, and demanded to have the *back* of the turkey – hardly to be considered the choicest piece!

Dr. Hope then invited Knight and the staff artist to ramble with him around the house and farm. Knight subsequently wrote:

"Passing through the rear of the main hall an open court was displayed. This was lined on either side by a long projection of wards, each room opening upon a long veranda, and commanding a clear view of the court as well as a convenient access to it. A well projected itself immediately in front of the open door and a large shade tree guarded the remote extremity of the left hand ward. This ward is occupied by the women and the one directly opposite is occupied by the men. Beyond the shade tree just mentioned a high water tank rises above the neighboring treetops and commands a lordly view of the surrounding country. This huge tank supplied water to farm for sanitary and other purposes and was constructed about two years ago.

"In the open court yard a number of children were playing in the snow. They were comfortably clad and seemed to enjoy the bracing atmosphere, for their cheeks were rosy and a merry din greeted the ears of those in the neighborhood.

"On the right veranda a group of old men were standing. As soon as they caught a glimpse of their visitors they hobbled off to their rooms and closed the doors." It was another instance of the well-known reclusiveness of almshouse inmates. Crushed down with a sense of failure, they did not wish to be seen, identified, and, as they imagined, humiliated, by acquaintances from "the outside world."

Despite the withdrawn attitude of so many of the inmates, Dr. Hope suggested that the three of them make rounds of individuals in their rooms, since he knew of some who would welcome visits by strangers. And so they called on not a few of the people, the reporter making notes all the while, and the artist doing his sketches.

The little dwarf, Jim Hill, was available as usual, and, as usual, he was living proof of the doctor's observation that the quiet life of the place was relieved by the "odd and unique characters." Wearing a coat that had long ago been discarded by its proper owner, Jim Hill was "a mixture of dirt and bristles."

Jim's infatuation with the buxom girl-convict called "Missouri," was not his only romantic flight, for the one which took place in the early 1880's has been recounted already (see pp. 180-81). He had also succumbed recently to the wiles of other female convicts. Indeed, he had "manifested an amazing aptitude for falling in love" with them. The part of it all that was so amusing to reporter Knight was that all of the girls with whom Jim fell in love were so much larger than he!

"Missouri" seemed to be Jim's great fascination now. He had not gotten over a trick played on him, concerning Missouri. Mr. Jim Collins, a member of the board of county commissioners, had told Jim Hill, as previously related, that he would get him a marriage license, so that he could marry Missouri. Little Jim was very excited, but Collins' promise had been only a cruel practical joke. The license was never produced.

As Dr. Hope and the two reporters accosted Jim Hill out at a spot where hogs were being skinned and their flesh boiled, the misshapen little man showed his bitterness. When the name of commissioner Collins was mentioned in his hearing, Jim Hill, till that moment not speaking, suddenly broke his silence.

"He's no good. He's the biggest liar in the county. He promised to get a license for me and Missouri and he never brought it. The Devil take him, he's no good."

Having delivered himself of that speech, Hill stooped in front of one of the pork cauldrons, transferred a glowing coal from the fire under it, to the bowl of his pipe. Puffing away, he walked off and disappeared.

"That," remarked the doctor, "is a funny fellow. He is absolutely harmless and one of the most singular characters I ever encountered."

A tour of the vegetable garden, the poultry yard, and the buggy stables followed. The men poked their heads into the almshouse kitchen and dining room, Knight jotting such comments as, "Dr. Hope is greatly assisted by his good wife and by his matron, Mrs. Williams."

It had been years since Poor House food had been criticized, in a political ploy against the superintendent. L.L. Knight probably had that in mind, for he was careful to write, "Everything is well seasoned and prepared in such abundance and variety as to satisfy the appetites of all."

The reporter especially noticed the condition of the rooms. They were "comfortably furnished - - bedsteads fashioned of wrought iron - - covered with good warm bedding."

"The walls," he said, "are tastefully ornamented with decorative designs, and chairs, tables, Testaments and other articles constitute the furnishings of each room."

Knight rode back into Atlanta that afternoon with a highly favorable opinion of the almshouse, and the way it was being operated. The city, too, had great pride in its almshouse. Indeed, it had now become Atlanta's most admired public facility. The newspaper gave the place recognition by printing Knight's compliments in an extremely lengthy and thorough article. To add icing to the cake, the article was mounted within a *gold border*, and it glowed with praise in every paragraph.

*   *   *   *   *

The praise kept coming. The popularity of the almshouse, Atlanta's unlikely jewel, was never higher.

During the same year that L.L. Knight visited the almshouse, 1895, another reporter, who signed himself simply, "B.M.B.," came to visit.[161] He had stopped over at Joseph Thompson's Brookwood estate on the way. He took the opportunity to tour the home, and write up his findings. He wrote that he was convinced that this showcase Atlanta home was <u>the</u> ideal house, and that it had been placed on property developed into "one vast undulating plot of beauty."

Apparently B.M.B. was in a good mood, and, continuing on out to the almshouse, he was in the jolly company of the county commissioners. They arrived at the Poor House at about 1 P.M., and B.M.B. recounted that they were "extended a hospitable welcome by Dr. Hope, the efficient superintendent.." The visitors toured the Poor House first, then, at close of day, Della served them "a magnificent dinner."

A lot that B.M.B. said about the Poor House, and about Dr. Hope's good and wise administration of it simply repeated or overlapped L.L. Knight's description. He added a compliment, however, concerning the conditions afforded the black inmates:

"The negro paupers live in nice, comfortable cottages, and raise their chickens and cultivate their garden spots just as they would if they owned the premises."

The reporter's assessment of the almshouse was, in sum, "an ideal place of comfort and cleanliness." So, once again, a reporter had led his readers to the question, "Should a place this nice really be called a 'Poor House'?" It did seem a drastic misnomer.

* * * * *

As this is being written, modern Atlanta is wrestling with the vast problems that are inherent in an American metropolis' efforts to provide for the sick, the homeless, and the otherwise needy. The city recently has passed through a time of decision on bankrupt Grady Hospital, its vast public emergency facility.[162] It is at least encouraging to realize that historically Atlanta has always shown great interest in benevolent works. That interest continues, but the community's ability to solve the problems is dangerously impaired at points.

In 1895, there were many interested partisans of charity in general, in Atlanta, and more and more were gaining interest in the almshouse in particular. Accordingly, L.L. Knight had led into his glowing article on the almshouse with the words, "The giving of alms is one of the highest duties enjoined upon a civilized community." "Civilized" was a catch-word of the Darwin-influenced Victorians, with their onward-and-upward-forever mind set. With many of them, "civilized" was misused as a near synonym of "Christian."

Today's journalists seldom appeal to Holy Writ directly, to support positions they take. In 1895, L.L. Knight was less reticent.[163] He plunged forward to quote Proverbs 19:17, "He who has pity on the poor lends to the Lord." From there he went on to allude to the New Testament, pointing to Jesus' example in His treatment of the poor and outcast.

Having thus applied both the Old and New Testaments to the case, Knight embraced Atlanta's then-limited religious pluralism: "The Jew and the Gentile, therefore, can meet on common ground in the mutual acceptance of this great law of charity - -." Many good

Jewish citizens had dwelt in Atlanta almost from its beginning. Knight knew, of course, that some downtown Jewish storeowners, at Dr. Hope's request, had contributed to the Poor House.

In newspaper article after article, it is clear that, by 1895, Atlanta admired the almshouse with the fervency of "fans." Somehow, out there beyond the horizon, beyond the small village of Buckhead, the doctor/superintendent had managed to create something of worth. The Poor House now matched everyone's vision of an idyllic "haven for the golden years."

CHAPTER TWENTY-SEVEN

BUILDING A JAIL

"No young man believes he shall ever die."
           - The Feeling of Immortality in Youth
           William Hazlitt

*   *   *   *   *

By 1896, R. L. Hope had been elected to the building committee of the Fulton County Board of Commissioners.[164] He had been put on the building committee simply because it was felt that his expertise in supervising construction had been demonstrated. Had he not turned the Poor House into "the finest institution of its kind in the country"? Well, if he had, the commission could make good use of him. The task confronting the building committee went beyond construction of Poor House facilities. The Poor House superintendent would be called on to leave the institution in other hands for extended periods, while he and other committee members went on the road. The mission? A new county jail must be planned and built.[165]

The old Fulton County jail, twenty-five years old, had been built during Reconstruction times. It was now inadequate. The County Commission laid plans for a junket to be made to major cities of the eastern United States. Building committee members would look at the jails in those places, and get ideas for the new one for Fulton County.

The trip was taken by four members of the Commission: Mssrs. Walter R. Brown, Forrest Adair, Dr. R.L. Hope, and Grant Wilkins, in the winter of 1897. To begin their tour, the four visited several of the largest jails in the South, and in the West. They then moved north. On February 17, from Cincinnati, Ohio, a telegram from the building committee was received by the <u>Atlanta Constitution</u>, and it was printed in the newspaper the next day:

> "Mssrs. Hope, Brown, Wilkins, and Adair, who are here to inspect jails and prisons, visited the county jail and the state prison today. Speaking of the jail, Mr. Brown said:
>
> 'We have visited a great many jails so far on this trip and have found but one jail as well, but none better, arranged, than the jail in this city. Your jail here (note: evidently at this point he was addressing the Cincinnati authorities) is kept well and arranged and the locking process is perfect. At Indianapolis we were well pleased with the arrangement of the jail, yet the Columbus institution has some good points not to be found at Indianapolis. I think your jail is a model one.'"

Continuing, the telegram disclosed the information that the four gentlemen had visited Atlantan Lewis Redwine, who was incarcerated in the Columbus penitentiary.[166] All four men had been acquainted with him previously, and the meeting was a poignant episode of their trip. It was the first time that this noted prisoner had had to see anyone from his native city, other than a few friends. He was visibly humiliated by having to appear before them in stripes.

Redwine's running afoul of the law had been Atlanta's scandal story just four years before.

*   *   *   *   *

Lewis Redwine, in February, 1893, had been the assistant cashier at the Gate City National Bank, in Atlanta. He was a thirty-two year old bachelor, and was a respected citizen of the city. He was also, of course, a trusted employee of the bank. He had joined the Capital City Club on, or soon after, its inception in 1883.

Redwine was a big spender, and as this was noted, it created the suspicion that he might be embezzling. He was known as quite a social lion, paying handsome sums for his clothing. He often laid out plenty of cash to entertain his friends and acquaintances at extravagant dinners and theater parties. He lived at the Kimball House, Atlanta's top hotel, and he associated with the cream of Atlanta society. There could be no doubt, to a knowledgeable close observer, that he was living well beyond his annual salary of $1,500.

On February 22, Redwine, already fearing that he might be suspected, was directed to go to the office of bank president L. J. Hill. He did not go. Instead, he headed downstairs, and went into Buckalew's saloon, on the ground floor of the bank. There he bought a stiff drink, tossed it down in one gulp, and walked out. He disappeared, as it were, "into thin air."

President Hill, drumming his fingers on his desk, was informed that Redwine was nowhere to be found. Immediately he, the vice-president, and the cashier issued a public statement that the assistant cashier had defaulted, but that his shortage would not cripple the bank's capital.

This reassurance to the public proved to be a grossly over-optimistic statement. A feverish investigation was conducted in the bank throughout that day, and on into the night. That thorough survey caused increasing consternation, for it showed that Redwine's felony could indeed cause a breakdown, despite the bank's early denial. The amount that he had embezzled was going to reach $66,000. This would be considered a serious loss in any era, but in 1897 it was a fortune. The ghastly truth was read in the newspapers the next morning: "The Doors Closed – The Gate City National Bank Will Do Business No Longer."

The bank was put into the hands of the U.S. bank examiner, and it suspended its operations. However, to the great and lasting praise of its officers and directors, the Gate City Bank paid back every cent that had been on deposit at the time of the embezzlement. Those men made up many of the thousands out of their own pockets.

They did not want a crime by one of their bank employees to make suffering for any depositor. Theirs was the kind of action that made the Atlanta business leaders so very special down through decades.

While the bank was agonizing on February 22, the police threw out the dragnet for Redwine. They were knocking on doors, following up every lead. Their efforts were intensified by the promise of a $1,000 reward for the fugitive's capture. Throughout the 23rd the search continued. Police combed the smoky, so-called "Pittsburgh" section of the city, also called, "Mechanicsville," south of Georgia Avenue, and just few blocks west of the present-day Turner Field. On the 24th, officers entered a boarding house at 97 Rockwell Street, in "Pittsburgh." No forced entry was needed, to find Redwine in one of the rooms. He was unshaven, disheveled, living under an assumed name. The friends were no more, the parties were over, his game was up.

The assistant cashier never accounted for the money he had stolen. He was tried in court, amid great publicity. The result of the open and shut case was Redwine's being sentenced to the penitentiary.

By the time that superintendent Robert Hope and the others visited Redwine in the Ohio pen, four years after his crime, he was in a bad state of health. All four of the committee members who saw him were impressed that he needed a pardon, such was the extreme degree of his illness. In Atlanta, too, the prevailing sentiment was for a pardon for him, since it was reported that he was so sick that he might die in prison. President Grover Cleveland was already reviewing the case, and he granted the pardon.

Thus it was that Redwine was released after serving only four years in prison. His freedom, however, lasted only three more. He moved to Texas, then to Bowie, Louisiana, where he was employed as the bookkeeper for a lumber concern. He died there on April 10, 1900, only forty years of age. His body was brought back to Atlanta, and it lies today in an unmarked grave in Oakland Cemetery.

* * * * *

The Redwine story furnished Robert Hope with yet another sad tale, of the kind with which, in later years, he loved to regale his grandchildren. One such narration was that of the time the Yankees burned down his house. Neither did he spare for the youngsters' tears when he told of his and his brothers' placement in the orphanage, after the war. And there was the occasion on which everybody forgot him, and went to the circus without him. There was something within the Poor House superintendent that drew forth an interest in poignancy. That fascination with sadness perhaps made him the very sympathetic Poor House governor that he became.

* * * * *

After leaving Ohio, the four-man building committee headed north to Pennsylvania, and thence onward to Buffalo, New York. After work there, they proceeded on the theory that "all work and no play makes Jack a dull boy." They took in Niagara Falls.

Niagara Falls, then, as now, was a well-developed tourist spot that most people in the United States knew about, and would have liked to see. Nowadays, a paying visitor is given a raincoat and boots to begin his tour. He is then led on a walk through the underground corridors behind the falls. From viewing ports, he sees the mighty cascading waters thundering down past him. The certain drenchings make him thankful for the raincoat and boots. But in February, the committeemen discovered, there were no drenchings. When they passed beneath the falls, they were a frozen curtain of ice.

* * * * *

Within a few more days, the committee had seen jails in the northeast, and headed south. The last stop on their fact-finding mission was Baltimore. Then the four returned to Atlanta, chock-full of good ideas.

Committee member Grant Wilkins at once prepared a set of drawings and plans, and bids were sought on the new jail. What was built was the famous Fulton Tower.[167] This jail was grim, grey, and forbidding, when this author first laid eyes on it. When it had been new, however, it was called by the <u>Atlanta</u> <u>Constitution</u>, "a colossal structure with an elegant interior, the finest, perhaps, on earth." It was completed during the late summer of 1898, and stood on Butler Street.

The Constitution had a field day, bragging on the brand, spanking, new Fulton Tower.

It was termed, "this great, modern prison," and the newspaper gave its dimensions, reporting, too, that it had 190 "toilet apartments." On every floor were electric lights, and the best of sanitary fixtures. Cells were made of the finest chilled steel, and were arranged with outside corridors, and the best of patent prison locks. Floors were of cement, and could be flushed and drained in a few minutes. The basement consisted of rooms of machinery connected with the heating and lighting, the ventilation, and the elevator.

The cost of the building, not counting the fortress-like outside walls, was $175,000.

To assess the 1898 size of this price, one must remember that only $66,000 had broken the Gate City Bank.

Somewhere in there is a moral about the high cost of crime.

CHAPTER TWENTY-EIGHT

HOUSES AND LANDS

"You may buy land now as cheap as stinking mackerel."
King Henry IV, Part I – Act
II, Scene 4, Line 399
- William Shakespeare

Quite early in his management of the Poor House, the super-intendent began "joining house to house and field to field," evaluating and acquiring real property for personal gain. His first purchases were of lands adjacent to the Poor House grounds. As his land-purchase hobby continued through the succeeding years, people came to recognize that real estate speculation was definitely one of his gifts.[168]

Not surprisingly, Dr. Hope's life-long habit of saving every nickel of his earnings that he could, gave him the wherewithal for making land purchases. When he and Della married, in 1881, they had a nice little nest-egg in the bank. His Poor House salary added to it, and additional income came through practice as a private physician. Former patients, and new ones, who lived in the Buckhead and Peachtree-Piedmont neighborhoods, repaired to him for treatment.

The Poor House superintendent's real estate sideline never attracted direct criticism, since his management of the Poor House and inmates continued to be thorough and efficient. And, time after time, when there happened to be a good piece of available land on which he wanted to spend it, he came up with the cash. This became much easier as Dr. Hope's affluence advanced, along with the years.

Robert Hope had thought throughout his life that strength was in the land. Land would stay there, in good times and bad. On each occasion when the best times returned, and market conditions were right, land could be sold for a nice profit. During the bad times, if one had a little carefully hoarded money, the best thing that could be bought with it was a piece of land – cheap.

As years passed, Robert was sometimes able to improve land by the addition of rental dwellings or business buildings, causing the property to climb upwards in value. The secret was the farmer's eye for land, joined to dollar-wise common sense, with a dash of vision for an expanding Atlanta.

The vision was there. As the Twentieth Century advanced, and he bought more property, Robert Hope made a prediction which was quite impressive. Atlanta, he said, would someday "grow all the way out to Norcross."[169] In the 1920's that possibility seemed remote, and it was still somewhat distant as late as 1960. Today, expanding Atlanta, no longer just a city, but more like a region, has rendered the forecast quaint.

By sticking a tentative toe into the waters of estate dealing, purchasing some lots adjacent to Poor House property, young Dr. Hope apparently confused newspaper reporters. They variously quoted the size of the Poor House's lands throughout Hope's twenty-nine years at the helm. It was said to consist of 200, 280, 300, or 330 acres, in reports made at different times. Some of the discrepancies may be explained by the superintendent's additions to the property, or reductions of the same, through the years. Moreover, some of the reports obviously dealt in round figures.

The superintendent's love of the Poor House and its purpose added somewhat to these news errors. His personal property was counted more than once as Poor House property. He had allowed the county the free use of his own land, when this would benefit the Poor House in some way. He did not ask a penny for its use.

So, Dr. Hope, patently fascinated by land and land trades, never stopped his dealing for the rest of his days. One of his early windfalls was the acquisition of some of the Peachtree-Piedmont District lands. This territory had been part of the 1,316-acre plantation of Benjamin Plaster, of whom Dr. Hope's wife was a direct descendant. Plaster had owned the plantation from 1822 to his death in 1836, at which time his property was divided up among his heirs.

In 1864, the U.S. Army Corps of Engineers had published a map for the use of Sherman's forces.[170] That map shows three Plaster farms occupying Benjamin Plaster's old territory. The widow Plaster had a rustic estate south of the present Lindbergh Drive. It included the site of Benjamin Plaster's old plantation house. Stretching across Peachtree Creek to Rock Spring Road, this property embraced much of what, after Robert Hope's days on earth, became known as Monroe Office park.

A second farm inhabited by Plaster descendants lay to the north of Lindbergh. It ran westward from Plaster's Bridge Road, presently known as Piedmont Road. The western limit of this farm was Peachtree Road. The farm occupied the area south and east of the current locations of Christ the King Cathedral and Second Ponce de Leon Baptist Church.

The third Plaster spread was to the east side of Piedmont, taking in the forest and fields south of the Southern Railroad, and it ran eastward to the south fork of Clear Creek.

Some of this area became available to Dr. Hope through the failure of an in-law. In the 1990's a descendant of that man met this author in another state, where the descendant still lives. He told the author that the man in question simply had been "no good."[171] His excitement had not lain in the direction of making and saving money. As his inherited fortune dwindled, times had become hard for him and his family. His answer was to sell off his land. Robert Hope, as his kinsman by marriage, had the inside track to buy some of it. This sale kept the wolf away from the ne'er-do-well's door, and Robert Hope eventually acquired much of the land on both sides of Piedmont, running north from Rock Spring. He especially took possession of lots on the east side of that road, with the exception of some few plots already having private dwellings.

All of the lands described above were similar, in that they were generally timbered, with clearing here and there for farming. It was good land, and, far different from its condition today, it was thinly populated.

One might say that Dr. Hope lived and worked in the wrong decades. Had he been alive in the 1950's and 1960's, when areas north of Buckhead were coming to life, he would doubtless have taken advantage of his opportunities. He no doubt would have made many *more* purchases, leading to lucrative sales in Sandy Springs, Dunwoody, and other places. He is not remembered as a tycoon, but he did amass a fortune estimated at over $750,000, whose worth was $11 million, in 2006 dollars, with purchasing power doubtless vastly greater.

And he lived at the Poor House.

*   *   *   *   *

Newspaper artists often sketched flattering portraits

Amid his land bargains and coups, Dr. Hope made one in 1894 that had repercussions.[172] In 1890 he had purchased a section of land north of the Poor Farm, along the Roswell Road, and bordering the area now known as Chastain Park. On its south side, it touched the Poor House property near the present Old Ivy Road. It was a very extensive tract of some 279 acres, running north and south between the Roswell Road and the present Lake Forest Drive. In 1894, Dr. Hope convinced County Commission chairman Charles Collier that the county needed this land. He was willing to sell; would the Commission buy?

Collier was a good friend. His lands, also considerable, joined the Hope-Plaster properties, being situated to the west of them. The association of the families was cordial and of long standing. Collier went before the Commission and sponsored the purchase of the property the doctor wanted to sell. The commissioners agreed, and the deal went through. Hope, having bought the 279 acres in 1890 for $8,250, and now selling it in 1894 for $18,000, turned a profit of $9,750 – six and one-half times his annual salary as superintendent of the Poor House.

The deal started to go sour, however, when the new commission came into office in 1895. The Fulton County Grand Jury, as always, had recommendations for the commission. The Grand Jury said that, from the Poor House property 150 to 200 acres should be sold. This seemed quite a drastic proposal!

In the newspaper, the area to be sold was quoted to be that of "the Poor House property fronting on Peachtree." That description, however, was only intended to remind the public of the street address of the Poor Farm. The Grand Jury was not specifying that the property to be sold off had to be that part along Peachtree. It might be taken from any part of the institution's extensive land.

The proceeds of the sale, on the Grand Jury's plan, could be used to build new buildings for the so-called "imbeciles." These structures would be located near the main building of the Poor House, a short way down Piedmont Road. The Grand Jury made the additional suggestion that the money gained from selling this land would be sufficient to build suitable quarters for the convicts as well. They felt that the wholesale amputation of half of the Poor House's land left enough to meet all the needs of the institution.

No sooner were these recommendations made than the <u>Atlanta Constitution</u> raised sensational questions. Why was the Grand Jury now contradicting the recent action of the Fulton County Commission? Specifically, why was the Grand Jury saying that *less* land was needed by the Commission for its Poor House? The Commission, not many months before, had bought 279 acres of privately-owned land, which adjoined the Poor House property. Presumably, this acreage was meant to be added to the Poor House lands.

More to the point, said the <u>Constitution,</u> the county's money had been used to buy Dr. Hope's 279 acres, which was not yet part of Poor House land. That money might have been used instead to build the desired new buildings for the Poor House. But, no, the Grand Jury now wanted to sell off land which *was* Poor House property all along, to get the money. It made no sense.

The newspaper said that, between the Grand Jury and the County Commission, "it appears there is a difference of opinion somewhere - -." However, it quickly stated that it was not raising a journalistic eyebrow at Dr. Hope. In the same column, it made this disclaimer:

"The almshouse was examined and is pronounced to be the finest institution of its kind in the country. The management is admirable, and Dr. Hope, the superintendent, has devoted his entire attention to the improvement of the institution and the care of the unfortunates who find an asylum there."

*　*　*　*　*

Freshman commissioner Forrest Adair took the <u>Constitution's</u> questions very seriously. At the first meeting of the new commission, in January, 1895, he tossed a bombshell of a motion:

"Whereas, from an inspection of the minutes of the board of county commissioners it appears that the law was not complied with, in that they failed to submit to a vote of the people of the county the contemplated indebtedness for the purchase of the almshouse property (Note: the "almshouse property," 279 acres, so far belonged to the county, not to the almshouse), therefore be it ordered, that the chairman of this board be instructed to make a quit claim deed to Dr. R. L. Hope and demand from him a surrender of the two notes given by the county for the purchase of said land and that said sale be declared void and that the almshouse committee (a subcommittee of the County Commission) be instructed to withdraw the hands from the property at once if any have been placed there."

Forrest Adair, young, good-looking, neat as a pin, the ends of his handlebar moustache properly waxed, was displaying the newcomer's reforming zeal. It was not merely that.

Adair was a man of his convictions, and courageous, too. In all the years of his service on the County Commission, he would show himself to be "Mr. Clean," and one who was usually striving to be fair.

Having made his motion, Adair spoke to it. It was only necessary, he said, to defend the land purchase on the grounds of legality. Had the purchase been made in accordance with what the law prescribed, or not? But then Adair weakened his argument by adding his opinion that the county had made a bad trade. Property costing only $8,250 in 1890 had been bought for $18,000.

Chairman Collier was sitting there listening, grimly aware that he had led the Commission to make the land purchase. When Adair opined that this had been a poor trade, Collier pounced: If the purchase was illegal, as Adair had wondered, then his motion should carry. But, Collier said, if the contention was simply that the purchase was not a *wise* one, then it should carry no weight, even if it might possibly be true.

Collier continued, saying that one thing that the Commission must not do was to put Fulton County in the position of repudiating her obligations. If the purchase had been made, it should stand. And on the issue of legality, he did not believe that the purchase had been illegal. It had been made under the advice of the county attorney, Colonel Thomson.

Adair answered him warmly. He had thoroughly checked the records, and could not find any mention that Colonel Thomson had recommended the purchase. Had he really done so? He, Adair, was doubtful of it.

On top of that, Adair said that the original mention of the property showed 300 acres offered by Dr. Hope for $18,000. But, on the entry of purchase the acreage was shown as 280 acres more or less, while the price was still $18,000. So Adair was attacking all along the line.

Just as tenaciously, Collier defended all along the line. "If we are to attack the actions of the old Board, Mr. Adair," he said, "and are to begin with the almshouse property, why don't you bring in the Heinz property? That was purchased in just the same way. Why didn't you bring that in? The principle is the same in both instances."

Collier's last rebuttal had dampened Adair's zeal somewhat, and after this exchange of salvoes, the meeting smoothed out. It was decided that nothing illegal had been done, and whether the purchase had been wise or not, it was allowed to stand. The almost-soured deal had again been sweetened.

Some amount of damage had been done to Dr. Hope, however. He remained unpopular with a few Atlanta politicos. They were leery of a county official who could make money with such apparent ease, and through a sideline, too. Attempts to punish him lay just ahead. These would be done by reducing his salary, and they seem to have been motivated, in part, by this envy. They were an ineffective penalty, since Robert Hope's real estate income was so far in excess of his Poor House earnings.

As for Forrest Adair, he was following no hidden political agenda. True, he did open his service on the Commission by criticizing the previous Commission's land purchase.

However, he simply had to be sure that everything was on the up-and-up. He and Dr. Hope became good friends. Adair was elected chairman of the Commission in 1897, and in the role, and later, he was Dr. Hope's champion, first blocking attempts to cut the superintendent's salary, and later battling for its restoration after it was cut.

Robert Hope had learned a savvy thing or two from the stir that his land deal had caused. A decade and a half later, when he sold the land that became North Fulton Park (later renamed Chastain Park), he did not sell it directly to the county. Instead he sought out Troy G. Chastain, and sold it to him. Mr. Chastain, whose membership on the Commission was yet in the future, could sell it to the county, and did. In that way, all was acceptable. The county had acquired the land from one who was not an employee of the county. One could say that the Chastain property was, in a sense, "laundered land."

It was on the Chastain property that the next Poor House was built, in 1909. It was located on what became West Wieuca Road. At this writing both of the buildings which housed the white and black divisions not only exist, but still are used, though not as a Poor House. In the decades that followed, North Fulton Park was developed around the institution, with walking trails, ball fields, picnic grounds, and a golf course.

The doctor who had built up the Poor House complex between the Peachtree and Roswell roads never served in the new West Wieuca location. He had just retired, and had begun to build a home for himself and his family on some of his land. Happily this new family dwelling was located at Piedmont and Rock Spring, just across the road from the church that the superintendent and his family had always continued to attend.

*   *   *   *   *

Both before and after retirement, the doctor had bought up properties in downtown Atlanta. He carefully purchased rental properties in areas populated by Negroes and poor whites. Some were black people's dwellings in the teeming valley just east of Peachtree Street downtown. Other properties housed poor white families along old Plum Street, near the Coca-Cola headquarters. Plum Street is now totally engulfed by the expanding campus of Georgia Tech, and half its length has been destroyed, and recast.

So Dr. Hope became what would later be dubbed, a "slum lord." This name, often unjustly applied to property owners, was made a protest cry in the 1960's. The slur implied that unfeeling owners were getting rich on rents, while failing to improve shabby property. Some were, but others genuinely cared for the people who rented from them. If they provided low-rent housing, and kept it up to standard, they performed a humanitarian service.

It would be difficult to find a more compassionate slum lord than Robert Hope. He was a curious mixture of toughness and soft touch. During his twenty-nine years of active retirement equaling the length of time that he served the Poor House, 1909-1938, he owned a series of automobiles. In the 1930's, in a tan Buick, he would sit behind chauffeur Dave, sometimes with grandchildren loaded aboard.[173] As they rode across neighborhoods in the north of downtown Atlanta, his mission was to inspect his property and collect the rents.

The children waited and played in the car or on the sidewalk, while "Granddaddy"

talked interminably with the tenants. He listened to complaints of broken commodes, fallen plaster, termite-eaten floor boards, uncloseable doors, torn-out screens. He would make commitments to repair whatever needed it, and would then come back on another day, to watch the work being done.

Care and maintenance seemed to be his strong suit with these people, and with their houses. He found it easy to identify with them, for he had not forgotten seeing his own childhood house burned to the ground. He also remembered the discomforts of his refugeeing from Sherman, and his years in the orphanage. Mostly, he must have recalled all those poor people he had cared for at the Poor House.

CHAPTER TWENTY-NINE

POLITICS AND A SALARY CUT

"Many of the injuries that we have suffered in life were inflicted by people who had no idea that they were doing it."

Willis Timmer, Fund-raising expert

Wednesday, January 6, 1897: On this Epiphany night the lights at the Fulton County Court House blazed for almost three hours. This was the first after-dark meeting of the Fulton County Board of Commissioners in a very long time.[174]But other things were different, too.

Two new commissioners were coming on the board, men who were unknown, as to what direction they would try to take the Commission. There was Judge Howard E. W. Palmer, the same man who had been for a short while the organizing director-general of the Cotton Exposition (see Page 149). Palmer, he of the heavy body, he of the puffing cigar, was one of the two freshmen. The other was bald, bespectacled Judge E. B. Rosser, a man considerably older than Palmer. Both of these men, as it turned out, wanted to make reforms that would cut costs. "Economy" was to be their watchword on the commission from this time forward.

As the commissioners scraped their chairs up to the table, Palmer was seen whispering to commissioner Spalding, who nodded in reply.

The meeting was convened promptly at 7:30 P.M. At Spalding's suggestion, Rosser took over as temporary chairman. Then veterans Forrest Adair and Walter Brown were elected permanent chairman, and vice-chairman, respectively. All was routine thus far. From this point on, nothing was routine.

Palmer, knowing that Rosser would be his ally, proposed sweeping salary cuts for those employed by the commission, including the superintendent of the Poor House. The cuts would be specified by a committee to be appointed.

Chairman Adair and Vice-Chairman Brown were scandalized at the proposal. Adair:

> "Can such cuts be sustained morally?" Brown: "Your resolution puts the cart before the horse, Judge Palmer. A committee should first be appointed to examine the matter, before we commit to making cuts."

Palmer simply answered them with the argument, "times are hard." Indeed, he was right. The South's economy, and, in particular, Atlanta's, had boomed since the end of Reconstruction, but then had come the Panic (recession) of 1893. The recession continued, and in 1897, things were still slow, although this year would see the end of the trouble. Meantime, the price of cotton, still an economic weathervane in the South, had hit rock bottom. Other prices had followed it downward. With money short, Palmer knew that a tax reduction would be popular throughout the county. A way to get to the tax reduction would be to cut salaries.

Adair yielded. "Well, I see that we must do *something*." He appointed Palmer, Brown, and Spalding to examine the county payroll, and recommend what salaries might be reduced. The three withdrew from the meeting room, leaving Adair, Rosser, and two newsmen sitting there.

Atlanta newspapers followed politics
of the County Commission

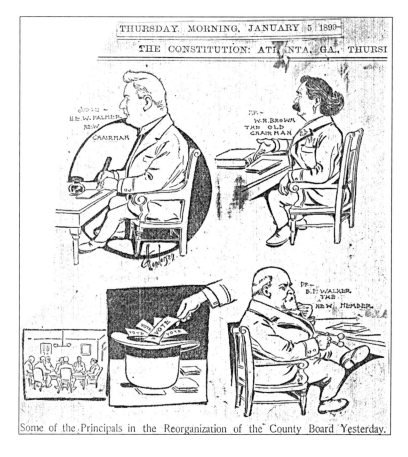

Newspaper artists caricatured Commission members

Newspaper cartoons of County Commission

They were going to have to spend several minutes looking at the salaries of seven county officers. In the anteroom, Palmer showed that he had done his homework, and he jumped to recommendations, but the other two were not ready to jump with him. At length, they filed back into the meeting room, and said that they thought it best for the full committee to decide the matter.

The full Commission, therefore, started down the list. The highest paid officer was the superintendent of public works, at $2,400 per year. Brown moved that this officer's salary be continued at the same level in 1897. Economy-minded Rosser wanted to know how long such a salary would remain in effect. He was told that salaries were normally set for the whole year, but that the Commission could change them at any time, just as it could hire or fire at any time. The matter was discussed additionally for a moment or two. The vote was then taken, and the salary of the public works superintendent, Captain T. J. Donaldson, was continued at the same level.

It may seem odd that newsmen were permitted in a meeting whose task was as sensitive as that of setting salaries. However, they had been present at the table from the very start. Never had the public's right to know been more highly honored! Now the reporters leaned forward to catch each word as the next name came up.

Palmer: "Now I move that the salary of Dr. Hope, the superintendent of the almshouse, be cut from $1,500 per year, to $1,200 per year."

Rosser: "I second the motion."

Brown reacted: "Just a moment. I know that you new men on the board are keen to reduce costs. But I object to the proposed cuts. Dr. Hope deserves every dollar he receives. He is one of the busiest men in the county, and consistently, year by year, the amounts of food grown on the Poor Farm have increased, so that the institution is very largely self-supported. Under Dr. Hope's care, the number of deaths of inmates in the Poor House has drastically decreased. They get excellent care. As for the general improvement of the place, just look at it! With the new buildings added and the beautification of the grounds, the poor House has become, the sixteen years of Dr. Hope's leadership, a model of its kind."

Palmer: "I don't want to be misunderstood - -"

Brown: "All the things I have pointed out about the Poor House are true. They're a matter of the public record. If any change is made in Dr. Hope's salary, I think it ought to be in the direction of an *increase*, not a decrease."

Adair: "I agree. I have here figures showing the totals of inmates in the Poor House for the last several years. In general, you can count on about 60-80 people being in the home at any given time. In the course of a year, the turnover is larger than that, with a total of more than a hundred admitted and discharged. Many people, I am glad to say, don't have to stay long."

Brown: "And about the quality of the care?"

Adair: "Very good indeed. The hiring of Mrs. D. Gallagher almost a decade ago to superintend the imbecile section has proved over the years to have been a stroke of genius. She is the finest that can be found. And the section of the grounds confining the woman convicts is also in good shape."

Palmer: "I believe you gentlemen, and I don't want to be misunderstood as reflecting on the present incumbent, Dr. Hope. I am aware of his faithful and efficient service. But I repeat what I said earlier – the times are hard, and the people of our county would appreciate a lowering of the tax rate. If that is to be done, it must be done by saving the county from heavy expenses such as salaries that are too high."

Adair: "Would you relieve the taxpayer by injuring our county officials?"

Palmer: "No. This would be no injury. After all, money
                 has *twice* the purchasing power today that it had
                 two years ago, so it seems to me that a salary of
                 $1,500 two years ago is equal to $3,000, taking
                 into consideration the condition of the commer-
                 cial world."

The discussion went on and on, with Palmer continuing to insist
that he was "not making a fight on Dr. Hope, the almshouse, or any
officer or department under this board." Rosser, of course, took his
side, with Brown and Adair making the opposite argument.

Finally, Spalding declared that in his opinion, any salary cut
would be "unconscionable." The vote was taken at last, and Palmer
lost. The status quo prevailed, three votes to two.

*   *   *   *   *

When 1898 dawned, with the same board re-elected, Palmer still
had economy through salary-cutting as his prime objective.[175] He
had no chance of reducing Dr. Hope's salary, for the Poor House
superintendent had just been congratulated and endorsed by the
Fulton County Grand Jury, two weeks earlier.

The Grand Jury had taken this action as a Christmastime statement, because of a report rendered to it. A three-man committee of
jurymen, Garland S. Prior, J.A. Norris, and A.C. Woolley had stayed
an entire day at the Poor House, and had reported that it was exceedingly well managed. "The management could not be improved upon,
and there are no criticisms to be made," was their conclusion.

Palmer, blocked in that direction, switched his assault to two
other county officers.

He proposed that the county physician, Dr. J. L. McDaniel, and
the county custodian of public buildings, John Corrigan, both have
their salaries reduced. Again, Rosser joined him, and again they
were defeated, three to two.

*   *   *   *   *

218

On January 5, 1899, men from the <u>Journal</u> and <u>Constitution</u> newspapers were again present at the meeting of the Fulton County Commission. This time, Palmer's hour struck.[176]

The old board met this day at 3:00 P.M., for just a few minutes, then was replaced by the newly-elected board. The only change in personnel between the two boards was that Dr.B.F. Walker came on to replace Spalding, who had served out his term.

Dr. Walker was a former Fulton County surveyor, whose old home place had been turned into the Gentlemen's Driving Club in 1887. This club was later renamed, becoming the exclusive Piedmont Driving Club. Dr. Hope and his wife Della were afterwards invited to join this club, but for undisclosed reasons declined the invitation.

As a Confederate veteran, and an older citizen, Dr. Walker was a known quantity, with whom many felt comfortable. He, together with Adair and Brown, had run for this year's Commission posts virtually as a three-man faction. On the other side of the fence, during the political race, Palmer's faction were candidates Peters, Sanders, and Anderson.

As the race had developed, powerful Atlanta business leader and transportation executive Joel Hurt openly opposed Adair, and it was also said that he backed the Peters-Sanders-Anderson trio. In the mind of the public, that crystallized the two groups. The group backed by Joel Hurt were the odds-on favorites.

Surprise! Joel Hurt's political power in that election seemed to run out at about the same places as did his Atlanta streetcar lines. Out in the county at large, he did not have the votes, and the Adair threesome won their seats on the Commission.

Surprise number two! B.F. Walker turned out to be no known quantity at all. All along, he had been economy minded, but that stance had not been brought to light during the election. In this first meeting of the 1899 Commission, Walker flipped to the Palmer side. This shift enabled Palmer's election as chairman, on the third ballot. Then he further used his new-found 3-2 voting advantage.

In the words of the <u>Atlanta Constitution</u>, Palmer drew "his big knife,"[177] and went for the heads of some county officials. He also went for the salaries of nearly all. Dr. Robert Hope was praised by Palmer, then his salary was cut from $1,500 to $1,200.

"Doc" B.F. Walker was so eager to cut expenses that he proposed to cut into the clerical force of the Commissioners' office. At that proposal, Adair roundly scolded him:

"Do you know that four years ago, this adequate office staff was set up, and that before that time, there was no system, and everything was chaos?"

Adair forced Walker to admit that he had never even casually examined the books kept before and after the staff was increased. Walker retreated.

Within just a few months, old Dr. B.F. Walker was dead. He had been alive just long enough to be the catalyst enabling a new austerity to take shape.

* * * * *

Dr. Robert Hope went through 1899 and 1900 with the lowered salary. By a little extrapolation, it may be seen that a reduction of $300 per annum, with Palmer's estimate of its double worth in those deflation times (see Page 243), was a yearly loss of $600. And in terms of today's money, it was a loss of 20-30 times that.

However, the superintendent hardly missed it, except that it had been a tangible confirmation of the board's good opinion of him, and of the job he was doing. Quite apart from his Poor House salary, he was making most of his money now on land deals.

Adair and Brown continued to think that the salary cut had to been unfair to Dr. Hope, and they battled in his behalf. Palmer, on the other hand, made further complimentary remarks about the doctor's work, but stuck to his guns for economizing, and outvoted Adair and Brown, 3 to 2, both in 1899 and 1900. He appears to have been an earnest man with honorable motives. His single thought, though, was cutting costs by keeping salaries low. He thus seemed to be the enemy of every elected official in the county.

In the board meetings, everything had been politeness and deference. Despite that, Adair and Brown were smarting under their repeated defeats. In the organizational meeting of 1901, they took off the velvet gloves and got tough.

Adair and Brown lost the vote on the salaries once again, but for the rest of the meeting, they won a victory of sorts. They did it by outgeneraling the majority on the elections of the board's various committee chairmen. They had come to the meeting prepared to stick together on every vote that would be taken concerning the composition of the committees. They won victory after victory, as the majority was split, first one way, then another.

Case in point: they prevented Captain Clifford L. Anderson's election as chairman of the Commission. They wished to block his chairmanship because his views were regarded as the most extreme among the opposition. Anderson's name was the only one in nomination. Since the vote was taken in alphabetical order of the names of the voters, Adair voted first. He voted for the nominee, Anderson, even though he knew that he was on the opposite side, on many important issues. It was a ruse.

Anderson voted second, and would not vote for himself, for that would have run against the grain of the ultra-polite parliamentary manners of those Edwardian times. Anderson voted for Palmer; it was a vote intended to be no more than a compliment to the chairman of two years before. Brown, voting third in the alphabetical order, voted for Palmer also. Instantly, Adair spoke up to change his vote to Palmer, simulating a well-worn parliamentary courtesy. But this time, the "courtesy" elected Palmer with the necessary three votes!

The maneuver had caught the majority completely by surprise, for they could do nothing to retrieve the situation. Anderson could not gracefully change his vote, and vote for himself! The majority had been denied the extremist whom they wanted.

So it went throughout the meeting, with the foxy minority winning vote after vote, through a switch of Adair's or Brown's choice. They had figured out, in advance, the whole sequence of votes, and they followed their plan. The three majority members, Rosser, Palmer, and Anderson, were left in confusion. Adair and Brown just sat and smiled, at least inwardly. It was chicanery, it was obvious collusion, but it was legal.

The majority did have the last word in the meeting, however. Rosser, the retiring chairman, performed his duty of appointing the personnel to the board's committees. In the newspaper language of the time, he gave "the marble heart" to Adair and Brown.

That is, he showed them no mercy. Instead, he made sure, in his appointments, that the minority were outnumbered two to one on each committee, so that they controlled nothing.

To stack the committees in this way, Rosser had to give multiple appointments to the three majority members. For example, the extreme Anderson, who had been denied the board's chairmanship, was placed on every single committee – a unique distinction among the commissioners.

Despite the obvious one-upmanship displayed throughout the meeting, there was no overt expression of rancor. This gentlemanliness was a notable feature of the commissioners' meetings of that era.

*   *   *   *   *

So how did the Poor House superintendent like being a political football? In later years he said that it had not mattered. "Went with the territory," we would say today. And if he lost $300, with its vastly greater purchasing power than the same amount would possess today, what of that? It would not prevent his wife's having a new dress!

As a large landowner in the north part of Fulton County, he was constantly showing his very pronounced gift for land speculation. He would continue in this second vocation until he died.

The superintendent would certainly have liked to have had the salary level restored, merely as a tangible affirmation of him, and his work. The commissioners' words of praise were all very well, but did the gentlemen really mean what they said? Or were theirs only "political words" for the consumption of a public whose very eyes told them that the Poor House was in excellent shape?

Other men had sought the post of poor House superintendent, especially now that the place had been expanded and improved. The job was considered rather a plum. Dr. Hope thought long thoughts: suppose that another man did succeed in winning the place? Would the county commissioners turn right around and favor the new man with a salary increase, which they had been unwilling to give to *him*? If they did that, would they justify their move by noting that, after all, the job's duties had increased?

So, the doctor, having started in the work at ago twenty-two, and now forty-two years old, wondered if the County Commission really wanted him around any longer. His doubts were much more than paranoia. His health had begun to show the strain of the high-stress job. He had been under the political pressures for several years. Meanwhile, the constant, often sleepless routine of the Poor House did not relent, but rather became more demanding. Under these circumstances, he made his next move. He made a decision that caught the Fulton County Commission completely off guard.

CHAPTER THIRTY

ONE HONEST OFFICIAL

"A wit's a feather, and a chief a rod;
An honest man's the noblest work of God."
Essay on Man, Epistle IV, Line 215
Alexander Pope

The "bombshell" that Dr. Hope threw at the Fulton County Commission was an attempt at resignation. As it turned out, however, this man had a hard time resigning and dying. He made a pass at both events, in this first decade of the Twentieth Century, but he had to wait years for the one, and decades for the other.

He had suffered ill health for some time. He reluctantly decided it was time to go.

Once his wife Della had been told, and they had prayed it over for some little while, he seemed to have peace about the decision. He felt he could no longer perform his duties well, at the Poor House.

Doctor Hope told his wife that he thought it was unfair to the county for him to stay on.[178] He argued that Fulton County did not need "an old, sick man caring for old, sick people." She laughed at him, telling him that he was not old, but adding that she did not want him to be trying to do things that he did not feel well enough to do.

If he could just get his health back, really get back on his feet, he would not feel that he was cheating anybody out of a good day's work. His wife, sensing his blue mood, replied to it with practicality: Sometimes, it simply took time to recover. He needed to take care of himself. It was not the end of the world. Of money, they had enough, and more than enough. In addition, she was fond of his oft-expressed idea to quit the Poor House, and build a place over at Rock Spring. All the burden would be off of him.

So, down-spirited, he continued to ponder. Maybe it was the lack of energy, the circles under his eyes, the prematurely grey hair, but he decided he *did* feel old. The rat-gnawing, mid-life doubts had loosened his resolve. At least, amid Job's troubles, he had so far maintained Job's faithfulness. He was far from shaking his fist at God, as if He had brought all this about. But he was nonetheless at the end of his tether.

Dr. Hope was too much a man of action to wait longer. That very afternoon, he sat down and wrote a letter of resignation[179] to the chairman of the almshouse committee of the Fulton County Commission. That chairman was none other than Captain Clifford L. Anderson, the disappointed would-be Commission chairman.

On the following Wednesday, Robert dragged himself over to the Commission meeting, and sat there, pale and haggard. Newspaper reporters were sitting in on the meeting, as usual. In due time, Anderson dropped the bombshell:

"Dr. Hope has sent his letter of resignation to me."

He then read the letter to the board, whose members were aghast. Especially upset were the two members who had sought, for the past two years, to be the superintendent's allies, seeking restoration of his salary. But the economy-minded majority seemed equally dismayed.

"Well! This is certainly not something that any of us expected," the papers quoted Palmer as saying, at that point.

"I think we had better ask Dr. Hope to explain why he has submitted this letter, offered Anderson, and all eyes were turned to the Poor House superintendent.

"I regretted to have to resign. I have been at the Poor House in the capacity of superintendent for 20 years now. I love the institution, the inmates, and my work.

But, you see, I have been in very poor health for some time now. I feel that I cannot perform my duties well. If I don't do well, then I shall be drawing a salary for work that I am failing to do. This will be known, and might well bring criticism of myself and of this board. I wish to avoid that, so I thought it best to resign."

"I appreciate what you have said, Dr. Hope," responded commissioner Rosser. "Your attitude is exemplary. But I wonder if there is not some other alternative to your resigning? In my opinion, we cannot spare you."

Others on the board were heartily in agreement. The things that Dr. Hope had accomplished in his twenty years of directing the Poor House were cited once again. Regrets that he had offered his resignation were expressed all around. Suddenly faced with the resignation, and with the necessity of replacing this man, the board felt themselves on the brink of a chasm. Unwilling to attempt to leap it, they hesitated.

"It would take some time to find someone with Dr. Hope's knowledge of the Poor House routine and system," ventured Anderson.

"That is not very surprising," rejoined Rosser. "He developed that system. He knows the Poor House inside and out. In fact, he knows the *inmates* inside and out!" The quip brought laughter.

Commissioner Adair, the doctor's staunchest friend on the board, then proposed his solution. "Mr. Chairman, I move that this board grant Dr. Hope two months' leave of absence, and appoint someone in his place until he has sufficiently regained his health."

Would that be acceptable, Dr. Hope? The board wanted to know. The superintendent nodded. Clearly, he had not gone into the meeting intending to plead his case, but his ears had been attuned to the verdict, and he was pleased. In addition to his wife, this board was his life's Significant Other. He knew, now, that they really approved of him. He was accepted by what Friedrich Nietsche called, "the herd."

The doctor told the board that, given two months' leave, he would withdraw his resignation. A motion was made, and the board promptly voted it.

The superintendent was going to stay, and the reporters made the most of it, in the next day's newspapers. It could be seen that his dominant motive was pure – a desire to do an honest day's work for an honest day's pay. Consequently, the next day's headline proclaimed, "Board Finds One Honest Official."[180] The article began, "The board of county commissioners has found an honest official, and without a lantern, too. He is Dr. R.L. Hope, superintendent of the county almshouse."

R.L. Hope took his leave of absence, and did get well. He would continue as Poor House superintendent for nearly nine more years. When he finally resigned, that time, in 1909, he would be gone from the Poor House for good.

*   *   *   *   *

Life plays its pranks. When Robert again resigned, in 1909, his reason was again, poor health. Yet, once again, he was not near death. The bad health proved to be not nearly as bad as some other physicians led him to believe.

Before that second resignation, the superintendent had begun to feel much under the weather for several months. He seemed to go from bad to worse. Suspecting that he might be seriously ill, he repaired to his colleagues of the medical profession. Three physicians examined him. After checking his heart, the point of complaint, the consensus of the three of them was that he had only six months to live![181]

"Set your house in order, for you shall die and not live." (2 Kings 20.1) On the advice of these doctors, Robert Hope resigned for real, this time. He said "goodbye" to the Poor House, its pleasures and its pressures. He decided that he would spend the rest of his days on this planet working at half speed. He would work at private practice, would pursue his beloved real estate avocation, and would build that house in the Rock Spring community.

Done. But the three doctors' forecast was far too gloomy. In his active retirement, Robert would not die. In fact, for each month that these three medical Cassandras gave him, he lived *fifty-eight* months! That's right. After they said that he had just six months to live, R.L. Hope lived for *three hundred and forty-eight months* – 29 more years.

It was said that, sober and sad-eyed, he recalled their somber prediction three times over the years, standing beside their graves. He reportedly served as pallbearer for each of the physicians in turn.[182]

CHAPTER THIRTY-ONE

THE SCHOOL BOARD

"Just children on their way to school again?
Nay, it is ours to watch a greater thing.
These are the World's Rebuilders!"

The Rebuilders
Theodosia Garrison

The health problems that had precipitated the superintendent's first and second resignations from the Poor House, were in large part the result of overstrain. The work of Poor House duties of medication and management was heavy, yet, as an activist, the doctor had taken on more. Already, he had been dealing successfully in real estate for years. To that, he added his service to the public schools.

His public school involvement came about in the following way.[183] The year 1898 was only a twelve-month after Mr. Palmer's first, unsuccessful attempt to cut the salaries of county employees. Palmer had alleged "hard times" as the reason for reducing salaries. Perhaps he knew that there was going to be other county expense, shortly, and a lot of it. In 1898, the county needed a new elementary school in Buckhead.

The Buckhead district, otherwise known by the elegant name of "Atlanta Heights," had grown in population. The county owned much land adjacent to, and including, the Poor House grounds, and it seemed good to put a school somewhere on it. To accomplish this, a summer morning's meeting was held in the office of county school commissioner Glenn. In that meeting, the County Commission duly voted to give a portion of its land to the Board of Education, for the school. However, for economy's sake, it was further decided that the land should be carved from existing Poor House property.

Cost-cutting in this case would be achieved by using the former Poor House lunatic asylum to house the school. This building was positioned at some distance from the rest of the Poor House quarters. All of the insane persons who had been housed there had been moved to the state insane asylum at Milledgeville, so the building was available.

The new school, to be opened October 31, 1898, would be known as "R. L. Hope School," simply to honor the now widely-respected and beloved Poor House superintendent. He had long shown great interest in the county's schools, and, as the Atlanta Journal reported, he had "contributed liberally to their support."[184] Though he had no position on the Fulton County School Board at this time, that would come two years later.

Notwithstanding that Commission discussions had spoken of cutting salaries, including Dr. Hope's, he had been riding a wave of popularity for several years. He was highly touted for the school board post.

Shortly after the meeting in the school commissioner's office, which decided on opening a new school, eight members of the County Commission, and the Board of Education, visited the Poor House. They were there to make final plans to implement the decision. They came, they saw, and they agreed on what they must do. As the earlier meeting had decided, the former insane asylum would now indeed be a school. In 1898 or 1950, school teachers might well have smiled at the comparison of their classrooms to madhouses. In 2008, the humor in such a comparison is less clear!

It was not until the first Wednesday in September that the Board of County Commissioners actually passed a resolution giving the asylum building to the Board of Education.[185] After this was done, the structure was moved southward onto a hill some considerable distance from its original location, and was extensively remodeled.

Consolidation of its schools was a prime concern of the Board of Education at this time. The board mandated that several smaller schools in that section of the county were to be absorbed by R. L. Hope School. These were mostly of the one-room schoolhouse type. The nearest was only a mile away, the most distant some four miles from the new school. Once all were combined, said the <u>Atlanta Journal</u>, R.L. Hope School would be a school "which will probably outrank in equipment and thoroughness any other school of the county."[186]

"Thoroughness"! Ah, that was where the 1898 educational planners excelled. They were being as thorough as they could be, with the funds they had available. The <u>Constitution</u> uttered no more than the truth, in saying,

> "There is no other county in the state that can boast of as complete and thorough a system of public schools as that in Fulton County, and few counties in other states have the same instruction for the children of rural districts as the county of Fulton. Time, work, money, and thought have been expended to build up the present system, and the intelligence and culture of the children of the country districts stand as an example of the splendid methods used in the schools."[187]

The "splendid methods" were centered around a unified view of life, so foreign to the split mindset currently popular in public education. While moderns theorize that "education is about *public facts*, while Christianity is about *private values*," most of the 1898 educators thought that *values* belonged in the classroom too. However, it is mostly in Bible-centered Christian schools, and in family home schooling situations that this view survives today, albeit to the great benefit of the pupils, and of society at large.

The <u>Constitution</u> article gushed on for another hundred words or so, making the point that the development of the school system was the outstanding achievement of the county's public advancement. Also, it proudly proclaimed that no other school system had been more completely overhauled.

This editorializing, of course, was all about bigness and improvement of physical facilities, within Fulton County. The newspaper did perhaps embellish a bit too much, if its words were applied to R.L. Hope School only. The new equipment emplaced in the school was first-rate, but the building itself, having been Poor House quarters, was not designed to be a school. It would need remodeling, and in twenty-seven years would be replaced by a second R.L. Hope School which would dwarf the first one in size.

There was no mention by the newspaper of any philosophy of education, or of what direction the education might take. Probably the reason for the omission was that the "received wisdom" was simply the unified life view, as it had always been. Only in the minds of a few theorizers in some American universities did the public school experiments of the future exist.

Demonstrating its commitment to education and the further development of the system, the school board laid big plans. The annual county teachers institute in October, getting the teachers ready for their task, would be followed by the opening of R.L. Hope School, along with the other county schools, on October 31. City schools would open earlier. The late opening of the county schools was standard: farm children had to help get the harvest in.

Next in line after the teachers' institute, and the school's opening day, there was to be a series of rallies for parents and grandparents. These rallies were harbingers of the P.T.A., but in this case, they were to be held in different schools. The first of the rallies was set for the new R.L. Hope School on November 5. It would be a daytime meeting. The newspaper exulted, "This will be one of the largest gatherings of the people in the interest of education that has ever been held in the county."[188]

The paper's prediction was correct. *Everybody*, it seemed, was at that first meeting.

There were the members of the Fulton County Board of Education, the teachers from all the schools in the county, the people from the northern part of the county, the Fulton County Board of Commissioners, the Fulton County Grand Jury, plus a lengthy list of prominent persons, including Georgia ex-governor W.J. Northen.

They jammed R.L. Hope School, "wall-to-wall, and hanging from the rafters." It was well that the meeting was in November, rather than in a steamy Georgia August, because of the numbers of people who could not get inside. They had to endure the long meeting standing around on the grounds.

But the people had come to be informed, prepared to give the day. They got satisfaction: no fewer then nine addresses were delivered during the day. Some were papers read in the morning by teachers who held forth on subjects vital to the schools: Miss Fannie Brown spoke on, "What Should Be the Teacher's Contribution to the Community?" (emphasis on helping make good, responsible citizens of the children) Miss Mamie Tolbert's message was, "The Importance of Promptly Supplying New School Books to Teachers When Needed." Mr. Walker White spoke on, "The Moral Element in the Teacher's Equipment" (again, morality taking center stage in the public schools).

The truth-seeking crowd saw none of this as stuffy and pedantic. They were ready to be challenged, and had not long to wait for it.

At noon, there was a barbecue basket lunch, furnished by the Buckhead ladies. Then, as the afternoon session began, Mrs. J.K. Ottley delivered the most ringing challenge of the meeting thus far. She spoke convincingly on the need for libraries in the schools.

Not stopping there, she called for immediate action to meet the need!

Here was something that those in attendance could get their teeth into. When Mrs. Ottley sat down, someone moved that a library be established "for this school in which we are meeting." At this, A.P. Stewart, "Uncle Andy" Stewart, prominent landowner, the tax collector of Fulton County, and the man for whom Stewart Avenue is named, rose to volunteer. He said that he would take care of the cost of a good, small library for R.L. Hope School, all by himself. E.H. Thornton then said that he would donate an additional twenty volumes to the library, and Posey Foster agreed to furnish a bookcase. So a "good, small library" got its start, then and there. It would grow.

The Hon. Walter R. Brown, Mr. Hubert L. Culberson, Mr. W.P. Patillo, and R.J. Guinn all made addresses. Somewhere along the way, there was a proposal to take the appointment of teachers out of the hands of the Fulton County Grand Jury, and put it into the hands of the people. This got nowhere. It was thought that such a measure would lead to interference by politics, and cause the good school system to deteriorate. Better to leave the responsibility for teacher appointments in the hands of a few leaders.

Capping off the huge success, the news reporter noted, "Dr. Hope was present - - - and added much to the pleasure of the visitors." If one had taken the trouble to come to the school, it was a thrill to shake hands with the man after whom the place was named.

*　*　*　*　*

After seventeen years in command of the Poor House, Robert Hope rode high, on his greatest popularity to date. Just fourteen months later, in 1899, his salary would be cut, but, as previously told, his attitude was, What of it? So was everyone else's salary cut.

The following year, on March 7, 1900, the busy superintendent was elected by the Grand Jury, along with Major R.J. Guinn, to succeed ex-Governor Northen, and W.P. Patillo on the school board.[189] The news column heralding the election mentioned R.L. Hope's considerable accomplishments as superintendent and resident physician at the Poor House. It added,

"Dr. Hope has also manifested a deep interest in the county schools and has contributed liberally to their support. He will be a valuable acquisition to the board."

He proved to be a valuable acquisition indeed. Three years later, he was elected President of the Fulton County Board of Education.[190] Other board members were impressed with his unstinting attention to school board matters. All realized the heavy responsibilities residing in business management of the Poor House, medical care of its inmates, avocation as real estate speculator, and fulltime duty as a father, and husband of a crippled wife. He got it all done, but remarked, "I only wish that a week had eight days instead of seven. Then I might give enough time to this board."

Dr. Hope's greatest interest now was in public education. He had enough labors to consume a man, yet he did not slacken them.

Eventually, the overwork again caught up with him. The first time, in 1901, after he had been on the school board for 15 months, he had sought to resign the Poor House.

Two months' leave instead, had brought back the sparkle to his eyes. But, now, in 1904 and 1905, as school board president, he was beginning to feel the old pressure in his chest again. He asked not to be considered for another term, and this time the Commission acceded to his request.[191]

"Whereas our esteemed President, Dr. R.L. Hope, has resigned on account of ill health, be it "Resolved, that - - - deep appreciation - - - faithful and very efficient services - - -profound regret - - - deprives us of his wisdom and experience - - - extend our sympathy in his affliction - - -.""

Robert was free from the school board. Yet, the heavier responsibility, that of the Poor House superintendence, remained. In four more years, as heart problems recurred, and with the aforementioned doleful warning of the three medical colleagues, he made a third attempt at resignation. This time, the resignation was accepted, and was final. The Fulton County Commission, accepting it, November 3, 1909, entered its letter of acceptance and regret, as did the Fulton County Board of Education, from whose presidency he also resigned.[192]

The doctor relocated his family three miles nearer to Atlanta proper, down Piedmont Road. They settled in the old Rock Spring community whence had come Dr. Hope's wife, Della. This was the neighborhood of the old settlers' families, the Johnsons, the Plasters, the Cheshires, the Pedens, and others. The Hopes started building the rambling red-brick house on 20 acres at the corner of Piedmont and Rock Spring Road, completing it in 1910. On this spot, Dr. Hope was a gentleman farmer until his death 28 years afterwards. He also continued in real estate, as an active church elder, and as the patron saint of the R.L. Hope elementary school, and of the county's public school system.

Dr. Hope continued to be a heavy contributor to public education. He treated "his school," R.L. Hope School, in a loving and fatherly manner. In his life of active retirement, he was an easily-recognized figure, attending important meetings, graduations, and other events.

*   *   *   *   *

Seventeen years after his retirement into the private sector, the former superintendent saw the building of a second R.L. Hope elementary school. The year was 1926, and the need for a larger, better equipped school was absolute. After all, the old R.L. Hope School was merely that remodeled hospital for the insane. It had now served as a school for twenty-seven years. Moreover, further population growth mandated rebuilding. Atlanta in 1900 had had a population of 89,872, but by 1920 that figure had grown to 200,616. A huge share of that growth was in the direction of Buckhead.

An impressive dedicatory exercise was held for the new, red-brick school when it was completed in 1927.[193] Dr. Frederick Stevenson, pastor of Peachtree Road Presbyterian Church (named now: Peachtree Presbyterian) lifted the invocation. Then Mrs. Howell Dodd, P.T.A. president, extended a cordial welcome, and offered the 300 seat auditorium to the community for its future uses. Two Girl Scout troops conducted a ceremony which officially dedicated the room.

Brief speeches were made by a select list of dignitaries, most of whom live in the memory of people still alive today. They included: Miss Ida Williams, past principal of the school, Jere A. Wells, the current superintendent of Fulton County schools, Edwin Johnson, County Commission member, and Hope relative, W.J.J. Chase, the architect who designed the school, Senator Walter C. Hendrix, and Dr. Willis Sutton, the superintendent of Atlanta City schools.

Interestingly, the reporter from the <u>Atlanta Constitution</u> recorded that on this special evening, Miss Ida Williams, Miss Kathleen Mitchell, and Dr. R.L. Hope were in a mood of reminiscence. In the course of the proceedings they drew pictures and diagrams of the old R.L. Hope School. They noted that when the older school had first opened, it had been quite small, compared to this new edition. That school had consisted of only two very large rooms. At its outset it had only two teachers responsible for teaching no fewer than *nine grades* from 8:00 A.M. to 4:00 P.M. every day.

The oddity of the evening's memories concerned the first R.L. Hope School student body. It was revealed that the pupils in that school initially ranged in age from five years old, to thirty!

The second R.L. Hope School stood there facing Piedmont Road, on what had been Poor House land in the old days. It was situated 400 feet northwest of Peachtree, until well into the 1980's. When the school was phased out of existence, the building was at first sold to Renaissance Antiques, and was used as a warehouse. It was demolished in the middle 1980's, its demise signaling the close of yet another era in the life of that neighborhood, and of Fulton County public education.

* * * * *

To record the retirement life of the ex-superintendent, Dr. Robert Hope, with its great wealth of anecdotes and incidents, would be to range too far afield from this book's subject. Before Dr. Hope is dismissed to history, however, some closing remarks must be made.

The doctor continued private practice as a physician after he retired. Already, he had dabbled in private practice even while working at the Poor House. His children related what seemed humorous to them: a man would come to Dr. Hope needing a tooth extracted. The physician would perform the job out on his back porch, with a pair of dental forceps. Because of the man's groans and hollers, the kids questioned whether their father had used an anesthetic!

The physician journeyed through fatherhood from 1882 to 1936. This spanned the time from the birth of his first child to the marriage of his last. None of the children born in the first decade of his and Della's marriage survived to adulthood, although one did reach the age of twelve. The five children who lived to become adults were born from 1890 to 1914.

Robert Hope dominated his children's lives, a necessary relationship, since their mother had been crippled by poliomyelitis as a young woman. He was obliged to demand instant obedience, and got it. He carried out his leadership in such a way, however, that all five children loved him supremely. It was to him that they always went, even as adults, for every kind of advice. They thought that he knew everything.

The doctor did not like to administer corporal punishment, though he sometimes reluctantly did it. He shrank from inflicting physical pain, but was a good talker. His corrective lectures to his children included a scolding, then a review of the child's past history, the reasons for doing right, his own worthy example, his love for the child, hopes for the child's future, his disappointment over their misdemeanor, etc., etc.

After a full twenty minutes of this barrage, the child's guilt-burden was heavy, and his self-esteem low. The switching then followed. No wonder that his next-to-youngest daughter told him, "Dad, I wish you'd just go ahead and *spank* me, instead of going on with all these words!"[194]

CHAPTER THIRTY-TWO

A NEW POOR HOUSE

"A new house has no sense of the have-beens."
The Two Houses, Stanza 5
Thomas Hardy

After R.L. Hope moved from the Fulton County Poor House, neither he nor it would ever be the same. Yet God in His providence saw to it that the institution, after the doctor's departure, was blessed with further good leadership.

Following Robert's migration with his family to the Rock Spring section, the Poor House itself changed location. The County Commission had already decided that, as sound as the Poor House buildings had been, they were becoming a bit creaky. They had been on the Piedmont Road property since shortly after the end of the Civil War. Although Dr. Hope had presided over the construction of new ones, that event had taken place in the early 'Eighties, a full quarter of a century earlier.

Not only so, but the R.L. Hope School was now on the formerly Poor House land, and right next door to the property that the Poor House still occupied. The placement of an elementary school hard by a poor peoples' shelter seemed incongruous to many parents.

The Commission thus began to explore the possibilities open to them, to move the Poor House, and begin selling its land to private home builders. The school would stay where it was.

The County Commission members did not have to search long or far. Dr. Hope still had their ear. While he was still superintendent he was speaking to the Commission about some property that he owned, which would be a good place for a new Poor House. The Commission looked at the land, and became interested. The suggested location was what is now known as Chastain Park. The Poor House could be located in a particular spot fronting on West Wieuca Road.[195]

The present Chastain Park area has an interesting background. It had been the site of a Muscogee Creek Indian settlement until 1821.[196] These peaceful Indians lived in the flood plain of Nancy Creek, and farmed the land that is today the Chastain Golf Course. The Creek Indian village was located where the park's ball fields are now.

The Muscogee Creek Indians were living in a politically untenable area, however. They were the northernmost extension of the large Creek Nation, which mostly occupied Middle Georgia. Very near to the north of them was the powerful Cherokee Nation, which occupied most of the rest of north Georgia. To the south and east of them, the white people were expanding. So life was quite dangerous and uncertain for the Creeks. To maintain peace, they sold off their land, piece by piece, to vast Henry County, before this portion of it became DeKalb County, then Fulton County. Finally, the Creeks sold the last of it. Though a few were permitted to continue living there, they were no longer the masters of the domain. Most others, of course, had been forced to trek, in the celebrated "Trail of Tears," to Oklahoma, giving their name to Muscogee County in that state.

It seems that Robert L. Hope, in beginning his land speculation, bought 300 acres of this very property, cheaply, as early as 1878. He was not quite 20 years old, and still in medical school, but he may have been lent the money by his older brother, Captain George M. Hope.

Dr. Hope was wary of the uproar that might arise if he sold the land directly to the Fulton County Commission. He had not yet departed from the Poor House, and was its superintendent. His memory of the furor that his lucrative property sale to the Commission had created fifteen years before, checked his impulse to sell, this time. What to do?

Hope sought out a friend, Troy Green Chastain, who had the good of the Poor House at heart, and was himself a land speculator of the first rank. If he could sell the property to Chastain, thought Dr. Hope, the latter could then sell it to the county, and all would be legal and blameless. Chastain was not connected with the Commission in any way at this time, although he would at last become a member of it in 1938.

A deal was struck between Dr. Hope and Mr. Chastain. Chastain then duly sold the designated property to the Commission, who were only too willing to have it. The transfer of the Poor House was to begin once a new Poor House could be constructed on the former Chastain land.

The plan for the Poor House, 215 West Wieuca Road, went forward throughout most of 1910, and on into the following year. The construct of the second Poor House, the Piedmont one, once it was improved, had been of brick. This third Poor House would be of brick also. As in the building of the previous Poor House, this one's bricks would be made by convicts. They produced the brick in the area now occupied by the ball fields of Chastain Park.[197]

The new Wieuca Road Poor House was completed in 1911, its plan having been drawn by the Atlanta architectural firm of Morgan and Dillon.[198] In architectural form, it resembled its Piedmont Road predecessor, but there were important differences. This Poor House was built in the neo-Classical style, with a horseshoe shape, having a courtyard between the two wings. In the front, looking up at it from Wieuca Road, one would have seen the imposing two-storey structure of red brick, with its tall white columns. The building extended back for half a block. On its east side, a subsidiary road climbed upward, and turned left, giving access to the rear of the Poor House.

Like the former Poor House, this one had superintendent's quarters in the bricked front part, while the paupers' rooms were located in the rearward extensions. A long banistered porch flanked these rooms, and overlooked a courtyard between the two wings. It was built to accommodate 145 residents.

Behind the Poor House rose a very steep wooded hill. Forest was all around the place on every side except the east, where lay a broad, undulating field. Much later, this would become a children's playground, as the Chastain property was developed, piece by piece, into North Fulton Park.

The indigents were moved over to their lodgings, and once there, most were delighted,

but some dragged their feet. One elderly woman said that if her next home were to be Heaven, the move to that location could not be too soon for her!

As at the previous Poor House, the African-American inmates had a separate building, about 150 yards from that of the whites, at 135 West Wieuca. The two buildings were on one, ten-acre property, with eight acres allotted to the whites, two to the blacks. The vegetable garden plots here helped to feed the inmates, although, unlike the previous 330-acre Poor House, this one was not to be self-sustaining through a farm. Instead, the county increased direct gifts to it.

Racial segregation would go on for many more decades in the South. Regardless, the Negro division was well equipped. There were facilities for at least 40 hospital patients, and for 85 residents in all. The Negro Poor House, like its neighbor which housed the whites, was built in the Classical Revival tradition. It featured a covered portico around its L-shaped layout.

The new home, still popularly called, "the Poor House," or, "the almshouse," was furnished with a more entrancing view from its front porch, than had been the case at the Piedmont Road predecessor. As inmates sat on the front porch of the new Poor House, and many did, they looked across the rolling green expanse of farmland that stretched away one-third of a mile. In future, it would be the golf course, but for now it was only a rustic scene. The peaceful and beautiful outlook gave the old and tired a perpetual vacation. Many preferred the long veranda to the rear, to sit, rock, and share stories of the old times.

*   *   *   *   *

The new Poor House could accommodate as many inmates as there had been at the older place. Yet the Fulton County Commission, as mentioned, limited its property to ten acres, denying it a farm. The Commission planned a different kind of development for the hundreds of acres. Still owning the entire tract purchased in the land deal involving Hope, Chastain, and the Commission, they thought to develop a park on the bulk of this property. Perhaps sell off parcels of it, as well, to private businesses.

Moreover, the Commission wished to bring some of the indigent Confederate veterans over to this West Weiuca location, and house them here. So it was done, and part of the property was used for that. For many years visitors to the Poor House saw the old fellows sitting in front of their quarters, or conversing on the front steps of the Poor House itself.

Another reason for giving only ten acres for this Poor House was the Commission's decision to separate the convict unit from the institution. Like it or not, the prisoners would not have their camp on the grounds, as they had over at the Piedmont establishment. They would go to live in the jail instead.

As the Commission's plans were implemented, the privately owned or leased businesses were developed within the park. Today, the magnificent Chastain Park Golf Course is laid out where the woods and fields used to be viewed from the Poor House front porch. The great music shell stands a quarter of a mile, just over a hill, to the north of the Poor House. Here, many special productions have been staged.

Years afterward, ball fields for baseball, softball, football, and soccer were developed down the hill and across West Weiuca, to the left of the Poor House. Day in, and day out, year around, these fields now draw far more patrons, players and parents, than all other attractions of the park combined.

*　*　*　*　*

The 1911 opening of the Poor House on West Weiuca preceded the start of the Great War by just four years. In only three more years after that, sons of the Fulton County commissioners went away to

France, to join two million other American soldiers who served there. In late 1918, it was all over, with Germany defeated. The impact of the war on the Poor House was almost nil. Only two or three pitiful wounded came to live there, following the end of the conflict.

CHAPTER THIRTY-THREE

BEST AND WORST OF TIMES

"Indeed seven years of great plenty will come throughout all the land of Egypt; but after them seven years of famine will arise - -."

Genesis 41.29-30a

Following the horrors of the First World War, ending in the Allies' victory, the United States of America had a new confidence. The Civil War and the Spanish-American War had both concluded with the U.S.A.'s powerful military frightening European rulers away from interference in North America. Now the outcome of the World War brought further power. For the first time, the United States stood forth as one of the leaders on the world stage.

With the power came great prosperity. Wall Street now rivaled the Bank of England as the weathervane of world economy. New York and Hollywood grew to become the prime centers of entertainment in the world. People had money to spend, and the sports world prospered. It was "the Roaring 'Twenties."

Even so, the Poor House on West Weiuca Road was needed, for, as Jesus had said, "the poor you have always with you." Moreover, this Poor House was the only one in the Atlanta area. No matter the good times, people who were old, disabled, without family, without hope of income, had to resort there.

In 1925, Mr. A.Q. Turner became the new superintendent of the Poor House. He seems to have done a creditable job, though his best work was done in organizing the Fulton County Police Department.[199] At the Poor House, he needed to manage far fewer inmates than the one hundred and forty-five that the building for the whites could accommodate. The same was true in the black division; there were many empty rooms.

Mr. Turner quit the Poor House, to seek other employment, after just three years at its helm. He had considered his oversight of the Poor House to be a "holding operation." Ironically, the end of his directorship in 1928 came in the last full year of the country's unprecedented wealth. After 1929 the Poor House would be needed more than ever.

* * * * *

With the departure of A.Q. Turner, the Poor House needed a new superintendent. The man selected for the job, by the Fulton County Commission, was Henry C. Clark.[200] He brought with him his wife, Jessie, who was officially employed by the Commission also. Mrs. Clark was given the position of assistant superintendent.

The Clarks, continuing to serve in the well-established tradition of the Poor House, throughout the year 1928, never imagined the great change that was to come. Through the first nine months, almost ten, of 1929, they served the indigents. The work was no easier than it had ever been, but the Poor House had plenty of room for newcomers. Soon there would be no room.

On October 24, to be known ever after, as "Black Thursday," the financial bottom dropped out, on Wall Street. The fears of a decline had started building several weeks before, when reports spread that managers of large trusts were liquidating many of their securities. On Black Thursday, fear became reality. There were spectacular declines in individual stocks in the middle of the day. General Electric, Johns-Manville, Montgomery Ward stocks all tumbled precipitously. Those and other companies recovered later in the afternoon, but still posted significant losses for the day.

It was a nightmare day. Neither brokers on the floor of the stock exchange, nor their machines, could keep up with the market's losses. The shocks spread to other exchanges and markets. There was near-panic on the Chicago commodities exchange. Rumor was rife, on and off the exchange. One report said that at least eleven speculators had committed suicide.

The market stabilized in the afternoon, but that was too late for many smaller investors. Prices did start to rise as soon as word spread that a meeting was being held at J.P. Morgan and Co. From that meeting, bankers emerged to assure investors that the market, despite the unprecedented losses, was essentially sound. They also indicated they would prop up the exchange to prevent it from dropping further.

The "Coolidge Boom" was obviously over. Some analysts had been warning that the buying spree had to stop somewhere. They said that stock prices had been pushed too high, with some of them selling at 15 to 150 times their actual earnings.

Thousands of foreign investors had recently sold their portfolios, and were reinvesting at home, as their countries continued to recover from the Great War. That contributed to the downturn.

The crash continued, also, because of the psychology of the investors some two weeks after Black Thursday. They had hoped for some life in the market. When it stayed in the doldrums, they started calling their brokers with sell orders.

Some analysts even said that weather played a part. Many Western cities were blanketed by snow and sleet, which made communication with New York more difficult. With all the uncertainties, the Westerners did not want to be left out in the cold. They also decided to sell.

In succeeding years, the Great Depression only deepened. Many middle class Americans were lightly affected by it, as far as their lifestyle was concerned. Many others were out of work. This reality made a dramatic change in the Poor House.

*   *   *   *   *

Henry and Jessie Clark found more and more people coming to the door of the Poor House, seeking shelter. Sometimes, they only wanted some temporary lodging, or a handout of food to keep them going for one more day. These people would shuffle along West Weiuca Road from Peachtree, singly, or in groups, their slumping shoulders showing their despair. Often, it was Mrs. Clark who met them, and invariably did something, gave something, to help.

Mr. and Mrs. Clark found their Poor House filling up with new residents, especially as 1930-1932 saw little improvement in the economy. President Herbert Hoover, though a smart and energetic man, turned out to be one of America's most unappreciated presidents. He made strenuous efforts to "keep business on an even keel," as he said, to stimulate wages, to create jobs, but he could not win against the financial undertow.

Many years later, Mrs. Clark reminisced,

"The home really served Fulton County during the Depression. There were no nursing homes and we were pioneers in the field."[201]

Of course, to state the matter more accurately, the Weiuca Poor House was simply following along in the path of what the Piedmont Poor House had pioneered. However, in West Weiuca's Depression era floods of needy people were coming – an influx never before seen in so short a period of time.

Asking the County for more aid, the Clarks sometimes got it, and often did not. Nonetheless, Jessie Clark later recalled,

"We furnished everything from shoes and drugs to a fully staffed beauty shop."[202]

Before long the Poor House was harboring as many residents as the Piedmont Poor House had done. In a home and medical clinic built to serve 145, there were 200 present! The condition of overcrowding continued until well after the Depression was just a memory. In fact, it would not level off until the Second World War brought the final end to the poor economic times. In the early 1940's the Poor House finally regained its normal population quota.

Changes in the various divisions of the Poor House had always been the order of the day. Now, the order came down from the Commission that a Negro women's convict camp would be opened near the Poor House property. This was done, and the convict women worked a farm situated to the north of Nancy Creek.[203]

Indigents who died in the Poor House were often buried in the tract of land which became North Fulton (later, Chastain) Park. These people, homeless, rootless, had no other burial ground. A dirt road led south to the almshouse cemetery beside Lake Forest Drive. It was located at approximately the place where the third green of the golf course is today.[204] Few, if any, relics can be found at what would, without the golf course, be a melancholy location. The remains of the deceased inmates who were buried there have long since gone to dust.

Another historic site that has never been discovered in these acres is that of the Creek Indian village. Once situated where the NYO ball fields are now located, it too, is long gone. An archaeologist has been quoted as saying that he believes there may be evidences of the village existing yet, but they may be as much as 10-15 feet under the present surface of the ground.[205]

*   *   *   *   *

In 1932, Franklin Delano Roosevelt was elected President of the United States, and, once in office, began to present more radical solutions to the curse of the Depression.

Unfortunately, he was never really able to get rid of it. Ultimately, the only way to exorcise the demon was with another, unintended demon – war. The Second World War swept millions of American men into uniform, and created war manufacture jobs for millions of other people. It was unimaginably expensive, but unemployment was cured.

Years before that unwelcome answer to the domestic problem was found, the Poor House, as noted, was bursting at the seams. Suddenly, the institution had a bigger problem than its overcrowding: In 1932 the Poor House superintendent, died. He had been the boss of the County's home for only four years, since 1928.

Henry C. Clark, though his tenure was relatively brief, had lived through some of the worst times in Poor House history. He had not known, when he took the job in 1928, that the nation's all-time worst economic crisis would strike the very next year. He could not have foreseen the overwhelming difficulties, not only of caring for the inmates and patients, but also of the daily scraping for space to house the additional people. He served for four years under great pressure. Since he was a Christian man, one may hope that death came to him as a sweet relief.

* * * * *

The Fulton County Commission, and its almshouse committee, now had a large problem: Who could be gotten to replace Henry Clark? Once the Poor House was considered a choice political job in the county. But now? Would a worthy individual wish to accept such a place, and if so, would the Commission want him?

Mrs. Clark, Jessie, had borne much of the responsibility at the Poor House, as paid assistant superintendent. She was still doing it, and she now unexpectedly applied to the Commission for the position of superintendent.

The Commission was surprised. The members received Jessie Clark's application with due admiration for the young woman's spunk, and self-confidence. They knew that she had done excellent work for four years. It was just the idea of a woman's heading the Poor House that made them hesitate. Never had a woman been appointed by the County Commission to head any County department.

Sitting once again in solemn session, the Commission batted Mrs. Clark's proposal back and forth. Finally, they agreed to interview her. The result of that interview was unprecedented in Fulton County's experience. She got the job!

As the first female head of a county department, she owned quite a distinction.[206] She was to prove more than equal to it, in the ensuing years. Jessie remained in her position as Poor House superintendent until 1963. Her four years as assistant superintendent (1928-32), followed by thirty-one more years as superintendent made her the most durable of all the people who ever occupied the position.

CHAPTER THIRTY-FOUR

POOR HOUSE IN A PARK

"In Xanadu did Kubla Khan
A stately pleasure-dome decree;"

Kubla Khan
Samuel Taylor Coleridge

A year after Jessie Clark was given the headship of the Poor House, the Fulton County Commission began to plan for the use of lands around it.[207]Eventually, though not immediately, this would result in what became Chastain Park.

The year was 1933. Many years earlier, the Commission had bought a total of 1,000 acres in this Poor House vicinity. Now they designated 268 of those acres around the Poor House for the gradual development of a park. The rest of the huge acreage would be put up for sale for private homes.

In 1936, young widow Jessie Clark remarried.[208]She was wed to Charles F. Boynton, who came to live with her at the indigents' home, while she continued to manage it. She and her family lived in the two-storey front section of the building, which overlooked the road.

That same year, the institution, which had always been known as "the Poor House," or, "the almshouse," had a name change. Thereafter, with the approval of the Fulton County Commission, it would be called, "Haven Home."[209]

After she had at last retired, almost three decades later, Mrs. Boynton would re-tell to newspapermen her greatest distinction:

"I was the first woman ever appointed by the county commission to head a department, and I still am the only one that has ever been appointed."[210]

She described what the home was, and how it was operated:

"It was a home for people of any age who were non-employable and who had no one to care for them.

Of all the people whom they had the privilege of serving at the Poor House in her 35-years' (1928-1963) tenure, the youngest was only fourteen. This was an afflicted child.

The oldest inmate had been a person who was nearly 100, she said.

"We always took them if the county said they were eligible," Jessie Boynton said.

The Commission's almshouse committee had arranged a form which Poor House applicants were assisted to fill out. They must show that they had absolutely no means of support, in order to be accepted into the institution.

The Poor House on West Wieuca was much more fully staffed than the Poor House on Piedmont had been. A lot of the staff were part-time people from outside the institution. Two doctors visited the home each week. A Dr. Moyer supplied eyeglasses for the inmates. In addition to the doctors, three nurses and a dentist were on call.

ONCE A HAVEN, NOW A STOREHOUSE

Old Home Has New Role

WEEDS, AGE OVERTAKE OLD HAVEN HOME
Former Indigent Care Center Now Storehouse

The Poor House in the present Chastain Park served from 1911 into the 1960's. The director of the previous (Piedmont Road) Poor House played golf in retirement

For entertainment for the inmates, the piano was played every day by Miss Ollie Brown, a blind pianist. Mostly, however, inmates sat on the front porch, when the weather was clement, and rocked away the hours.

While Mrs. Boynton was there, the door to the Poor House was always open.

"I never locked the front door.[211] That was one of my rules. There was always the chance that someone was out late and I never wanted them to be left outside."

Thus Mrs. Boynton stood as a second mother to all the people, mostly elderly, who passed through the home.

*   *   *   *   *

Nineteen Thirty-Eight was an important year in the saga of the Poor House. Robert L. Hope, its 1881-1909 superintendent and rebuilder, died.[212] He was lauded by the press, and his home was visited by Mayor William Hartsfield and other political and clerical dignitaries. After the memorial service, Hope's body was laid to rest in Oakland Cemetery. The grave is right under the shadow of the historical marker which tells that Confederate General John Bell Hood observed the battle of Atlanta from that point.

This same year, the man to whom Dr. Hope had sold the Poor House land twenty-nine years before, Troy G. Chastain, at last became a Fulton County Commission member.[213]

Mr. Chastain came aboard with very big ideas for the development of all that land surrounding the Poor House. He was joined by others with the same opinions. The idea was to encourage residential development in that north-of-Buckhead area. Chastain still owned some property adjacent to the county-owned spread. On it he had built himself a cabin. From that place he would glowingly oversee the step-by-step blossoming of the park.

Chastain used all the influence at his command. He became the major person promoting the creation of a recreation facility that would be a showplace of fun and leisure. A great deal of what North Fulton Park eventually became was done during Chastain's service on the Commission, 1938-1942, and in the years immediately afterwards. The pool, bathhouse, stables, tennis center, picnic areas, lakes, one-by-one became realities in this period just prior to, and during, World War Two. Workers of the WPA, and prison farm laborers, were used to do the building.

William L. Monroe, owner of Monroe Landscaping, was on retainer to the Commission to supervise the workers.[214] The quality stone masonry that they produced compared beautifully with that which already enhanced the grounds of Monroe Gardens, at the end of Monroe Drive, near the Rock Spring neighborhood. The laborers built the grills and walls, the decorative stonework that still remains, together with the picnic areas north of West Wieuca Road.

Already, in 1935, the eighteen hole North Fulton Golf Course had been built.[215] It was designed by H. Chandler Egan, in collaboration with Perry Maxwell, in 1934. As was customary with such projects, the labor was performed by prisoners of the county. In this case, they were living in a temporary prison camp which was established on the site of the present ball fields. It was the same area where, more than a century before, the Creek Indian village had been located.[216]

The golf course, having seen a number of changes, is still very much in operation. The first most famous event held there was the USGA National Amateur Public Links Golf Championship.

In 1942, the tennis center was built, and in 1944, after a tour of six U.S. cities, by two Commission members, and former member Chastain, the great amphitheater was constructed.[217] Attendance at the first year's productions was poor, because of the continuing strain of World War Two. The amphitheater's offerings very quickly caught on with the public after the war, however. In the late 1950's, a run of fifteen years of musicals began. The "Theater Under the Stars" was an overwhelmingly popular attraction, before its venue was changed. To escape from often inclement spring weather, the company changed the name to "Theater Of the Stars," and moved the productions inside, to the Fox Theater, on Peachtree Street, downtown. Company equipment was kept at the North Fulton Park location, however.[218] For a long while after 1967 it was stored in the old Haven Home, after that institution's relocation left the West Wieuca building vacant.

North Fulton Park's riding stables were opened in 1945.[219]These were established to provide housing for the animals used by rival polo clubs in the area. Residents around the park typically had stables and horses on their private property. A polo field was created where the NYO ball fields are now located. A riding ring made there provided a place for fine horse shows.

*   *   *   *   *

In that same year, 1945, Troy Chastain died.[220] There was much sadness in Atlanta because of the loss. Grateful that Mr. Chastain had been the prime mover who began the development of North Fulton Park, the Commission declared that the park should be renamed, "Chastain Park."[221] This was done, and the park was dedicated under this name in 1946.

In 1952, the City of Atlanta expanded its limits once again, in the largest area expansion it had ever made. With this action, Chastain Park was swept into the city.

Eight years later, the Northside Youth Organization ball fields were built.[222] Where formerly boys played sandlot baseball, football, and soccer, the fields were now improved, lime-striped, and fenced. Boys' teams and girls' teams began drawing hundreds of parents to the park daily, to see their offspring play. During their respective seasons, several baseball or softball games, and at least two football games, could be played simultaneously.

Changes did not halt for Haven Home, either.[223]In 1961 the sick people among the white inmates were moved away from it entirely. These patients were taken to Highview Hospital, at 2800 Springdale Road, SW. The Negro division continued to function, as always, on its two acres of land, where it had been since 1910.

*   *   *   *   *

Now Mrs. Charles Boynton, the Poor House's beloved Jessie, knew that her time was up. She retired in summer, 1963, after 35 years of service.[224]In going, she testified,

"Some of the sweetest memories of my life are the people I knew at the home. I have always been interested in elderly people. They have fascinated me since childhood."

Mrs. Boynton admitted that there was a lot of work involved in running a large establishment, but denied that her labors were ever drudgery.

"The people always appreciated what was done for them and it was very rewarding. I always had full 100 percent cooperation from all the county departments.

"And when you retire it's the people you work(ed) with that you really miss.

"The home is still my life. It can't help but be when you spend so much of your life with so many interesting people..

"Even though I have a beautiful family and love them dearly, I was, nevertheless, very close to my people at the home."

The former superintendent did, however, have fulfillment in her retired state. She and Mr. Boynton moved several miles from "Haven Home." In their new home, Jessie Boynton got to see much of her grandchildren. One of her five daughters and her young family lived right next door to the Boyntons.

Four years after Mrs. Boynton's retirement, the County Commission decided to move Haven Home.[225]Hal Patterson had worked for Mrs. Boynton as custodial manager. When she retired, he was made the new superintendent, but his work would not be on West Wieuca.

The white inmates were moved to a place called, "Happy Haven," west of Atlanta. The white Poor House, in a sense, had come full circle. Starting before the Civil War near the present entrance to Westview Cemetery, it was now not far from that first location.

The African-American division of Haven Home was kept on West Wieuca, and was still operating there in 1968.[226] Just the previous year, however, the City of Atlanta had acquired the building by swapping some land for it.[227]The land lay behind the former white division of Haven Home, and the city gave that property to the county, in exchange for the county's former Poor House buildings. The African-American inmates were moved elsewhere, probably to the west, to the new Happy Haven.

With both buildings now empty, the city government used the former black division's building to house the Chastain Arts and Crafts Center.[228] This center is still in operation, there at 135 West Wieuca, almost forty years later.

*   *   *   *   *

As for the former building of Haven Home's white division, it, too, was still used.[229] In September, 1963, just following Mrs. Boynton's retirement, the County, which still owned the building, gave permission to the City of Atlanta public school system to use parts of the old almshouse. It was used as an annex to Tuxedo Elementary School. This use continued for four years, through the spring of 1967.

After the elementary school ceased to use it, Municipal Theater leased the building, at no cost, from Fulton County.[230] As mentioned earlier, the theater company used it to store stage props for its Theater Under the Stars productions.

During its time as a storage bin, the old Haven Home seemed lonely and desolate. It did harbor a vast pigeon population on its roof tops, and enormous Egyptian statues and scenery belonging to Municipal Theater were found in its corridors. Human beings, however, normally stayed in the building only long enough to move things in and out. Outside, the stately oak trees stood in contrast with high weeds and unpruned shrubbery.

Revitalization came to the old Haven Home building in 1969, though, when Elliott Galloway began to refurbish the badly vandalized place. He did this in order to establish a new school there. Today the Galloway School occupies the same building,[231] renovated and enlarged, that once housed the Poor House inmates. Galloway School is a mixed high school and college institution – a liberal arts school, comprising ages Pre-K through Grade 12.

With the city's ownership of the two Haven Home buildings, better use of them seemingly has been made than what the county could have done. Now both buildings are places of teachers, young adults, children, and learning. Both within them and all around them outdoors, is vibrant life.

Happy Haven, coming into being in 1963, continued for some time. Fourteen years later, it was ready for phasing out. Government entitlements, nursing homes, and a generally stronger economy, had all conspired to make "poor houses," as such, obsolete.

At least in that century, in that place, they were mostly being superseded.

*   *   *   *   *

The successive almshouses in the Atlanta area had been administered by no fewer than four counties. The first one, at the present Westview Cemetery site, had been controlled by the vast Henry County. Fayette County then became the overseer, as counties, including Henry, were carved up into smaller units. DeKalb County next took over, and the last county to rule the place was Fulton, when it was created out of DeKalb.

The Poor Houses history stands as one of the finer traditions of Western civilization.

One moves back, and back, from the American South, to New England, to Old England, the European Continent, the abbeys, the Christians of the late Roman Empire. The end of the journey is Jesus Christ Himself.

The key thing to perceive about Jesus is not His role as Exemplar, although His own walk in right paths as a Man is important as one's perfect guide. Of infinitely greater importance is the *saving* significance of His sinless life and sacrificial death. "Only believe," says the Bible. "Believe, and be saved, through having all your sins washed away by that one, terrible, bloody death, died in your stead." And believe, and be saved also by having your whole life of daily sinning replaced by His perfect, sinless life. This is known as "the blessed exchange" – one's sinful record exchanged for Christ's perfect record. By His life and by His death, both accounted by God to us individually, we are redeemed for eternity.

As the individual *believes*, he is given the Holy Spirit, to enable him to *live* in a way pleasing to God. One example: the Savior of mankind taught that the strong must help the weak. The Poor House principle of doing good to those who were unable to give anything in return, was a reflection of this teaching of Christ. This principle was carried out only through the caregivers' self-sacrifice, which was sometimes extreme. One may even say that it was a faint portrayal and reminder of Christ's sacrificial *dying* to provide eternal salvation for the many.

THE END

NOTES

These endnotes are thorough, lacking only the day and month dates of some of the newspaper articles noted. The original compiler of the newspaper clippings, two generations ago, failed to join the dates to the articles. Please accept the author's apology for these omissions, which are indicated throughout the notes.

FOREWORD

1 The number of - - poorhouses - - exceeded 2,000: "Poorhouses," Wikipedia Free Encyclopedia (2007).

CHAPTER ONE: A POOR HOUSE INDEED!

2 Rude hovels - - without sufficient cover - -: Cited in Editorial Staff, *A Glimpse Into the Life of Fulton County's Poor* (Atlanta Constitution, Sunday, January 6, 1895), 11.
3 The obvious culprit in its rundown condition - -: Ibid., 10.
4 You have to do it - - Ibid., 10.
5 The philosophy of Aristotle replaced it: Nancy R. Pearcey, *Total Truth* (Wheaton, Ill.: Crossway Books, 2004), 77.
6 It was a mistaken and dangerous route: Ibid., 74.
7 They were mystics, ascetics, and hermits.: Ibid., 76.
8 Anthony- - he is credited with establishing the first monastery: Philip Schaff, *History of the Christian Church*, vol. III (Grand Rapids: William B. Eerdmans, 1950), 181-189.
9 Germans' actions- - mild compared to the actions of the Vikings: Ralph D. Winter, *Perspectives On the World Christian Movement*, Ed., Ralph D. Winter and Steven Hawthorne (Pasadena, CA: William Carey Library, 1981, 1992), B-11.

10 Christianity tamed the Vikings into - - the Christian kingdoms of Denmark, Sweden, and Norway: Ibid., B-14,15.

11 The ideas - - advanced by Colet: John R. Green, *Nations of the World,* vol. I (New York: Peter Fenelon Collier & Son, 1900), 93-94.

12 Let every man have his own doctor, but this man is the doctor for me!: Cited in ibid., 93.

13 The brothers are on good terms - -: Ibid., 134.

14 400 abbeys were dissolved: Ibid., 168.

15 Henry made - - only supreme head of the Church of England: *Encyclopedia Brittanica*, vol. 1 (1953), 439.

CHAPTER TWO: FROM THE VIRGIN QUEEN TO THE WIDOW AT WINDSOR

16 England was - - a nest of singing birds: Green, *Nations of the World*, vol. II (New York: Peter Fenelon Collier & Son, 1900), 494.

17 The influx of religious refugees - -: Green, *Nations - -,* vol. I, 407.

18 Oxford - - became a hotbed of Calvinism: Ibid., 408.

19 The queen was forced to fill the English bishoprics quietly and steadily with men whose creed in almost every case was Calvinist: Green, *Nations - -,* vol. III, 21.

20 The numbers of the vagrants had increased - -: "Poor Laws," *Encyclopedia Brittanica*, vol. 18 (1953), 214.

21 This measure was called, "The Act For the Relief of the Poor.": "Elizabethan Poor Law 1601," *Wikipedia Free Encyclopedia*, (2007).

22 The rates were used as well to assist those persons who were unable to work because of age, sickness, injury, or war wounds: "Poor Laws," *Encyclopedia Brittanica*, vol. 18 (1953), 214.

23 They had no rights to the land: Ibid., 214.

24 Like politicos elected by dead men's votes: Ibid., 214

25 English handicraftsmen provided their exquisite china, glass, and silverplate: "English History," *Compton's Pictured Encyclopedia*, vol. 4 (Chicago: F.E. Compton & Co., 1957), 439.

26 Dear, droll, distracting town - -: "A Farewell to London," *Poetical Works of Alexander Pope*, (New York, Hurst & Co.) 361.

27 I will venture to say, there is more learning and science - - : Cited in James Boswell, *Boswell's Life of Johnson*, (New York: Thomas Y. Crowell & Co.) 332..

28 The nemesis of the Napoleonic Empire was Great Britain: *A Survey of European Civilization*, vol. II (Cambridge, MA: Houghton Mifflin Company, 1939), 190.

29 Get into the House of Commons - -: Sherwood E. Wirt, *The Social Conscience of the Evangelical*, (New York, Evanston, & London: Harper & Row, 1968) 35.

30 - - that execrable villainy - -: Cited in ibid., 159.

31 All the poor laborers - - confined to workhouses - -: "Elizabethan Poor Law 1601," *Wikipedia* - -(2007).

32 They continued, nevertheless, to be so bad that a public investigation by a royal commission was made as late as 1905-09: "Poor Laws," *Encyclopedia Brittanica*, vol. 18 (1953) 215.

CHAPTER THREE: POOR HOUSES IN AMERICA

33 Where did all these ungodly men come from?: Cited by Carl W. Wilson, "America's Need For Revival," (Speech to Central Ga. Presbytery men at Vineville Presbyterian Church, Macon, Georgia, 1978).

34 - - the subject of the poor in our county is one that demands consideration and action: Cited in Franklin M. Garrett, *Atlanta and Its Environs*, vol. I (Lewis Historical Publishing Co., Inc., 1954) 428.

35 - - tends to concentrate many who are unable to provide for their own support: Cited in ibid.

36 - - many, who though able to work, are far from willing - -: Cited in ibid.

37 - - candidates for the jails, penitentiaries, and gallows: Cited in ibid.

CHAPTER FOUR: JOE BROWN, MONEY, AND WAR

38 Joseph Emerson Brown - - received the Democratic Party's nomination for governor: Ibid., 423.

39 At the outset, the aristocrats hated him - -: Ibid., 423.

40 Atlanta merchants owed less than their counterparts in the North: Ibid., 424.

41 - - a Southern belief that the South was being plundered by the "imperial North": "Federal Economic Policy," Speech to Georgia Legislature, by Robert Toombs, Cited by Kenneth M. Stampp, Ed., *The Causes of the Civil War*, (Englewood Cliffs, NJ: Prentice-Hall, Inc., 1974) 63-65.

CHAPTER FIVE: THE POOR HOUSE DESTROYED

42 As a first lieutenant in the U.S. Army, he had visited this very area, at age twenty-three, in the year 1844: Garrett, *Atlanta and Its Environs*, vol. I (1954) 211-212.

43 It was the battle in which Atlanta's first Poor House was destroyed: Ibid., 624.

44 - - the men then torched the house and burned it to the ground: Cited in Robert Lawson Hope, *Personal Recollections of Dr. R.L. Hope*, Library of Atlanta Historical Society.

CHAPTER SIX: RESURGENCE

45 She was playing with her puppy when a Federal shell fell that morning of July 20, at the corner of Ivy and Ellis, and blew her to Kingdom come: William Key, *The Battle of Atlanta and the Georgia Campaign*, (New York, Twayne Publishers, 1958) 67. See also, Franklin M. Garrett, *Atlanta and Its Environs*, vol. I (Lewis Historical Publishing Co., Inc. 1954) 626.

46 - - some wounded were put on trains, carts, wagons, or drays, and sent away: Ibid., Key, *The Battle of Atlanta and the Georgia Campaign,* 70.

47 They continued to be killed and maimed, both day and night: Ibid., 71.

48 The children were dressed only in tow sacks, with openings cut at the corners for armholes: Garrett, *Atlanta and Its Environs,* vol. I 662.

49 The children had a haven: Ibid., 752-753.

CHAPTER SEVEN: AFRICAN-AMERICANS

50 By 1867, Atlanta, with the bulk of the county's population, had seen its own numbers shift to fifty-four percent white, forty-six percent black: Ibid., 730.

51 Many former slaves did change: Ibid., 740-741.

52 - - forty acres and a mule - -: Ibid., 689.

53 Others were resorting to vagabondage - -: Ibid., 689

54 Before we censure these people too harshly - -: Cited in Robert Lawson Hope, *Personal Recollections of Dr. R.L. Hope*, Library of Atlanta Historical Society.

55 The Poor House would be at the corner of Piedmont and Peachtree roads, and a scant half-mile from the new railroad: Garrett, *Atlanta and Its Environs*, vol. I, 730, 816.

CHAPTER EIGHT: RECONSTRUCTION: WHO NEEDED IT?

56 "Reconstruction," as it was dubbed, would have been better named, "Restructuring" - -: Ibid., 669-875.

57 Civil War historian Fletcher Pratt wrote that the Radicals, by their harsh terms of Reconstruction, "disgraced themselves": Fletcher Pratt, *Ordeal By Fire*, (New York: William Sloane Associates, 1948) 373.

58 Franklin Garrett, Atlanta's all-time leading chronicler, wrote of Reconstruction in colors of disgust: Garrett, *Atlanta and Its Environs*, vol. I 733.

59 Union soldiers were surprised that a few Confederates captured at Gettysburg were black- -: Ervin L. Jordan, Jr., *Black Confederates and Afro-Yankees in Civil War Virginia*, (Charlottesville and London: University Press of Virginia, 1995) 223-224.

60 Reconstruction promised to receive a state back into the Union if it followed a rather tortuous, seven-step route: Garrett, *Atlanta and - -* vol. I 733-734.

61 For the white majority, this seemed a nightmare time: Ibid., 734.

62 Amazingly, Georgia fared much better through the trauma of Reconstruction than she expected: Garrett, *Atlanta and - -* vol. I 776-780.

CHAPTER NINE: THE POOR HOUSE REOPENS

63 It became Atlanta's queen of stores - - had a book written about it: Celestine Sibley, *Dear Store*, (Garden City, NY: Doubleday, 1967).

64 - - Fulton County Grand Jury to report in May, 1869 - -: Garrett, *Atlanta and - -* vol. I 807.

65 Fulton County at that time assumed full oversight: Ibid., 985.

66 It was the Creek Indians who, much earlier in the century, had occupied it: Ibid., 3-6; 11-12; 55.

67 So it was that the new Poor House property, whose location is described above, lay largely in Land Lot Number 62, with a smaller portion in Land Lot Number 98: Wall Map in Atlanta History Center, 1992.

68 We are unable to say that the management of the Poor House reflects the utmost credit on its keeper, Mr. Jesse M. Cook: Garrett, *Atlanta and - -* vol. I 513.

CHAPTER TEN: A NEW DIRECTOR

69 As it turned out, Calhoun had a young friend, Captain George M. Hope - -: *History of Fulton County, Georgia*, Library of Atlanta History Center 328. George Hope's life and achievements are fully outlined in this article within the *History*. A picture of him at age 55 or 60 is also included on p. 329.

70 Ultimately, he attended and graduated from the Georgia Eclectic Medical College: "Medical Profession," *Atlanta and Its Builders*, in Library of Atlanta History Center 357.

71 But besides individuals, you will benefit the whole community, too: Cited in Robert Lawson Hope, *Personal Recollections of Dr. R.L. Hope*, Library of Atlanta History Center.

72 - - in 1887 it would be increased to $900: Editorial Staff, "The Grand Jury – The General Presentments Submitted to the Court," *Atlanta Constitution* Autumn Report on Grand Jury, 1887.

73 His was the oldest recorded will of DeKalb County - -: Garrett, *Atlanta and - -* vol. I 141-143.

74 - - one of the busiest men in the county: "Wants a Low Rate," *Atlanta Constitution* January Report on Fulton County Commission, 1895.

75 He was then baptized there: Cited in Robert Lawson Hope, *Personal Recollections of Dr. R.L. Hope*, Library of Atlanta History Center.

CHAPTER ELEVEN: POOR HOUSE MEDICAL CARE

76 - - Robert Hope, who was a recent graduate of the little school which became Atlanta Boys High: Garrett, *Atlanta and* - - vol. I 876-879.

77 The college of the Eclectic opinion - - was opened at Forsyth, Georgia, in 1839: "Medical Profession," *Atlanta and Its Builders*, Library of Atlanta History Center 357.

78 His college was "closely allied to the Thomsonian and Eclectic Schools of medicine": Editorial, *The Eclectic Star*, July, 1970 1. "Drugs and Pharmacy in the Life of Georgia," Emory University Library, Decatur, Ga. 266.

79 Biochemistry - - developed by Antoine Lavoisier, at the end of the Eighteenth Century: "Biochemistry," *Encyclopedia Brittanica*, vol. 3 (1953) 589-593. Also see Ibid., "Lavoisier, Antoine Laurent," Vol. 13, 777-778.

80 A Creek Indian medicine man - -: Cited in Robert Lawson Hope, *Personal Recollections of Dr. R.L. Hope*, Library of Atlanta History Center.

CHAPTER TWELVE: MEETING THE PEOPLE

81 I must provide a haven for the paupers - -: Cited in Robert Lawson Hope, *Personal Recollections of Dr. R.L.* Hope, Library of Atlanta History Center.

82 Jim Hill - - a dwarf in size, and little better than half-witted: "Poor-House," *Atlanta Journal*, 1894.

83 This led to a cruel practical joke's being played on him: "A Glimpse Into the Life of Fulton County's Poor," *The Constitution*, Atlanta, Ga., Sunday, January 6, 1895, 11.

84 Another very special inmate at the Poor House was S.F. Billings: Ibid., 11.

85 One phenomenon - - was the extreme retiring nature of so many of the inmates: Ibid., 11.

86 They are almost all like that, was Dr. Hope's comment: Ibid., 11.

87 He had established a schedule that took him into the city every few days - -: Ibid., 11.

88 Five decades later, his grandchildren saw the potions - -: Cited in Robert Lawson Hope, *Personal Recollections of Dr. R.L. Hope,* Library of Atlanta History Center.

89 The ancient Egyptians and Greeks, in fact, had them - -: "Ancient Medicine," *Encyclopedia Brittanica*, vol. 15 (1953) 197.

90 As the result of this individual care - - no disease of any kind - -: A Glimpse Into the Life of Fulton County's Poor," *The Constitution*, Atlanta, Ga., Sunday, January 6, 1895, 10.

91 American life expectancy as late as 1900 was just 47 years: "Life expectancy," *Windows Internet Explorer,* National Center For Health Statistics, Faststats, January 5, 2008.

CHAPTER THIRTEEN: MAKING THE PLANS

92 By his arithmetic it would cost eight-and-a-half cents per day - -: Cited in "Letters to Editor," G.T. Dodd, A.M. Perkerson, R.L. Hope, *Atlanta Constitution,* 1884.

93 Dr. Hope reported to the Grand Jury that one inmate had recently injured his leg when a rotten floor board broke: Review cited in part, in "A Glimpse into the Life of Fulton County's Poor," *The Constitution*, Atlanta, Ga., Sunday, January 6, 1895, 10.

94 This will permit us to make enough money on the food we raise, to be self-supporting: Ibid.

95 I have come today to look upon these buildings where once we had battlefields: Cited in Franklin M. Garrett, *Atlanta and Its Environs*, vol. II (Lewis Historical Publishing Co. 1954) 32-33.

96 They recommended new buildings but first suggest that the 300 acres now owned be sold - -: "The County Institutions," *The Constitution*, Atlanta, Ga., 1882.

97 - - the county already has 50 acres of land near the Exposition grounds - -: "The County Commissioners," *The Constitution*, Atlanta, Ga., 1882.

98 The inside walls would be plastered, to make them suitable all-weather dwellings: "New Quarters For Colored," *Atlanta Capitol*, Atlanta, Ga., 1882.

CHAPTER FOURTEEN: TRIAL BY GOSSIP

99 In this column someone was always in trouble, and this time it was Perkerson: "Let the Responsibility Rest Where It Belongs," Daily complaint column, *The Constitution*, Atlanta, Ga., December 9, 1883.

100 - - the fact is sufficient to damn its author in the estimation of every man, woman, and child - -: "Let the Responsibility Rest Where It Belongs," Daily complaint column, *The Constitution*, Atlanta, Ga., December 11, 1883.

101 The sheriff may think differently. Respectfully, R.L. Hope: "Let the Responsibility Rest Where It Belongs," Daily complaint column, *The Constitution*, Atlanta, Ga., December 13, 1883.

102 Two such investigators found the average meals simple, but nourishing and adequate: "A Woman Whipped," Subtitled, "A Man Tells Some More Stories About the County Poor House Troubles," *The Constitution*, Atlanta, Ga., 1886. "Caught On the Fly," Subtitled, "The County's Poor," *The Constitution*, Atlanta, Ga., 1886.

103 Two inmates, it was said, had died in the Poor House under mysterious circumstances: "Coroner Hilburn Replies," *Atlanta Post-Appeal*, Atlanta, Ga., April 26, 1883.

104 The coroner - - had wanted only to relate the events: Ibid., cited in *Atlanta Post-Appeal*, April 27, 1883.

105 At this hinge moment Mr. J.T. Cooper - - stepped forward like the surprise rescuer in a stage play: "The Matter Settled," *Atlanta Post-Appeal*, April 30, 1883.

106 I hope this little matter is now settled to the entire satisfaction of all. Yours respectfully, J.T. Cooper: Cited in Ibid.

CHAPTER FIFTEEN: BUILDING BLOCKS OF PROGRESS

107 A force of sixteen convicts was brought to the Poor House property to live there temporarily, under guard: "The County Almshouse," Subtitled, "How the Work On the New Quarters Stands," *The Constitution*, Atlanta, Ga., September, 1884.

108 A sleepless moonlit night was a good time to walk and talk with God: Cited in Robert Lawson Hope, *Personal Recollections of Dr. R.L. Hope*, Library of Atlanta History Center.

109 The new quarters will then be given to the white inmates, and the quarters now used by the whites will be turned over to the colored inmates: Cited in Ibid., "The County Almshouse," *The Constitution*, 1884.

110 In November, the making of brick got started, and an interesting process it was: Cited in Ibid., "The County Almshouse," *The Constitution,* 1884. Brick-making methods consultation, Thomas Construction Company, Columbus, Ga., 1993.

111 The house is of splendid brick, and is almost if not fully as well built as any in Atlanta: "Dr. Hope Arrives," *Atlanta Capitol,* Atlanta, Ga. 1885.

112 The inmates appeared bright and cheerful - -: Cited in Ibid., 1885.

113 When that is done, the Poor House will be an honor to the county: Cited in Ibid., 1885 114 I expect in two or three years to make the place self-sustaining: Cited in Ibid., 1885.

115 - - Jefferson Davis, made his last visit to Atlanta from his home in Woodville, Mississippi: Cited in Franklin M. Garrett, *Atlanta and Its Environs*, vol. II (Lewis History Publishing Co. 1954) 116-117.

116 It was Coca-Cola, written in the flowing script of Pemberton's chemical company partner, Frank Mason Robinson: Garrett, *Atlanta and - -* 119-122.

CHAPTER SIXTEEN: NEW RUMORS

117 Only sixty days before - - Hamp Moss had made some sensational charges: "A Tale By Hamp Moss," Subtitle, "A Colored Citizen Makes Some Serious Charges," *The Constitution*, Atlanta, Ga., Date of publication separated from article, March, 1886.

118 As they talked, Hamp Moss' stories were shredded by the plain truth: Cited in Ibid.

119 The reign of terror that the sensation hunter was after did not appear to exist: Cited in Ibid.

120 Moss' impulse to strike out in revenge against cruel fate, plus the payment of money to him, triggered his wild stories: Cited in Ibid.

121 Dr. L.S. (sic) Hope, the superintendent, has an unblemished reputation in every respect: "Fulton County Alms House," *Atlanta Journal*, Atlanta, Ga., Date of publication separated from article, March, 1886.

CHAPTER SEVENTEEN: PRE-ELECTION SCRUTINY

122 The most extensive investigation of the Poor House was conducted by the Atlanta Evening Capitol: "Stories That Led to the Investigation – What the Inmates Say," *Atlanta Evening Capitol*, Atlanta, Ga., Date of publication separated from article, April, 1886.

123 She was the lady described by the Atlanta Constitution reporter a few days earlier as, "his very clever little wife": "Caught On the Fly," Subtitle, "The County's Poor," *The Constitution*, Atlanta, Ga., Date of publication separated from article, April, 1886.

CHAPTER EIGHTEEN: TRIUMPH AND TRAGEDY

124 In view of the impending election, one Capitol reporter was immediately dispatched - -: "Further Facts and Figures," *Atlanta Evening Capitol*, Atlanta, Ga., Date of publication separated from article, April, 1886

125 At the same moment, the Atlanta Journal was also supporting Dr. Hope: "Fulton County Alms House," *Atlanta Journal*, Atlanta, Ga., Date of publication separated from article, March, 1886.

CHAPTER NINETEEN: CONVICT CAMP

126 The colored people must be helped: Cited in Robert Lawson Hope, *Personal Recollections of Dr. R.L. Hope*, Library of Atlanta History Center.

127 There he prayed: Cited in Ibid.

128 We were like to hurt the negroes more than help them: Cited in Ibid.

129 Taking the establishment as a whole we think it is one of the best institutions of its kind - -: "A Racy Presentment," Subtitle, "The Grand Jury Presents to the Superior Court a Long Paper," *The Constitution*, Atlanta, Ga., January 7, 1888.

130 The full recommendation called for his services to be retained - -: "The Grand Jury," Subtitle, "The Alms House," *Atlanta Journal*, Atlanta, Ga. Date of publication separated from article. September, 1888.

131 - - the Grand Jury regarded the jail as a "blot upon the good name of Fulton County": "The Grand Jury," Subtitle, "The General Presentments Submitted to

the Court," *The Constitution*, Atlanta, Ga. Date of publication separated from article, September, 1888.

132 - - one of the busiest men in the county: "Wants a Low Rate," Subtitle, "Commissioner Palmer Favors an Economical Administration," *The Constitution*, Atlanta, Ga. Date of publication separated from article, January, 1889.

133 He just has insomnia: Cited in Robert Lawson Hope, *Personal Recollections of Dr. R.L. Hope*, Library of Atlanta History Center.

CHAPTER TWENTY: IMBECILES

134 Initially, one of the newspapers carried the story under the headline, "A Woman Whipped": Article cited in *The Constitution*, Atlanta, Ga. Date of publication separated from article, 1886.

135 - - the legislature shifted the "harmless lunatics" from Milledgeville - -: After-the-fact reference, "With Gloves Off," *The Constitution*, Atlanta, Ga. Date of publication separated from article, January, 1895.

136 There has to be a new, separate building, in which the imbeciles can be cared for: After-the-fact (1893) reference, "To Care For the Poor," Subtitle, "A Home For Imbeciles," *The Constitution*, Atlanta, Ga. January 22, 1896.

137 - - he made no mention of the need for a new unit for the insane: "The New County Board," Subtitle, "Interesting Reports From Superintendent Hope About the Alms House," *The Constitution*, Atlanta, Ga. January 2, 1895.

138 Those present were - -: "Feast at the Almshouse," Subtitle, "County Commissioners Partake of a Royal Meal In the Home of the Poor, *The Constitution*, Atlanta, Ga. Date of publication separated from article, 1895.

139 That confidence was restored - - by the - - Cotton States and International Exposition of 1895: Garrett, *Atlanta and Its Environs*, vol II 34.

140 At the Fulton County Commission's meeting - - the issue of improving facilities for the mentally deficient: Later reported, "To Care For the Poor," Subtitle, "The County Commissioners Will Be Asked To Make an Appropriation for the Unfortunates," *The Constitution*, Atl., Ga. December 28, 1895.

CHAPTER TWENTY-ONE: INMATE OF CONSEQUENCE

141 This man is Attorney-General Robert N. Ely: "A Glimpse Into the Life of Fulton County's Poor," *The Constitution*, Atlanta, Ga. January 6, 1895.

142 A more pathetic story I have never known: "Major Ely Dead," Subtitle, "Once Georgia's Attorney General," *The Constitution*, Atlanta, Ga. Date of publication separated from article, 1895.

143 The day after the funeral he received a hand-written, four-page letter - -: Letter held in box of Robert Lawson Hope, archives of Atlanta History Center.

144 He was for many years the physician of the Atlanta City Jail: Dr. Hollis F. Hope conducted his brother and his nephew (the present author) on tour through the jail in the 1940's.

CHAPTER TWENTY-TWO: INTERESTING INMATES

145 Back in the 'Eighties, a couple of <u>Constitution</u> reporters had toured - - gathering human interest material for the newspaper: "Poverty's Precinct," Subtitle, "The Home of the Halt, the Lame, and the Blind," *The Constitution*, Atlanta, Ga. Date of publication separated from article, 1884.
146 Hill's story is sorrowful, though predictable, given his deficient mentality: Cited in Ibid. Also cited in "A Glimpse Into the Life of Fulton County's Poor," *The Constitution*, Atlanta, Ga., 1895. Further cited in "Poor House," Subtitle, "Dwarf Jim Hill and His History," *The Constitution.*, Atlanta. Ga. 1894. 147 - - "Atlanta's most famous vagabond": Cited in Franklin M. Garrett, *Atlanta and Its Environs*, vol. II 106.
148 Three reporters from the <u>Atlanta</u> <u>Constitution</u> had been charmed with what they saw - -: "Poverty's Precinct," *The Constitution*, Atlanta, Ga. Date of publication separated from article, 1884.
149 Among the many Poor House episodes involving children, some were heartwrenching: News article lost or misplaced by author. Newspaper original to be researched in Library of Atlanta History Center.
150 Poor House feature articles appeared - -concerning two "famous" (or infamous) Atlanta prostitutes: "Objects to Paying the Wages of Sin," "The White Woman Must Don Stripes," "Woman Dons Stripes," *The Constitution*, Atlanta, Ga., *The Atlanta Journal*, articles cited in 1897.

CHAPTER TWENTY-THREE: OLD SOLDIERS

151 At one point in the 'Nineties there were ten of them residing there under the watchful eye of Dr. Hope: "Poor House," Subtitle, "Some Confederate Soldiers There," *The Constitution*, Atlanta, Ga. Date of publication separated from article, 1894.

CHAPTER TWENTY-FOUR: ONE WHO LOST A FORTUNE

152 Of all the tales of bitterness and loss - - none could top that of major Alexander Ratteree - -: "Major Ratterree (sic.) Tells of His Life," Subtitle, "His Story a Tale of Woe," *The Constitution*, Atlanta, Ga. Date of publication separated from article, 1897.
153 Garrett had checked the facts, and had written of them in his massive <u>Atlanta and Its Environs</u>: "Alexander Ratteree's litigations," Index listing, cited in *Atlanta and Its Environs*, vol. I 174-175.

CHAPTER TWENTY-FIVE: "POOR" HOUSE AND DIRECTOR

154 Despite the difficult prospect that travel presented, <u>Constitution</u> reporter L.L. Knight hitched his horses to his buggy: "A Glimpse Into the Life of Fulton County's Poor," *The Constitution*, Atlanta, Ga., Sunday, January 6, 1895.

155 - - "the old village of Buckhead, now designated by the more stylish name of Atlanta Heights": Cited in Ibid.

156 What did Knight see, instead of the poor visions he expected?: Cited in Ibid.

157 Robert Hope was not yet thirty-six years of age. Knight described him: Cited in Ibid.

158 The Poor House director told all - -: Cited in Ibid.

159 Do you encounter much difficulty in keeping (the inmates) under control?: Cited in Ibid.

CHAPTER TWENTY-SIX: POOR PEOPLE ON A RICH FARM

160 He pressed the doctor to relate something of the Poor House history of the last fourteen years: Cited in Ibid., Sunday, January 6, 1895.

161 - - another reporter, who signed himself simply, B.M.B, came to visit: "A Day At the Poor Farm," *Atlanta Journal*, Atlanta, Ga., Date of publication separated from article, 1895.

162 The city recently has passed through a time of decision on bankrupt Grady Hospital, its vast public emergency facility: Many articles in *Atlanta Journal-Constitution*, Atlanta, Ga., Late autumn, 2007, winter, 2008.

163 In 1895 L.L. Knight was less reticent: "A Glimpse Into the Life of Fulton County's Poor," *The Constitution*, Atlanta, Ga., Sunday, January 6, 1895.

CHAPTER TWENTY-SEVEN: BUILDING A JAIL

164 By 1896, R.L. Hope had been elected to the building committee of the Fulton County Board of Commissioners: "Talk With Redwine," *The Constitution*, Atlanta, Ga., Date of publication separated from article, 1896.

165 A new county jail must be planned and built: Cited in Ibid.

166 Continuing, the telegram disclosed the information that the four gentlemen had visited Atlantan Lewis Redwine - -: Cited in Ibid.

167 What was built was the famous Fulton Tower: Cited in Franklin M. Garrett, *Atlanta and Its Environs*, vol. II (Lewis Historical Publishing Co., Inc. 1954) 363-364.

CHAPTER TWENTY-EIGHT: HOUSES AND LANDS

168 - - real estate speculation was definitely a gift of his: Cited in Robert Lawson Hope, *Personal Recollections of Dr. R.L. Hope* Library of Atlanta History Center.
169 Atlanta, he said would someday grow "all the way out to Norcross": Ibid.
170 In 1864, the U.S. Army Corps of Engineers had published a map for the use of Sherman's forces: Davis, Major George B., *The Official Military Atlas of the Civil War*, "Map Illustrating the Fifth Epoch of the Atlanta Campaign," Plate LX, compiled by Edward Huger (New York, The Fairfax Press). Originals held in *Official Records of the War of the Rebellion*, Library of Congress, Washington, D.C.
171 He told the author that the man in question simply had been, "no good": Author's personal conversation, Miami, Florida, 1994; informant now resides in Keystone Heights, Florida, 2008.
172 Amid his land bargains and coups, Dr. Hope made one in 1894 that had repercussions: "Some Real Estate Figures Given," *The Constitution*, Atlanta, Ga., Date of publication separated from article, 1895.
173 In the 1930's, in a tan Buick, he would sit behind chauffeur Dave, sometimes with grandchildren loaded aboard: Cited in Robert Lawson Hope, *Personal Recollections of Dr. R.L. Hope*, Library of Atlanta History Center.

CHAPTER TWENTY-NINE: A SALARY CUT

174 This was the first after-dark meeting of the Fulton County Board of Commissioners in a very long time: "County Fathers Met Last Night," *The Constitution*, Atlanta, Ga., January 7, 1897.
175 - - Palmer still had economy through salary-cutting as his prime objective: Subtitle, "Brown Corrects an Interview," *The Constitution*, Atlanta, Ga., Date of publication separated from article, autumn, 1898.
176 This time, Palmer's hour struck: "Palmer Chairman of Board; a Big Cut Made in Salaries," Subtitle, Organization Meeting Held Yesterday Afternoon and Factional Lines Are Drawn –Spalding Goes Out,
Walker Comes In, *The Constitution*, Atlanta, Ga., Date of publication separated from article, Thursday edition, 1899
177 In the words of the Atlanta Constitution, Palmer drew "his big knife,": Cited in ibid.

CHAPTER THIRTY: ONE HONEST OFFICIAL

178 Dr. Hope told his wife that he thought it was unfair to the county for him to stay on: Cited in Robert Lawson Hope, *Personal Recollections of Dr. R.L. Hope*, Library of Atlanta History Center.

179 That very afternoon he sat down and wrote a letter of resignation - -: "Board Finds One Honest Official," Subtitle: "Dr. Hope, of Almshouse, Wanted to Resign Because of Health – Commissioners Grant Him Leave Instead," *The Atlanta Journal*, Atlanta, Ga. Date of publication separated from article, Wednesday edition, November, 1906.

180 Consequently, the next day's headline proclaimed, "Board Finds One Honest Official": Cited in Ibid.

181 After checking his heart, the point of complaint, the consensus of the three of them was that he had only six months to live!: Cited in Robert Lawson Hope, *Personal Recollections of Dr. R.L. Hope*, Library of Atlanta History Center.

182 He served as pallbearer for each of the physicians in turn: Cited in Ibid.

CHAPTER THIRTY-ONE: THE SCHOOL BOARD

183 His public school involvement came about in the following way: "Its Final Report," Subtitle, "County in Good Condition," *The Atlanta Journal*, Atlanta, Ga., Date of publication separated from article, Saturday evening edition, 1898; See also, "Commissioners Give School," *The Constitution*, Atlanta, Ga., same approximate date.

184 He had long shown great interest in the county's schools: "Two School Board Members Elected," *The Atlanta Journal*, Atlanta, Ga. After-the-fact, the article alluded to Dr. Hope's interest in the county's schools, March 8, 1900.

185 It was not until the first Wednesday in September that the Board of County Commissioners actually passed a resolution giving the asylum building to the Board of Education: "Commissioners Give School," *The Atlanta Journal*, Atlanta, Ga., Date of publication separated from article, September, 1898.

186 Once all were combined, said the <u>Atlanta Journal</u>, R.L. Hope School would be a school "which will probably outrank in equipment and thoroughness any other school of the county": Cited in Ibid.

187 There is no other county in the state that can boast of as complete and thorough a system of public schools - -: "Citizens Meet and Discuss Education," Subtitle, "Fulton's Public School System," *The Constitution*, Atlanta, Ga., Date of publication separated from article, 1898.

188 The newspaper exulted, "This will be one of the largest gatherings of the people in the interest of education that has ever been held in the county": "Teachers Named For County Schools," *The Constitution*, Atlanta, Ga., Date of publication separated from article, September, 1898.

189 The following year, on March 7, 1900, the busy superintendent was elected by the Grand Jury, along with Major R.J. Guinn, to succeed Georgia ex-Governor Northen and W.P. Patillo on the school board: Cited in Ibid., *Atlanta Journal*, March 8, 1900.

190 Three years later he was elected president of the Fulton County Board of Education: Cited in article, "Dr. R.L. Hope Rites To Be Held Today," *Atlanta Journal*, Atlanta, Ga., Date of publication separated from article, January, 1938.

191 He asked not to be considered for another term, and this time the Commission acceded to his request: *Letter over signature of Henry M. Wood, Clerk*, Office, Commissioners of Roads and Revenues, Fulton County, Ga., November 3, 1909.

192 The Fulton County Commission, accepting it, November 3, 1909, entered its letter of acceptance and regret, as did the Fulton County Board of Education, from whose presidency he also resigned: Cited in Ibid., *Letter - - of Henry Wood, - -* Commissioners of Roads and Revenues, - - November 3, 1909. Also cited, "Copy of Resolution in regard to resignation of Dr. R.L. Hope," *Letter from Board of Education, Fulton County, Ga.*, November, 1909.

193 An impressive dedicatory exercise was held for the new, red-brick school when it was completed in 1927: "Big School Rally For Tomorrow," Subtitles, "Programme is Arranged," "Board of Education and Board of Commissioners to Attend," "Teachers of County Will Be Present," "Day Will Be Spent at R.L. Hope School and Interest in Educational Matters Will Be Aroused," *The Constitution*, Atlanta, Ga., September, 1927. Cited in Ibid., Article furnished with report on the event: "Citizens Meet and Discuss Education," Subtitles, "Big Rally Held at R.L. Hope School Yesterday," "Enthusiasm Is Aroused," "Mr. A.P. Stewart To Furnish a Library For the School," "Great Crowd Enjoy a Barbecue," "Occasion Was the First of Series of Rallies To Be Held at the Schools in the County," September, 1927.

194 - - spank me, instead of going on with all these words!: These words reported by the person who spoke them, Martha Hope Scruggs (Mrs. Carlton Scruggs), Cited in Robert Lawson Hope, *Personal Recollections of Dr. R.L. Hope*, Library of Atlanta History Center.

CHAPTER THIRTY-TWO: A NEW POOR HOUSE

195 The Poor House could be located in a particular spot fronting on West Wieuca Road: "Old Home Has New Role," *The Constitution*, Atlanta, Ga., October 4, 1967.

196 It had been the site of a Muscogee Creek Indian settlement until 1821: "History," *Chastain Park Conservancy*, Windows Internet Explorer, 2008.

197 They produced the brick in the area now occupied by the ball fields of Chastain Park: Cited in Ibid.

198 The new Wieuca Road Poor House was completed in 1911 - -: Cited in Ibid.

CHAPTER THIRTY-THREE: BEST AND WORST OF TIMES

199 "- - his best work was done in organizing the Fulton County Police department: Cited in Harold H. Martin, *Atlanta and Environs*, vol. III (University of Georgia Press, Athens/London, and The Atlanta Historical Society, 1987) 65.

200 The man selected for the job - - was Henry C. Clark: "Old Home Has New Role," *The Constitution*, Atlanta, Ga., October 4, 1967.

201 "There were no nursing homes, and we were pioneers in the field": Cited in Ibid.

202 "We furnished everything from shoes and drugs to a fully staffed beauty shop": Cited in Ibid.

203 This was done, and the convict women worked on a farm situated to the north of Nancy Creek: "History," *Chastain Park Conservancy,* Windows Internet Explorer, 2008.

204 Indigents who died in the Poor House were often buried - - at approximately the place where the third green of the golf course is today: Cited in Ibid.

205 An archaeologist has been quoted as saying that he believes there may be evidences of the village existing yet - -: Cited in Ibid.

206 As the first female head of a county department, she owned quite a distinction: "Old Home Has New Role,"*The Constitution,* Atlanta, Ga., October 4, 1967.

CHAPTER THIRTY-FOUR: POOR HOUSE IN A PARK

207 A year after Jessie Clark was given the headship of the Poor House, the Fulton County Commission began to plan for the use of lands around it: "History," *Chastain Park Conservancy,* Windows Internet Explorer, 2008.

208 In 1936, young widow Jessie Clark remarried: Cited in Ibid., "Old Home Has New Role."

209 Thereafter, with the approval of the Fulton County Commission, it would be called, "Haven Home": Cited in Ibid.

210 "I was the first woman ever appointed by the county commission to head a department, and I still am the only one that has ever been appointed": Cited in Ibid.

211 "I never locked the front door": Cited in Ibid.

212 Nineteen-Thirty-Eight was an important year in the saga of the Poor House. Robert L. Hope, its 1881-1909 superintendent and rebuilder, died: "Dr. R.L. Hope Rites To Be held Today," *Atlanta Journal,* Atlanta, Ga., Date of publication separated from article, January, 1938.

213 - - Troy G. Chastain, at last became a Fulton County Commission member: "History," *Chastain Park Conservancy,* Windows Internet Explorer, 2008.

214 William L. Monroe, owner of Monroe Landscaping, was on retainer to the Commission, to supervise the workers: Cited in Ibid.

215 Already in 1935. the eighteen hole North Fulton Golf Course had been built: Cited in Ibid.

216 It was the same area where, more than a century before, the Creek Indian village had been located: Cited in Ibid.

217 In 1942, the tennis center was built, and in 1944 - - the great amphitheater was constructed: Cited in Ibid.

218 Company equipment was kept at the North Fulton Park location, however: Cited in Ibid., "Old Home Has New Role."

219 North Fulton Park's riding stables were opened in 1945: Cited in Ibid., *Chastain Park Conservancy.*

220 In that same year, 1945, Troy Chastain died: Cited in Ibid.

221 Grateful that Mr. Chastain had been the prime mover - - the Commission declared that the park should be renamed, "Chastain Park": Cited in Ibid.

222 Eight years later, the Northside Youth Organization ball fields were built: Cited in Ibid.

223 Changes did not halt for Haven Home either: Cited in Ibid., "Old Home Has New Role."

224 She (Jessie Boynton) retired in summer, 1963, after 35 years of service: Cited in Ibid.

225 Four years after Mrs. Boynton's retirement, the County Commission decided to move Haven Home:

226 The African-American division of haven home was kept on West Wieuca, and was still operating there in 1963: Cited in Ibid., "Old Home Has new Role."

227 Just the previous year, however, the City of Atlanta had acquired the building by swapping some land for it: Cited in Ibid., *Chastain Park Conservancy.*

228 With both buildings now empty, the city government used the former black division's building to house the Chastain Arts and Crafts Center: Cited in Ibid.

229 As for the former building of Happy Haven's white division, it, too, was still used: Cited in Ibid., "Old Home Has New Role."

230 After the elementary school ceased to use it, Municipal Theater leased the building, at no cost, from Fulton County: Cited in Ibid., *Chastain Park Conservancy.*

231 Today, the Galloway School occupies the same building - -: Author visited the school, December, 2007.

SOURCES

A Survey of European Civilization, Vol. II, Geoffrey Bruun & Carl L. Becker: Houghton Mifflin 1939.

Atlanta and Its Environs, Vol. I, II, Franklin Garrett: Lewis Historical Pub. Co., Inc., 1954.

Atlanta and Its Builders.

Atlanta Evening Capitol, Newspaper. Excerpts, 1882.

Atlanta Constitution, Newspaper. Excerpts, 1870's-1960's.

Atlanta Journal, Newspaper. Excerpts, 1883-1960's.

Atlanta Post-Appeal, Newspaper. Excerpts, 1883.

The Battle of Atlanta and the North Georgia Campaign, William Key: Twayne Publishers, N.Y. 1958.

Black Confederates and Afro-Yankees in Civil War Virginia, Ervin L. Jordan, Jr.: University Press of Virginia, 1999.

Boswell's Life of Johnson, James Boswell: Thos. Y. Crowell & Co., N.Y.

The Causes of the Civil War, Ed., Kenneth M. Stampp: Prentice-Hall, Inc., Englewood Cliffs, N.J.

Chastain Park Conservancy, Windows Internet Explorer, 2008

Compton's Pictured Encyclopedia, Vol. 4, F.E. Compton & Co., Chicago, 1957.

Dear Store, Celestine Sibley: Doubleday, Garden City, N.Y.

The Eclectic Star, Periodical.

Encyclopedia Brittanica, Vol. 1, 18, 1953.

History of the Christian Church, Vol III, Philip Schaff: Eerdmans, Grand Rapids.

History of Fulton County, Georgia,– Library, Atlanta History Center. Lecture: *"America's Need For Revival,"* Carl W. Wilson: Macon, Ga., 1978.

Letter From Commissioners of Roads and Revenues, Accepted R.L. Hope Resignation, 1909.

Nations of the World, Vol. I, II, III, Peter Fenelon Collier & Son, N.Y., 1900.

The Official Military Atlas of the Civil War, Fairfax Press, N.Y., 1983.

Ordeal By Fire, Fletcher Pratt: William Sloane Assoc., N.Y., 1948.

Personal Recollections of Dr.R.L. Hope, - Library, Atlanta History Center.

Perspectives On the World Christian Movement, Ed. Ralph D. Winter and Steven Hawthorne: William Carey Library, Pasadena, CA, 1992.

Poetical Works of Alexander Pope, Hurst & Co., N.Y.

The Social Conscience of the Evangelical, Sherwood Eliot Wirt: Harper & Row, N.Y., London, Evanston.

Total Truth, Nancy R. Pearcey: Crossway Books, Wheaton, Ill., 2004.

Wall Map of Atlanta Area Plats, Atlanta History Center.

Wikipedia, The Free Encyclopedia – Internet.

Windows Internet Explorer.

INDEX

LaVergne, TN USA
05 November 2010
203689LV00004B/1/P